McDougal Littell Science

Chemical Interactions

reactants ⟶ products

exothermic

CHEMICAL REACTION

PHYSICAL SCIENCE

A ▶ Matter and Energy
B ▶ Chemical Interactions
C ▶ Motion and Forces
D ▶ Waves, Sound, and Light
E ▶ Electricity and Magnetism

LIFE SCIENCE

A ▶ Cells and Heredity
B ▶ Life Over Time
C ▶ Diversity of Living Things
D ▶ Ecology
E ▶ Human Biology

EARTH SCIENCE

A ▶ Earth's Surface
B ▶ The Changing Earth
C ▶ Earth's Waters
D ▶ Earth's Atmosphere
E ▶ Space Science

Acknowledgments: Excerpts and adaptations from *National Science Education Standards* by the National Academy of Sciences. Copyright © 1996 by the National Academy of Sciences. Reprinted with permission from the National Academies Press, Washington, D.C.

Excerpts and adaptations from *Benchmarks for Science Literacy: Project 2061*. Copyright © 1993 by the American Association for the Advancement of Science. Reprinted with permission.

ISBN: 0-618-33438-6   2 3 4 5 6 7 8 VJM 08 07 06 05 04

Internet Web Site: http://www.mcdougallittell.com

Science Consultants

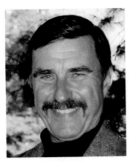

Chief Science Consultant

James Trefil, Ph.D. is the Clarence J. Robinson Professor of Physics at George Mason University. He is the author or co-author of more than 25 books, including *Science Matters* and *The Nature of Science*. Dr. Trefil is a member of the American Association for the Advancement of Science's Committee on the Public Understanding of Science and Technology. He is also a fellow of the World Economic Forum and a frequent contributor to *Smithsonian* magazine.

Rita Ann Calvo, Ph.D. is Senior Lecturer in Molecular Biology and Genetics at Cornell University, where for 12 years she also directed the Cornell Institute for Biology Teachers. Dr. Calvo is the 1999 recipient of the College and University Teaching Award from the National Association of Biology Teachers.

Kenneth Cutler, M.S. is the Education Coordinator for the Julius L. Chambers Biomedical Biotechnology Research Institute at North Carolina Central University. A former middle school and high school science teacher, he received a 1999 Presidential Award for Excellence in Science Teaching.

Instructional Design Consultants

Douglas Carnine, Ph.D. is Professor of Education and Director of the National Center for Improving the Tools of Educators at the University of Oregon. He is the author of seven books and over 100 other scholarly publications, primarily in the areas of instructional design and effective instructional strategies and tools for diverse learners. Dr. Carnine also serves as a member of the National Institute for Literacy Advisory Board.

Linda Carnine, Ph.D. consults with school districts on curriculum development and effective instruction for students struggling academically. A former teacher and school administrator, Dr. Carnine also co-authored a popular remedial reading program.

Donald Steely, Ph.D. serves as principal investigator at the Oregon Center for Applied Science (ORCAS) on federal grants for science and language arts programs. His background also includes teaching and authoring of print and multimedia programs in science, mathematics, history, and spelling.

Sam Miller, Ph.D. is a middle school science teacher and the Teacher Development Liaison for the Eugene, Oregon, Public Schools. He is the author of curricula for teaching science, mathematics, computer skills, and language arts.

Vicky Vachon, Ph.D. consults with school districts throughout the United States and Canada on improving overall academic achievement with a focus on literacy. She is also co-author of a widely used program for remedial readers.

Content Reviewers

John Beaver, Ph.D.
Ecology
Professor, Director of Science Education Center
College of Education and Human Services
Western Illinois University
Macomb, IL

Donald J. DeCoste, Ph.D.
Matter and Energy, Chemical Interactions
Chemistry Instructor
University of Illinois
Urbana-Champaign, IL

Dorothy Ann Fallows, Ph.D., MSc
Diversity of Living Things, Microbiology
Partners in Health
Boston, MA

Michael Foote, Ph.D.
The Changing Earth, Life Over Time
Associate Professor
Department of the Geophysical Sciences
The University of Chicago
Chicago, IL

Lucy Fortson, Ph.D.
Space Science
Director of Astronomy
Adler Planetarium and Astronomy Museum
Chicago, IL

Elizabeth Godrick, Ph.D.
Human Biology
Professor, CAS Biology
Boston University
Boston, MA

Isabelle Sacramento Grilo, M.S.
The Changing Earth
Lecturer, Department of the Geological Sciences
Montana State University
Bozeman, MT

David Harbster, MSc
Diversity of Living Things
Professor of Biology
Paradise Valley Community College
Phoenix, AZ

Richard D. Norris, Ph.D.
Earth's Waters
Professor of Paleobiology
Scripps Institution of Oceanography
University of California, San Diego
La Jolla, CA

Donald B. Peck, M.S.
*Motion and Forces; Waves, Sound, and Light;
Electricity and Magnetism*
Director of the Center for Science Education (retired)
Fairleigh Dickinson University
Madison, NJ

Javier Penalosa, Ph.D.
Diversity of Living Things, Plants
Associate Professor, Biology Department
Buffalo State College
Buffalo, NY

Raymond T. Pierrehumbert, Ph.D.
Earth's Atmosphere
Professor in Geophysical Sciences (Atmospheric Science)
The University of Chicago
Chicago, IL

Brian J. Skinner, Ph.D.
Earth's Surface
Eugene Higgins Professor of Geology and Geophysics
Yale University
New Haven, CT

Nancy E. Spaulding, M.S.
Earth's Surface, The Changing Earth, Earth's Waters
Earth Science Teacher (retired)
Elmira Free Academy
Elmira, NY

Steven S. Zumdahl, Ph.D.
Matter and Energy, Chemical Interactions
Professor Emeritus of Chemistry
University of Illinois
Urbana-Champaign, IL

Susan L. Zumdahl, M.S.
Matter and Energy, Chemical Interactions
Chemistry Education Specialist
University of Illinois
Urbana-Champaign, IL

Safety Consultant

Juliana Texley, Ph.D.
Former K–12 Science Teacher and School Superintendent
Boca Raton, FL

English Language Advisor

Judy Lewis, M.A.
Director, State and Federal Programs for reading proficiency
and high risk populations
Rancho Cordova, CA

Teacher Panel Members

Carol Arbour
Tallmadge Middle School,
Tallmadge, OH

Patty Belcher
Goodrich Middle School,
Akron, OH

Gwen Broestl
Luis Munoz Marin Middle School,
Cleveland, OH

Al Brofman
Tehipite Middle School,
Fresno, CA

John Cockrell
Clinton Middle School,
Columbus, OH

Jenifer Cox
Sylvan Middle School,
Citrus Heights, CA

Linda Culpepper
Martin Middle School,
Charlotte, NC

Kathleen Ann DeMatteo
Margate Middle School,
Margate, FL

Melvin Figueroa
New River Middle School,
Ft. Lauderdale, FL

Doretha Grier
Kannapolis Middle School,
Kannapolis, NC

Robert Hood
Alexander Hamilton Middle School,
Cleveland, OH

Scott Hudson
Coverdale Elementary School,
Cincinnati, OH

Loretta Langdon
Princeton Middle School,
Princeton, NC

Carlyn Little
Glades Middle School,
Miami, FL

Ann Marie Lynn
Amelia Earhart Middle School,
Riverside, CA

James Minogue
Lowe's Grove Middle School,
Durham, NC

Joann Myers
Buchanan Middle School,
Tampa, FL

Barbara Newell
Charles Evans Hughes Middle School,
Long Beach, CA

Anita Parker
Kannapolis Middle School,
Kannapolis, NC

Greg Pirolo
Golden Valley Middle School,
San Bernardino, CA

Laura Pottmyer
Apex Middle School,
Apex, NC

Lynn Prichard
Booker T. Washington Middle Magnet
School, Tampa, FL

Jacque Quick
Walter Williams High School,
Burlington, NC

Robert Glenn Reynolds
Hillman Middle School,
Youngstown, OH

Stacy Rinehart
Lufkin Road Middle School,
Apex, NC

Theresa Short
Abbott Middle School,
Fayetteville, NC

Rita Slivka
Alexander Hamilton Middle School,
Cleveland, OH

Marie Sofsak
B F Stanton Middle School,
Alliance, OH

Nancy Stubbs
Sweetwater Union Unified School District,
Chula Vista, CA

Sharon Stull
Quail Hollow Middle School,
Charlotte, NC

Donna Taylor
Okeeheelee Middle School,
West Palm Beach, FL

Sandi Thompson
Harding Middle School,
Lakewood, OH

Lori Walker
Audubon Middle School & Magnet Center,
Los Angeles, CA

Teacher Lab Evaluators

Andrew Boy
W.E.B. DuBois Academy,
Cincinnati, OH

Jill Brimm-Byrne
Albany Park Academy,
Chicago, IL

Gwen Broestl
Luis Munoz Marin Middle School,
Cleveland, OH

Al Brofman
Tehipite Middle School,
Fresno, CA

Michael A. Burstein
The Rashi School,
Newton, MA

Trudi Coutts
Madison Middle School,
Naperville, IL

Jenifer Cox
Sylvan Middle School,
Citrus Heights, CA

Larry Cwik
Madison Middle School,
Naperville, IL

Jennifer Donatelli
Kennedy Junior High School,
Lisle, IL

Melissa Dupree
Lakeside Middle School,
Evans, GA

Carl Fechko
Luis Munoz Marin Middle School,
Cleveland, OH

Paige Fullhart
Highland Middle School,
Libertyville, IL

Sue Hood
Glen Crest Middle School,
Glen Ellyn, IL

William Luzader
Plymouth Community Intermediate School,
Plymouth, MA

Ann Min
Beardsley Middle School,
Crystal Lake, IL

Aileen Mueller
Kennedy Junior High School,
Lisle, IL

Nancy Nega
Churchville Middle School,
Elmhurst, IL

Oscar Newman
Sumner Math and Science Academy,
Chicago, IL

Lynn Prichard
Booker T. Washington Middle Magnet
School, Tampa, FL

Jacque Quick
Walter Williams High School,
Burlington, NC

Stacy Rinehart
Lufkin Road Middle School,
Apex, NC

Seth Robey
Gwendolyn Brooks Middle School,
Oak Park, IL

Kevin Steele
Grissom Middle School,
Tinley Park, IL

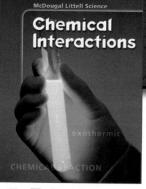

Chemical Interactions

eEdition

Unit Features

SCIENTIFIC AMERICAN

1 Atomic Structure and the Periodic Table   6

the BIG idea

A substance's atomic structure determines its physical and chemical properties.

2 Chemical Bonds and Compounds   38

the BIG idea

The properties of compounds depend on their atoms and chemical bonds.

How do these skydivers stay together? How is this similar to the way atoms stay together? page 38

What changes are happening in this chemical reaction?
page 66

Features

Visual Highlights

Internet Resources @ ClassZone.com

INVESTIGATIONS AND ACTIVITIES

Standards and Benchmarks

Each chapter in **Chemical Interactions** covers some of the learning goals that are described in the *National Science Education Standards* (NSES) and the Project 2061 *Benchmarks for Science Literacy*. Selected content and skill standards are shown below in shortened form. The following National Science Education Standards are covered on pages xii–xxvii, in Frontiers in Science, and in Timelines in Science, as well as in chapter features and laboratory investigations: Understandings About Scientific Inquiry (A.9), Understandings About Science and Technology (E.6), Science and Technology in Society (F.5), Science as a Human Endeavor (G.1), Nature of Science (G.2), and History of Science (G.3).

Content Standards

1 Atomic Structure and the Periodic Table

National Science Education Standards

B.1.b	Substances react chemically in characteristic ways with other substances to form new substances.
B.1.c	There are more than 100 known elements that combine to produce compounds.

Project 2061 Benchmarks

4.D.1	The atoms of any element are alike but are different from atoms of other elements.
4.D.6	There are groups of elements that have similar properties, including • highly reactive metals • less-reactive metals • highly reactive nonmetals • some almost completely nonreactive gases
10.F.2	Scientists are still learning about the basic kinds of matter and how they combine.
10.G.1	The discovery that minerals containing uranium darken photographic film led to the idea of radioactivity.
10.G.2	Scientists Marie Curie and Pierre Curie isolated the elements radium and polonium.

2 Chemical Bonds and Compounds

National Science Education Standards

B.1.b	Substances react chemically in characteristic ways with other substances to form new substances.

Project 2061 Benchmarks

4.D.1	Atoms may stick together in molecules or may be packed together in large arrays.
10.F.2	Scientists are still learning about the basic kinds of matter and how they combine.
11.B.1	Models are often used to explore processes that • happen too slowly, too quickly, or are on too small a scale to observe directly • are on too great a scale to be studied experimentally • are potentially dangerous
11.C.5	Symmetry or a lack of symmetry may determine the properties of many objects.

3 Chemical Reactions

National Science Education Standards

B.1.b	In chemical reactions, the total mass is conserved.
B.3.e	In most chemical reactions, energy is transferred into or out of a system.

	Project 2061 Benchmarks
4.D.4	The temperature and acidity of a solution influence reaction rates. Many substances dissolve in water, which may make reactions between them easier.
4.D.6	An important kind of reaction between substances involves a combination of oxygen with something else—as in burning and rusting.
4.D.7	No matter how substances in a system interact with one another, the total weight of the system remains the same.
10.F.3	The work of scientist Antoine Lavoisier led to the modern science of chemistry.
10.F.4	Lavoisier tested the concept of conservation of matter by measuring the substances involved in burning.

4 Solutions

	National Science Education Standards
B.1.a	A substance has characteristic properties, such as density, a boiling point, and solubility, all of which do not depend on the amount of the sample.
B.1.c	Chemical elements do not break down during normal reactions involving • heating • electric current • acids
D.1.h	The atmosphere is a mixture of nitrogen, oxygen, and small amounts of gases such as water vapor.
	Project 2061 Benchmarks
4.D.4	The temperature and acidity of a solution influence reaction rates. Many substances dissolve in water, which may make reactions between them easier.

5 Carbon in Life and Materials

	National Science Education Standards
B.1.c	There are more than 100 known elements that combine to produce compounds.
C.1.a	Living systems demonstrate the complementary nature of structure and function.
	Project 2061 Benchmarks
4.D.6	Carbon and hydrogen are essential elements of living matter.

Process and Skill Standards

	National Science Education Standards		**Project 2061 Benchmarks**
A.1	Identify questions that can be answered through investigation.	12.B.1	Find what percentage one number is of another.
A.2	Design and conduct a scientific investigation.	12.B.2	Use, interpret, and compare numbers in several equivalent forms, such as integers, fractions, decimals, and percents.
A.3	Use appropriate tools and techniques to gather and interpret data.		
A.4	Use evidence to describe, predict, explain, and model.	12.C.3	Using appropriate units, use and read instruments that measure length, volume, weight, time, rate, and temperature.
A.5	Use critical thinking to find relationships between results and interpretations.		
A.7	Communicate procedures, results, and conclusions.	12.D.1	Use tables and graphs to organize information and identify relationships.
E.1	Identify a problem to be solved.	12.D.2	Read, interpret, and describe tables and graphs.
E.2	Design a solution or product.		
E.3	Implement the proposed solution.	12.D.4	Understand information that includes different types of charts and graphs, including circle charts, bar graphs, line graphs, data tables, diagrams, and symbols.
E.4	Evaluate the solution or design.		

Introducing Physical Science

Scientists are curious. Since ancient times, they have been asking and answering questions about the world around them. Scientists are also very suspicious of the answers they get. They carefully collect evidence and test their answers many times before accepting an idea as correct.

In this book you will see how scientific knowledge keeps growing and changing as scientists ask new questions and rethink what was known before. The following sections will help get you started.

What Is Physical Science?

In the simplest terms, physical science is the study of what things are made of and how they change. It combines the studies of both physics and chemistry. Physics is the science of matter, energy, and forces. It includes the study of topics such as motion, light, and electricity and magnetism. Chemistry is the study of the structure and properties of matter, and it especially focuses on how substances change into different substances.

The text and pictures in this book will help you learn key concepts and important facts about physical science. A variety of activities will help you investigate these concepts. As you learn, it helps to have a big picture of physical science as a framework for this new information. The four unifying principles listed below will give you this big picture. Read the next few pages to get an overview of each of these principles and a sense of why they are so important.

- **Matter is made of particles too small to see.**

- **Matter changes form and moves from place to place.**

- **Energy changes from one form to another, but it cannot be created or destroyed.**

- **Physical forces affect the movement of all matter on Earth and throughout the universe.**

the BIG idea

Each chapter begins with a big idea. Keep in mind that each big idea relates to one or more of the unifying principles.

Matter is made of particles too small to see.

This simple statement is the basis for explaining an amazing variety of things about the world. For example, it explains why substances can exist as solids, liquids, and gases, and why wood burns but iron does not. Like the tiles that make up this mosaic picture, the particles that make up all substances combine to make patterns and structures that can be seen. Unlike these tiles, the individual particles themselves are far too small to see.

What It Means

To understand this principle better, let's take a closer look at the two key words: *matter* and *particles*.

Matter

Objects you can see and touch are all around you. The materials that these objects are made of are called **matter.** All living things—even you—are also matter. Even though you can't see it, the air around you is matter too. Scientists often say that matter is anything that has mass and takes up space. **Mass** is a measure of the amount of matter in an object. We use the word **volume** to refer to the amount of space an object or a substance takes up.

Particles

The tiny particles that make up all matter are called **atoms.** Just how tiny are atoms? They are far too small to see, even through a powerful microscope. In fact, an atom is more than a million times smaller than the period at the end of this sentence.

There are more than 100 basic kinds of matter called **elements.** For example, iron, gold, and oxygen are three common elements. Each element has its own unique kind of atom. The atoms of any element are all alike but different from the atoms of any other element.

Many familiar materials are made of particles called molecules. In a **molecule,** two or more atoms stick together to form a larger particle. For example, a water molecule is made of two atoms of hydrogen and one atom of oxygen.

Why It's Important

Understanding atoms and molecules makes it possible to explain and predict the behavior of matter. Among other things, this knowledge allows scientists to

• explain why different materials have different characteristics
• predict how a material will change when heated or cooled
• figure out how to combine atoms and molecules to make new and useful materials

Matter changes form and moves from place to place.

You see matter change form every day. You see the ice in your glass of juice disappear without a trace. You see a black metal gate slowly develop a flaky, orange coating. Matter is constantly changing and moving.

What It Means

Remember that matter is made of tiny particles called atoms. Atoms are constantly moving and combining with one another. All changes in matter are the result of atoms moving and combining in different ways.

Matter Changes and Moves

You can look at water to see how matter changes and moves. A block of ice is hard like a rock. Leave the ice out in sunlight, however, and it changes into a puddle of water. That puddle of water can eventually change into water vapor and disappear into the air. The water vapor in the air can become raindrops, which may fall on rocks, causing them to weather and wear away. The water that flows in rivers and streams picks up tiny bits of rock and carries them from one shore to another. Understanding how the world works requires an understanding of how matter changes and moves.

Matter Is Conserved

No matter was lost in any of the changes described above. The ice turned to water because its molecules began to move more quickly as they got warmer. The bits of rock carried away by the flowing river were not gone forever. They simply ended up farther down the river. The puddles of rainwater didn't really disappear; their molecules slowly mixed with molecules in the air.

Under ordinary conditions, when matter changes form, no matter is created or destroyed. The water created by melting ice has the same mass as the ice did. If you could measure the water vapor that mixes with the air, you would find it had the same mass as the water in the puddle did.

Why It's Important

Understanding how mass is conserved when matter changes form has helped scientists to

- describe changes they see in the world
- predict what will happen when two substances are mixed
- explain where matter goes when it seems to disappear

Energy changes from one form to another, but it cannot be created or destroyed.

When you use energy to warm your food or to turn on a flashlight, you may think that you "use up" the energy. Even though the camp-stove fuel is gone and the flashlight battery no longer functions, the energy they provided has not disappeared. It has been changed into a form you can no longer use. Understanding how energy changes forms is the basis for understanding how heat, light, and motion are produced.

What It Means

Changes that you see around you depend on energy. **Energy,** in fact, means the ability to cause change. The electrical energy from an outlet changes into light and heat in a light bulb. Plants change the light energy from the Sun into chemical energy, which animals use to power their muscles.

Energy Changes Forms

Using energy means changing energy. You probably have seen electric energy changing into light, heat, sound, and mechanical energy in household appliances. Fuels like wood, coal, and oil contain chemical energy that produces heat when burned. Electric power plants make electrical energy from a variety of energy sources, including falling water, nuclear energy, and fossil fuels.

Energy Is Conserved

Energy can be converted into forms that can be used for specific purposes. During the conversion, some of the original energy is converted into unwanted forms. For instance, when a power plant converts the energy of falling water into electrical energy, some of the energy is lost to friction and sound.

Similarly, when electrical energy is used to run an appliance, some of the energy is converted into forms that are not useful. Only a small percentage of the energy used in a light bulb, for instance, produces light; most of the energy becomes heat. Nonetheless, the total amount of energy remains the same through all these conversions.

The fact that energy does not disappear is a law of physical science. The **law of conservation of energy** states that energy cannot be created or destroyed. It can only change form.

Why It's Important

Understanding that energy changes form but does not disappear has helped scientists to

- predict how energy will change form
- manage energy conversions in useful ways
- build and improve machines

Physical forces affect the movement of all matter on Earth and throughout the universe.

What makes the world go around? The answer is simple: forces. Forces allow you to walk across the room, and forces keep the stars together in galaxies. Consider the forces acting on the rafts below. The rushing water is pushing the rafts forward. The force from the people paddling helps to steer the rafts.

What It Means

A **force** is a push or a pull. Every time you push or pull an object, you're applying a force to that object, whether or not the object moves. There are several forces—several pushes and pulls—acting on you right now. All these forces are necessary for you to do the things you do, even sitting and reading.

- You are already familiar with the force of gravity. **Gravity** is the force of attraction between two objects. Right now gravity is at work pulling you to Earth and Earth to you. The Moon stays in orbit around Earth because gravity holds it close.

- A contact force occurs when one object pushes or pulls another object by touching it. If you kick a soccer ball, for instance, you apply a contact force to the ball. You apply a contact force to a shopping cart that you push down a grocery aisle or a sled that you pull up a hill.

- **Friction** is the force that resists motion between two surfaces pressed together. If you've ever tried to walk on an icy sidewalk, you know how important friction can be. If you lightly rub your finger across a smooth page in a book and then across a piece of sandpaper, you can feel how the different surfaces produce different frictional forces. Which is easier to do?

- There are other forces at work in the world too. For example, a compass needle responds to the magnetic force exerted by Earth's magnetic field, and objects made of certain metals are attracted by magnets. In addition to magnetic forces, there are electrical forces operating between particles and between objects. For example, you can demonstrate electrical forces by rubbing an inflated balloon on your hair. The balloon will then stick to your head or to a wall without additional means of support.

Why It's Important

Although some of these forces are more obvious than others, physical forces at work in the world are necessary for you to do the things you do. Understanding forces allows scientists to

- predict how objects will move
- design machines that perform complex tasks
- predict where planets and stars will be in the sky from one night to the next

The Nature of Science

You may think of science as a body of knowledge or a collection of facts. More important, however, science is an active process that involves certain ways of looking at the world.

Scientific Habits of Mind

Scientists are curious. They are always asking questions. Scientists have asked questions such as, "What is the smallest form of matter?" and "How do the smallest particles behave?" These and other important questions are being investigated by scientists around the world.

Scientists are observant. They are always looking closely at the world around them. Scientists once thought the smallest parts of atoms were protons, neutrons, and electrons. Later, protons and neutrons were found to be made of even smaller particles called quarks.

Scientists are creative. They draw on what they know to form possible explanations for a pattern, an event, or an interesting phenomenon that they have observed. Then scientists create a plan for testing their ideas.

Scientists are skeptical. Scientists don't accept an explanation or answer unless it is based on evidence and logical reasoning. They continually question their own conclusions and the conclusions suggested by other scientists. Scientists trust only evidence that is confirmed by other people or methods.

Scientists cannot always make observations with their own eyes. They have developed technology, such as this particle detector, to help them gather information about the smallest particles of matter.

Scientists ask questions about the physical world and seek answers through carefully controlled procedures. Here a researcher works with supercooled magnets.

Science Processes at Work

You can think of science as a continuous cycle of asking and seeking answers to questions about the world. Although there are many processes that scientists use, scientists typically do each of the following:

- Observe and ask a question
- Determine what is known
- Investigate
- Interpret results
- Share results

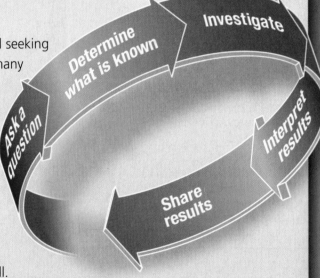

Observe and Ask a Question

It may surprise you that asking questions is an important skill. A scientific process may start when a scientist asks a question. Perhaps scientists observe an event or a process that they don't understand, or perhaps answering one question leads to another.

Determine What Is Known

When beginning an inquiry, scientists find out what is already known about a question. They study results from other scientific investigations, read journals, and talk with other scientists. A scientist working on subatomic particles is most likely a member of a large team using sophisticated equipment. Before beginning original research, the team analyzes results from previous studies.

Investigate

Investigating is the process of collecting evidence. Two important ways of investigating are observing and experimenting.

Observing is the act of noting and recording an event, a characteristic, or anything else detected with an instrument or with the senses. A researcher may study the properties of a substance by handling it, finding its mass, warming or cooling it, stretching it, and so on. For information about the behavior of subatomic particles, however, a researcher may rely on technology such as scanning tunneling microscopes, which produce images of structures that cannot be seen with the eye.

An **experiment** is an organized procedure to study something under controlled conditions. In order to study the effect of wing shape on the motion of a glider, for instance, a researcher would need to conduct controlled studies in which gliders made of the same materials and with the same masses differed only in the shape of their wings.

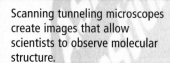

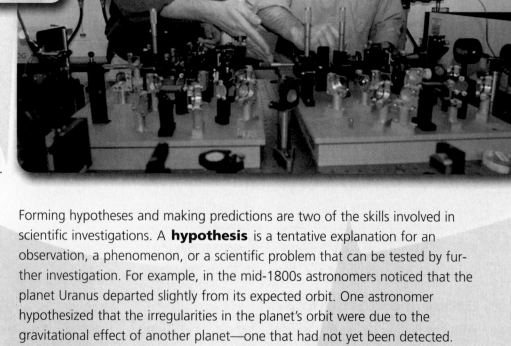

Scanning tunneling microscopes create images that allow scientists to observe molecular structure.

Physical chemists have found a way to observe chemical reactions at the atomic level. Using lasers, they can watch bonds breaking and new bonds forming.

Forming hypotheses and making predictions are two of the skills involved in scientific investigations. A **hypothesis** is a tentative explanation for an observation, a phenomenon, or a scientific problem that can be tested by further investigation. For example, in the mid-1800s astronomers noticed that the planet Uranus departed slightly from its expected orbit. One astronomer hypothesized that the irregularities in the planet's orbit were due to the gravitational effect of another planet—one that had not yet been detected. A **prediction** is an expectation of what will be observed or what will happen. A prediction can be used to test a hypothesis. The astronomers predicted that they would discover a new planet in the position calculated, and their prediction was confirmed with the discovery of the planet Neptune.

Interpret Results

As scientists investigate, they analyze their evidence, or data, and begin to draw conclusions. **Analyzing data** involves looking at the evidence gathered through observations or experiments and trying to identify any patterns that might exist in the data. Scientists often need to make additional observations or perform more experiments before they are sure of their conclusions. Many times scientists make new predictions or revise their hypotheses.

Often scientists use computers to help them analyze data. Computers reveal patterns that might otherwise be missed.

Scientists use computers to create models of objects or processes they are studying. This model shows carbon atoms forming a sphere.

Share Results

An important part of scientific investigation is sharing results of experiments. Scientists read and publish in journals and attend conferences to communicate with other scientists around the world. Sharing data and procedures gives them a way to test one another's results. They also share results with the public through newspapers, television, and other media.

The Nature of Technology

When you think of technology, you may think of cars, computers, and cell phones, as well as refrigerators, radios, and bicycles. Technology is not only the machines and devices that make modern lives easier, however. It is also a process in which new methods and devices are created. Technology makes use of scientific knowledge to design solutions to real-world problems.

Science and Technology

Science and technology go hand in hand. Each depends upon the other. Even designing a device as simple as a toaster requires knowledge of how heat flows and which materials are the best conductors of heat. Just as technology based on scientific knowledge makes our lives easier, some technology is used to advance scientific inquiry itself. For example, researchers use a number of specialized instruments to help them collect data. Microscopes, telescopes, spectrographs, and computers are just a few of the tools that help scientists learn more about the world. The more information these tools provide, the more devices can be developed to aid scientific research and to improve modern lives.

The Process of Technological Design

The process of technology involves many choices. For example, how does an automobile engineer design a better car? Is a better car faster? safer? cheaper? Before designing any new machine, the engineer must decide exactly what he or she wants the machine to do as well as what may be given up for the machine to do it. A faster car may get people to their destinations more quickly, but it may cost more and be less safe. As you study the techno-logical process, think about all the choices that were made to build the technologies you use.

Identify a Need

Successful technology fills a need; it helps us perform a task we need or want to do. For example, as more cars appear on the road, noise and air pollution become serious threats to the environment and to people's health. Gas consumption also depletes precious petroleum resources. There is a need to find a fuel source for a car that will not pollute the air and that will never run out.

Design and Develop

Hydrogen fuel cells are a potential solution to this need. These cells combine hydrogen and oxygen into water, producing electricity in the process. Engineers have found a way to make fuel cells small enough to fit into a car, yet able to produce enough electricity to power an electric motor. Before arriving at this final design, engineers tried many others.

Test and Improve

Just because a technology works doesn't mean it cannot be improved. A fuel-cell-powered car has been driven from San Francisco to Washington, D.C., but it probably will be a while before it's in dealer showrooms. Engineers won't know how these cars will perform until they're driven in real-world conditions. Engineers also won't know if the average driver will be able to handle the necessary maintenance on the car until the car is made available to ordinary drivers. Improvements in the future may well bring cars powered by fuel cells into garages everywhere.

Using McDougal Littell Science

Reading Text and Visuals

This book is organized to help you learn. Use these boxed
pointers as a path to help you learn and remember
the **Big Ideas** and **Key Concepts**.

Read the Big Idea.

As you read **Key Concepts** for
the chapter, relate them to
the Big Idea.

Take notes.

Use the strategies on the
Getting Ready to Learn page.

CHAPTER

1

Atomic
the Per

the **BIG** idea

A substance's atomic
structure determines its
physical and chemical
properties.

Key Concepts

SECTION
1.1 Atoms are the smallest
form of elements.
Learn about the structure
of atoms and how each
element's atoms are different.

SECTION
1.2 Elements make up the
periodic table.
Learn how the periodic table
of the elements is organized.

SECTION
1.3 The periodic table is a
map of the elements.
Learn more about the
groups of elements in
the periodic table.

Internet Preview

CLASSZONE.COM
Chapter 1 online resources:
Content Review, Simulation,
Visualization, three
Resource Centers, Math
Tutorial, Test Practice

CHAPTER 1

Getting Ready to Learn

CONCEPT REVIEW

- Matter is made of particles
  called atoms that are too
  small to see with the eyes.
- Matter can be an element,
  a compound, or a mixture.
- Matter can undergo physical
  and chemical changes.

VOCABULARY REVIEW

See Glossary for definitions.

atom

compound

element

CONTENT REVIEW
CLASSZONE.COM
Review concepts and vocabulary.

TAKING NOTES

MAIN IDEA WEB

Write each new blue
heading in a box. Then
write notes in boxes
around the center box
that give important terms
and details about that
blue heading.

**VOCABULARY
STRATEGY**

Write each new vocabulary
term in the center of a
frame game diagram.
Decide what information
to frame it with. Use
examples, descriptions,
parts, sentences that use
the term in context, or
pictures. You can change
the frame to fit each term.

See the Note-Taking Handbook
on pages R45–R51.

SCIENCE NOTEBOOK

Atoms are made of
protons, neutrons, and
electrons.

The atomic number is
the number of protons
in the nucleus.

Each element is made
of a different atom.

Every element has a
certain number of
protons in its nucleus.

Central part of atom

Contains
most of
an atom's
mass

NUCLEUS

Electrons
move
about it

Is made of protons and neutrons

Read each heading.

See how it fits into the outline of the chapter.

KEY CONCEPT

1.1 Atoms are the smallest form of elements.

◀ **BEFORE,** you learned

- All matter is made of atoms
- Elements are the simplest substances

▶ **NOW,** you will learn

- Where atoms are found and how they are named
- About the structure of atoms
- How ions are formed from atoms

Remember what you know.

Think about concepts you learned earlier and preview what you'll learn now.

VOCABULARY

proton p. 11
neutron p. 11
nucleus p. 11
electron p. 11
atomic number p. 12
atomic mass number p. 12
isotope p. 12
ion p. 14

EXPLORE The Size of Atoms

How small can you cut paper?

PROCEDURE

1. Cut the strip of paper in half. Cut one of these halves in half.

2. Continue cutting one piece of paper in half as many times as you can.

WHAT DO YOU THINK?

- How many cuts were you able to make?
- Do you think you could keep cutting the paper forever? Why or why not?

MATERIALS

- strip of paper about 30 centimeters long
- scissors

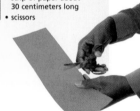

Try the activities.

They will introduce you to science concepts.

All matter is made of atoms.

Think of all the substances you see and touch every day. Are all of these substances the same? Obviously, the substances that make up this book you're reading are quite different from the substances in the air around you. So how many different substances can there be? This is a question people have been asking for thousands of years.

About 2400 years ago, Greek philosophers proposed that everything on Earth was made of only four basic substances—air, water, fire, and earth. Everything else contained a mixture of these four substances. As time went on, chemists came to realize that there had to be more than four basic substances. Today chemists know that about 100 basic substances, or elements, account for everything we see and touch. Sometimes these elements appear by themselves. Most often, however, these elements appear in combination with other elements to make new substances. In this section, you'll learn about the atoms of the elements that make up the world and how these atoms differ from one another.

READING TiP

The word *element* is related to *elementary*, which means "basic."

Learn the vocabulary.

Take notes on each term.

Chapter 1: **Atomic Structure and the Periodic Table 9** **B**

Reading Text and Visuals

Study the visuals.

- Read the title.
- Read all labels and captions.
- Figure out what the picture is showing. Notice colors, arrows, and lines.
- Answer the question. **Reading Visuals** questions will help you understand the picture.

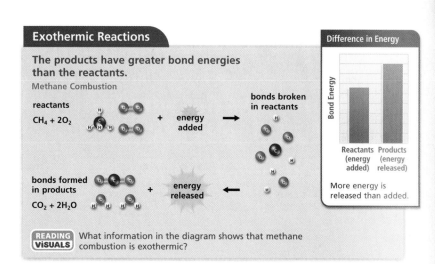

Exothermic Reactions

The products have greater bond energies than the reactants.

Methane Combustion

reactants
$CH_4 + 2O_2$ + energy added → bonds broken in reactants

bonds formed in products
$CO_2 + 2H_2O$ + energy released ←

Difference in Energy

Bond Energy

Reactants (energy added) Products (energy released)

More energy is released than added.

READING VISUALS What information in the diagram shows that methane combustion is exothermic?

Read one paragraph at a time.

Look for a topic sentence that explains the main idea of the paragraph. Figure out how the details relate to that idea. One paragraph might have several important ideas; you may have to reread to understand.

All common combustion reactions, such as the combustion of methane, are exothermic. To determine how energy changes in this reaction, the bond energies in the reactants—oxygen and methane—and in the products—carbon dioxide and water—can be added and compared. This process is illustrated by the diagram shown above. The difference in energy is released to the surrounding air as heat.

Some chemical reactions release excess energy as light instead of heat. For example, glow sticks work by a chemical reaction that releases energy as light. One of the reactants, a solution of hydrogen peroxide, is contained in a thin glass tube within the plastic stick. The rest of the stick is filled with a second chemical and a brightly colored dye. When you bend the stick, the glass tube inside it breaks and the two solutions mix. The result is a bright glow of light.

Exothermic chemical reactions also occur in living things. Some of these reactions release energy as heat, and others release energy as light. Fireflies light up due to a reaction that takes place between oxygen and a chemical called luciferin. This type of exothermic reaction is not unique to fireflies. In fact, similar reactions are found in several different species of fish, squid, jellyfish, and shrimp.

These cup coral polyps glow because of exothermic chemical reactions.

Answer the questions.

Check Your Reading questions will help you remember what you read.

CHECK YOUR READING In which ways might an exothermic reaction release energy?

B 88 Unit: **Chemical Interactions**

Doing Labs

To understand science, you have to see it in action. Doing labs helps you understand how things really work.

① **Read the entire lab first.**

② **Form a hypothesis.**

③ **Follow the procedure.**

④ **Record the data.**

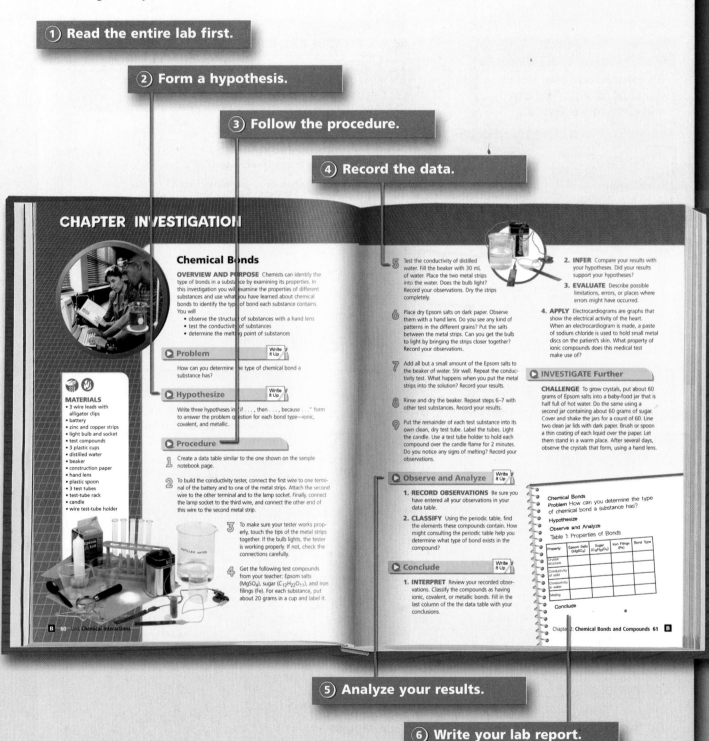

⑤ **Analyze your results.**

⑥ **Write your lab report.**

CHAPTER INVESTIGATION

Chemical Bonds

OVERVIEW AND PURPOSE Chemists can identify the type of bonds in a substance by examining its properties. In this investigation you will examine the properties of different substances and use what you have learned about chemical bonds to identify the type of bond each substance contains. You will
- observe the structure of substances with a hand lens
- test the conductivity of substances
- determine the melting point of substances

▶ **Problem**   Write It Up

How can you determine the type of chemical bond a substance has?

▶ **Hypothesize**   Write It Up

Write three hypotheses in "if . . . , then . . . , because . . ." form to answer the problem question for each bond type—ionic, covalent, and metallic.

▶ **Procedure**

1. Create a data table similar to the one shown on the sample notebook page.

2. To build the conductivity tester, connect the first wire to one terminal of the battery and to one of the metal strips. Attach the second wire to the other terminal and to the lamp socket. Finally, connect the lamp socket to the third wire, and connect the other end of this wire to the second metal strip.

3. To make sure your tester works properly, touch the tips of the metal strips together. If the bulb lights, the tester is working properly. If not, check the connections carefully.

4. Get the following test compounds from your teacher: Epsom salts (MgSO$_4$), sugar (C$_{12}$H$_{22}$O$_{11}$), and iron filings (Fe). For each substance, put about 20 grams in a cup and label it.

MATERIALS
- 3 wire leads with alligator clips
- battery
- zinc and copper strips
- light bulb and socket
- test compounds
- 3 plastic cups
- distilled water
- beaker
- construction paper
- hand lens
- plastic spoon
- 3 test tubes
- test-tube rack
- candle
- wire test-tube holder

5. Test the conductivity of distilled water. Fill the beaker with 30 mL of water. Place the two metal strips into the water. Does the bulb light? Record your observations. Dry the strips completely.

6. Place dry Epsom salts on dark paper. Observe them with a hand lens. Do you see any kind of patterns in the different grains? Put the salts between the metal strips. Can you get the bulb to light by bringing the strips closer together? Record your observations.

7. Add all but a small amount of the Epsom salts to the beaker of water. Stir well. Repeat the conductivity test. What happens when you put the metal strips into the solution? Record your results.

8. Rinse and dry the beaker. Repeat steps 6–7 with other test substances. Record your results.

9. Put the remainder of each test substance into its own clean, dry test tube. Label the tubes. Light the candle. Use a test tube holder to hold each compound over the candle flame for 2 minutes. Do you notice any signs of melting? Record your observations.

▶ **Observe and Analyze**   Write It Up

1. **RECORD OBSERVATIONS** Be sure you have entered all your observations in your data table.

2. **CLASSIFY** Using the periodic table, find the elements these compounds contain. How might consulting the periodic table help you determine what type of bond exists in the compound?

▶ **Conclude**   Write It Up

1. **INTERPRET** Review your recorded observations. Classify the compounds as having ionic, covalent, or metallic bonds. Fill in the last column of the the data table with your conclusions.

2. **INFER** Compare your results with your hypotheses. Did your results support your hypotheses?

3. **EVALUATE** Describe possible limitations, errors, or places where errors might have occurred.

4. **APPLY** Electrocardiograms are graphs that show the electrical activity of the heart. When an electrocardiogram is made, a paste of sodium chloride is used to hold small metal discs on the patient's skin. What property of ionic compounds does this medical test make use of?

▶ **INVESTIGATE Further**

CHALLENGE To grow crystals, put about 60 grams of Epsom salts into a baby-food jar that is half full of hot water. Do the same using a second jar containing about 60 grams of sugar. Cover and shake the jars for a count of 60. Line two clean jar lids with dark paper. Brush or spoon a thin coating of each liquid over the paper. Let them stand in a warm place. After several days, observe the crystals that form, using a hand lens.

Chemical Bonds
Problem How can you determine the type of chemical bond a substance has?

Hypothesize

Observe and Analyze

Table 1: Properties of Bonds

Property	Epsom Salts (MgSO$_4$)	Sugar (C$_{12}$H$_{22}$O$_{11}$)	Iron Filings (Fe)	Bond Type
Crystal structure				
Conductivity of solid				
Conductivity in water				
Melting				

Conclude

Chapter 2: Chemical Bonds and Compounds 61 **B**

B 60 Unit: Chemical Interactions

Using Technology

The Internet is a great source of information about up-to-date science.
The ClassZone Web site and SciLinks have exciting sites for you to
explore. Video clips and simulations can make science come alive.

Look for red banners.

Go to **classzone.com** to see
simulations, visualizations,
and content review.

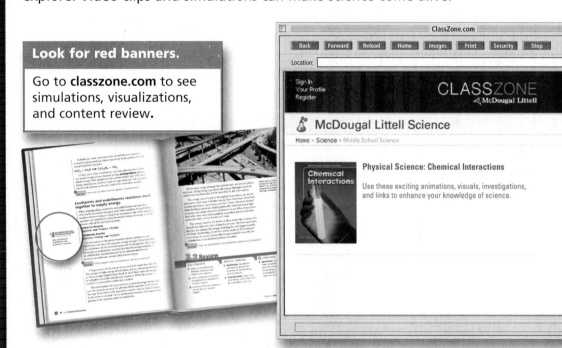

Watch the videos.

See science at work in
the **Scientific American
Frontiers video.**

Look up SciLinks.

Go to **scilinks.org** to explore
the topic.

Forces **Code: MDL005**

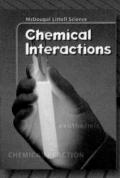

McDougal Littell Science
**Chemical
Interactions**

exothermic

CHEMICAL REACTION

Chemical Interactions
Contents Overview

B

Unit Features

1 Atomic Structure and the Periodic Table   6

2 Chemical Bonds and Compounds   38

3 Chemical Reactions   66

4 Solutions   108

5 Carbon in Life and Materials   144

Medicines from Nature

Where have people found medicines?

SCIENTIFIC AMERICAN FRONTIERS

View the "Endangered Wonder Drug" segment of your Scientific American Frontiers video to see how chemicals found in nature can improve the health of people.

In Brazil, extracts from plants are used to treat everything from Parkinson's Disease to arthritis.

Finding Natural Remedies

In the 1960s, people were searching desperately for new cancer-fighting agents. Scientists tested over 35,000 compounds, some of which came from the bark of the Pacific yew tree, long known to have strong effects on the body. The tests indicated that something in the bark stopped the growth of cancerous tumors. Scientists eventually derived the drug Taxol from the compounds found in the yew tree.

Natural medicines are much more than simple folk cures, like the sapi karta leaves that the Kuna people of Panama believe increase creativity. Many powerful medicines are based on compounds found in nature. But even though these natural compounds may be very effective at treating diseases, they can be limited in supply and can have harmful side effects. Organic chemists must find ways to make these compounds safer and produce them in greater amounts.

Modeling the Molecule

To make a compound, a chemist must know what its molecule looks like, atom by atom. Many useful drugs have structures that contain many atoms arranged in complicated ways. The chemist must know exactly how many atoms of each kind are in the molecule and how they are arranged. One atom in the wrong place might mean that the drug won't work the way it should.

To study the structures of molecules, chemists use a method called spectroscopy. Spectroscopy is a process that shows how the molecules of a compound respond to certain forms of radiation. Three important types of spectroscopy are

• NMR (nuclear magnetic resonance) spectroscopy, which allows chemists to identify small groups of atoms within larger molecules

• IR (infrared) spectroscopy, which shows the presence of certain types of bonds in molecules

• X-ray studies, which show details such as how much space there is between atoms and what the overall physical shapes of molecules are

Chemists put all this information together to determine the structure of a molecule. They might even build a model of the molecule.

Assembling the Puzzle

Once chemists know the structure of the molecule, they must figure out the starting reactants and the specific sequence of chemical reactions that will produce that molecule as a final product. It is a lot like doing a jigsaw puzzle when you know what the final picture looks like but still have to fit together all the pieces. Only in this case, the chemists may not even be sure what the little pieces look like.

Organic chemists often prefer to complete the process backward. They look at a model of the complete molecule and then figure out how they might build one just like it. How do chemists know what kinds of reactions might produce a certain molecule? Chemists have classified chemical reactions into different types. They determine how combinations of reactions will put the various kinds of atoms into their correct places in the molecule. Chemists may need to combine dozens of reactions to get the desired molecule.

Testing the Medicine

Once chemists have produced the desired drug molecule, the synthetic compound must be carefully tested to make sure it works like the natural substance does. The sequence of reactions must also be tested to make sure they produce the same compound when larger amounts of chemicals are used.

SCIENTIFIC AMERICAN FRONTIERS

View the "Endangered Wonder Drug" segment of your *Scientific American Frontiers* video to see how modern medicines can be developed from chemical compounds found in nature.

IN THIS SCENE FROM THE VIDEO ◯

A researcher works with a substance found in bark.

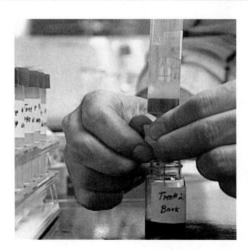

SAVING LIVES THROUGH NATURE AND CHEMISTRY
Medicines from plants and other natural sources have been used by different cultures around the world for thousands of years. The ephedra plant contains the raw material for many decongestants, which help shrink swollen nasal passages. It was used by the Chinese more than 5000 years ago. Today, the bark of the Pacific yew tree is being used as the source of the anticancer drug Taxol. A large amount of bark from the tree, however, is needed to make just one dose of the drug, and very few Pacific yew trees are available. Chemists, therefore, are trying to make this medicine in the laboratory.

Once a potential new drug is found in nature, it may take several years, or even decades, to figure out how to produce the drug synthetically and test it for safety. Only a small percentage of drugs tested ever goes to market, because the drugs must undergo several stages of testing on both animals and humans. Today, chemists routinely search the seas and the forests for marine organisms and rare plants that might have the power to fight cancer, heart disease, or viruses.

Chemists often use computers to make models of drug molecules. Computers allow the chemists to see how the drug molecules will interact with other molecules.

UNANSWERED Questions

The search for new chemical compounds that can be used to treat human illnesses raises many questions. Scientists need to find ways to investigate, produce, and test new, more powerful drugs.

- How might scientists more quickly test the safety and effectiveness of new medicines?
- Can easily synthesized compounds be just as effective as natural medicines?
- Might the processes that produce these drugs in nature be duplicated in a lab?
- Can we discover other new sources of medicines in the natural world?

UNIT PROJECTS

As you study this unit, work alone or with a group on one of these projects.

Medicines Around You

Present a report about a plant in your region that has medicinal properties.

- Collect samples of a plant that has medicinal properties.
- Bring your plant samples into your classroom. Prepare and present a report about the plant and the way it is used in medicine.

Model Medicine

Build a scale model of a molecule that is used to treat a certain illness.

- Using the Internet or an encyclopedia, determine the structure of a compound that interests you.
- Using foam balls, toothpicks, water colors, string, and other materials, construct a model of the molecule. Describe your model to the class.

Remedies

Write a news report about a popular herbal remedy, such as Saint John's Wort.

- To learn more about the herbal remedy, try interviewing a personal fitness trainer or an employee of a health-food store.
- Deliver a news report to the class telling of the advantages of the remedy and warning of its potential dangers.

CAREER CENTER
CLASSZONE.COM

Learn more about careers in chemistry.

Atomic Structure and the Periodic Table

the **BIG** idea

A substance's atomic structure determines its physical and chemical properties.

Key Concepts

SECTION
1.1 Atoms are the smallest form of elements.
Learn about the structure of atoms and how each element's atoms are different.

SECTION
1.2 Elements make up the periodic table.
Learn how the periodic table of the elements is organized.

SECTION
1.3 The periodic table is a map of the elements.
Learn more about the groups of elements in the periodic table.

Internet Preview

CLASSZONE.COM

Chapter 1 online resources: Content Review, Simulation, Visualization, three Resource Centers, Math Tutorial, Test Practice

You can't zoom in any closer than this! The picture is an extremely close-up view of nickel. How do things look different the closer you get to them?

EXPLORE (the BIG idea)

That's Far!

Place a baseball in the middle of a large field. Hold a dime and count off the number of steps from the baseball to the edge of the field. If the baseball were an atom's nucleus and the dime an electron, you would need to go about 6000 steps to walk the distance between the nucleus and the electrons.

Observe and Think How far were you able to go? How much farther would you need to go to model the proportion of an atom? What does this tell you about atomic structure?

Element Safari

Locate the following products in your home or in a grocery store: baking soda, vinegar, cereal flakes, and antacid tablets. You may examine other products if you wish. Look at the labels on the products. Can you recognize the names of any elements? Use your periodic table as a reference.

Observe and Think Which element names did you find?

Internet Activity: Periodic Table

Go to **ClassZone.com** to explore the periodic table. See different ways to set up the table and learn more about the listed elements.

Observe and Think How do atomic number and mass change as you move across the periodic table?

NSTA
scilinks.org

SCI LINKS

Atomic Theory **Code: MDL022**

Getting Ready to Learn

◀ CONCEPT REVIEW

- Matter is made of particles called atoms that are too small to see with the eyes.
- Matter can be an element, a compound, or a mixture.
- Matter can undergo physical and chemical changes.

◀ VOCABULARY REVIEW

See Glossary for definitions.

atom

compound

element

CONTENT REVIEW
CLASSZONE.COM
Review concepts and vocabulary.

▶ TAKING NOTES

MAIN IDEA WEB

Write each new blue heading in a box.
Then write notes in boxes around the center box that give important terms and details about that blue heading.

VOCABULARY STRATEGY

Write each new vocabulary term in the center of a **frame game** diagram. Decide what information to frame it with. Use examples, descriptions, parts, sentences that use the term in context, or pictures. You can change the frame to fit each term.

See the Note-Taking Handbook on pages R45–R51.

SCIENCE NOTEBOOK

Atoms are made of protons, neutrons, and electrons.

The atomic number is the number of protons in the nucleus.

Each element is made of a different atom.

Every element has a certain number of protons in its nucleus.

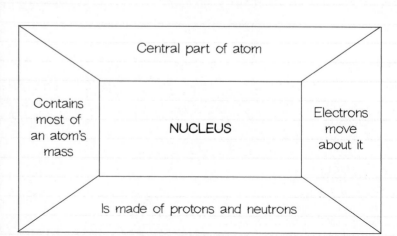

Central part of atom

Contains most of an atom's mass

NUCLEUS

Electrons move about it

Is made of protons and neutrons

KEY CONCEPT

Atoms are the smallest form of elements.

◀ **BEFORE**, you learned

- All matter is made of atoms
- Elements are the simplest substances

▶ **NOW**, you will learn

- Where atoms are found and how they are named
- About the structure of atoms
- How ions are formed from atoms

VOCABULARY

proton p. 11
neutron p. 11
nucleus p. 11
electron p. 11
atomic number p. 12
atomic mass number p. 12
isotope p. 12
ion p. 14

EXPLORE The Size of Atoms

How small can you cut paper?

PROCEDURE

① Cut the strip of paper in half. Cut one of these halves in half.

② Continue cutting one piece of paper in half as many times as you can.

WHAT DO YOU THINK?

- How many cuts were you able to make?
- Do you think you could keep cutting the paper forever? Why or why not?

MATERIALS

- strip of paper about 30 centimeters long
- scissors

All matter is made of atoms.

Think of all the substances you see and touch every day. Are all of these substances the same? Obviously, the substances that make up this book you're reading are quite different from the substances in the air around you. So how many different substances can there be? This is a question people have been asking for thousands of years.

About 2400 years ago, Greek philosophers proposed that everything on Earth was made of only four basic substances—air, water, fire, and earth. Everything else contained a mixture of these four substances. As time went on, chemists came to realize that there had to be more than four basic substances. Today chemists know that about 100 basic substances, or elements, account for everything we see and touch. Sometimes these elements appear by themselves. Most often, however, these elements appear in combination with other elements to make new substances. In this section, you'll learn about the atoms of the elements that make up the world and how these atoms differ from one another.

READING TiP

The word *element* is related to *elementary*, which means "basic."

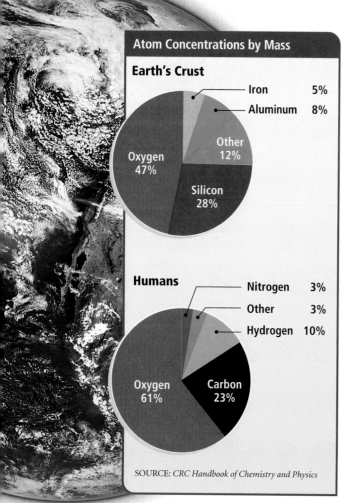

Atom Concentrations by Mass

Earth's Crust

- Iron — 5%
- Aluminum — 8%
- Other 12%
- Oxygen 47%
- Silicon 28%

Humans

- Nitrogen — 3%
- Other — 3%
- Hydrogen — 10%
- Oxygen 61%
- Carbon 23%

SOURCE: *CRC Handbook of Chemistry and Physics*

Types of Atoms in Earth's Crust and Living Things

Atoms of the element hydrogen account for about 90 percent of the total mass of the universe. Hydrogen atoms make up only about 1 percent of Earth's crust, however, and most of those hydrogen atoms are combined with oxygen atoms in the form of water. The graph on the left shows the types of atoms in approximately the top 100 kilometers of Earth's crust.

The distribution of the atoms of the elements in living things is very different from what it is in Earth's crust. Living things contain at least 25 types of atoms. Although the amounts of these atoms vary somewhat, all living things—animals, plants, and bacteria—are composed primarily of atoms of oxygen, carbon, hydrogen, and nitrogen. As you can see in the lower graph on the left, oxygen atoms account for more than half your body's mass.

CHECK YOUR READING What is the most common element in the universe?

Names and Symbols of Elements

Elements get their names in many different ways. Magnesium, for example, was named for the region in Greece known as Magnesia. Lithium comes from the Greek word *lithos,* which means "stone." Neptunium was named after the planet Neptune. The elements einsteinium and fermium were named after scientists Albert Einstein and Enrico Fermi.

Each element has its own unique symbol. For some elements, the symbol is simply the first letter of its name.

hydrogen (H)   sulfur (S)   carbon (C)

The symbols for other elements use the first letter plus one other letter of the element's name. Notice that the first letter is capitalized but the second letter is not.

aluminum (Al)   platinum (Pt)   cadmium (Cd)   zinc (Zn)

The origins of some symbols, however, are less obvious. The symbol for gold (Au), for example, doesn't seem to have anything to do with the element's name. The symbol refers instead to gold's name in Latin, *aurum.* Lead (Pb), iron (Fe), and copper (Cu) are a few other elements whose symbols come from Latin names.

Each element is made of a different atom.

In the early 1800s British scientist John Dalton proposed that each element is made of tiny particles called atoms. Dalton stated that all of the atoms of a particular element are identical but are different from atoms of all other elements. Every atom of silver, for example, is similar to every other atom of silver but different from an atom of iron.

Dalton's theory also assumed that atoms could not be divided into anything simpler. Scientists later discovered that this was not exactly true. They found that atoms are made of even smaller particles.

RESOURCE CENTER
CLASSZONE.COM

Learn more about the atom.

The Structure of an Atom

A key discovery leading to the current model of the atom was that atoms contain charged particles. The charge on a particle can be either positive or negative. Particles with the same type of charge repel each other—they are pushed apart. Particles with different charges attract each other—they are drawn toward each other.

Atoms are composed of three types of particles—electrons, protons, and neutrons. A **proton** is a positively charged particle, and a **neutron** is an uncharged particle. The neutron has approximately the same mass as a proton. The protons and neutrons of an atom are grouped together in the atom's center. This combination of protons and neutrons is called the **nucleus** of the atom. Because it contains protons, the nucleus has a positive charge. **Electrons** are negatively charged particles that move around outside the nucleus.

VOCABULARY
Remember to make a frame for *neutron, proton,* and *electron* and for other vocabulary terms.

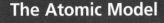

The Atomic Model

Atoms are made of protons, neutrons, and electrons.

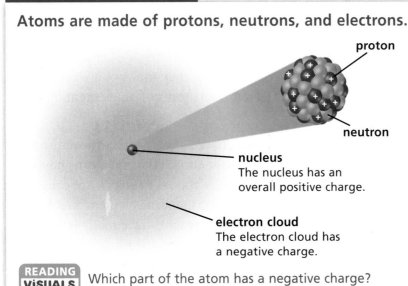

proton

neutron

nucleus
The nucleus has an overall positive charge.

electron cloud
The electron cloud has a negative charge.

Particle Charges and Mass		
Particle	Relative Mass	Relative Charge
Electron	1	−1
Proton	2000	+1
Neutron	2000	0

READING VISUALS Which part of the atom has a negative charge?

Atoms are extremely small, about 10^{-10} meters in diameter. This means that you could fit millions of atoms in the period at the end of this sentence. The diagram on page 11, picturing the basic structure of the atom, is not drawn to scale. In an atom the electron cloud is about 10,000 times the diameter of the nucleus.

Electrons are much smaller than protons or neutrons—about 2000 times smaller. Electrons also move about the nucleus very quickly. Scientists have found that it is not possible to determine their exact positions with any certainty. This is why we picture the electrons as being in a cloud around the nucleus.

The negative electrons remain associated with the nucleus because they are attracted to the positively charged protons. Also, because electrical charges that are alike (such as two negative charges) repel each other, electrons remain spread out in the electron cloud. Neutral atoms have no overall electrical charge because they have an equal number of protons and electrons.

Atom Size

Millions of atoms could fit in a space the size of this dot. It would take you 500 years to count the number of atoms in a grain of salt.

Atomic Numbers

If all atoms are composed of the same particles, how can there be more than 100 different elements? The identity of an atom is determined by the number of protons in its nucleus, called the **atomic number.** Every hydrogen atom—atomic number 1—has exactly one proton in its nucleus. Every gold atom has 79 protons, which means the atomic number of gold is 79.

Gold has 79 protons and 79 electrons.

Atomic Mass Numbers

The total number of protons and neutrons in an atom's nucleus is called its **atomic mass number.** While the atoms of a certain element always have the same number of protons, they may not always have the same number of neutrons, so not all atoms of an element have the same atomic mass number.

All chlorine atoms, for instance, have 17 protons. However, some chlorine atoms have 18 neutrons, while other chlorine atoms have 20 neutrons. Atoms of chlorine with 18 and 20 neutrons are called chlorine isotopes. **Isotopes** are atoms of the same element that have a different number of neutrons. Some elements have many isotopes, while other elements have just a few.

READING TiP

The *iso-* in *isotope* is from the Greek language, and it means "equal."

 CHECK YOUR READING How is atomic mass number different from atomic number?

Isotopes have different numbers of neutrons.

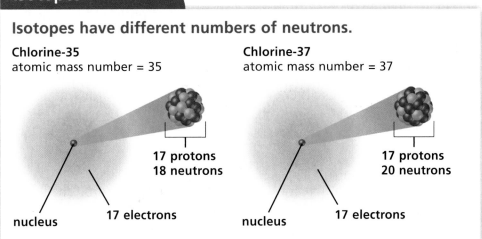

Chlorine-35
atomic mass number = 35

17 protons
18 neutrons

nucleus   17 electrons

Chlorine-37
atomic mass number = 37

17 protons
20 neutrons

nucleus   17 electrons

A particular isotope is designated by the name of the element and the total number of its protons and neutrons. You can find the number of neutrons in a particular isotope by subtracting the atomic number from the atomic mass number. For example, chlorine-35 indicates the isotope of chlorine that has 18 neutrons. Chlorine-37 has 20 neutrons. Every atom of a given element always has the same atomic number because it has the same number of protons. However, the atomic mass number varies depending on the number of neutrons.

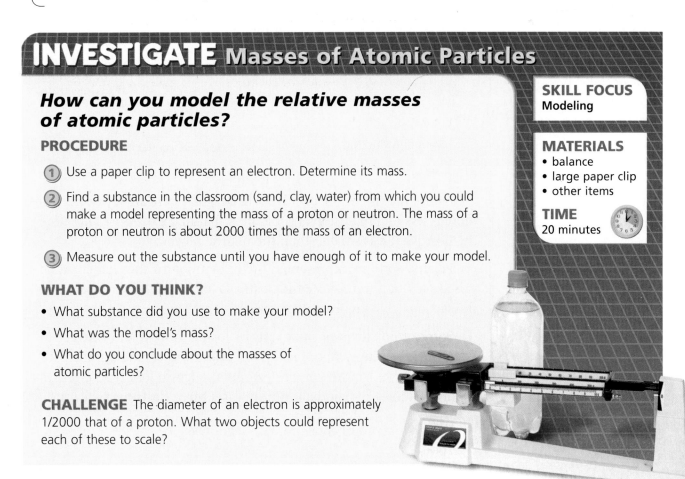

INVESTIGATE Masses of Atomic Particles

How can you model the relative masses of atomic particles?

PROCEDURE

SKILL FOCUS
Modeling

MATERIALS
• balance
• large paper clip
• other items

TIME
20 minutes

1. Use a paper clip to represent an electron. Determine its mass.

2. Find a substance in the classroom (sand, clay, water) from which you could make a model representing the mass of a proton or neutron. The mass of a proton or neutron is about 2000 times the mass of an electron.

3. Measure out the substance until you have enough of it to make your model.

WHAT DO YOU THINK?

• What substance did you use to make your model?

• What was the model's mass?

• What do you conclude about the masses of atomic particles?

CHALLENGE The diameter of an electron is approximately 1/2000 that of a proton. What two objects could represent each of these to scale?

MAIN IDEA WEB
Make a main idea web to
organize what you know
about ions.

Atoms form ions.

An atom has an equal number of electrons and protons. Since each electron has one negative charge and each proton has one positive charge, atoms have no overall electrical charge. An **ion** is formed when an atom loses or gains one or more electrons. Because the number of electrons in an ion is different from the number of protons, an ion does have an overall electric charge.

Formation of Positive Ions

Consider how a positive ion can be formed from an atom. The left side of the illustration below represents a sodium (Na) atom. Its nucleus contains 11 protons and some neutrons. Because the electron cloud surrounding the nucleus consists of 11 electrons, there is no overall charge on the atom. If the atom loses one electron, however, the charges are no longer balanced. There is now one more proton than there are electrons. The ion formed, therefore, has a positive charge.

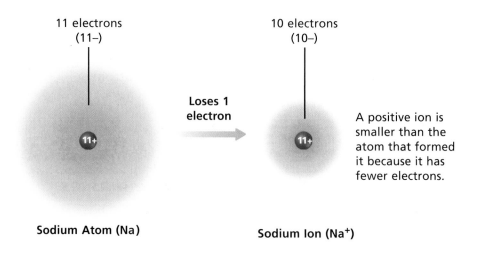

11 electrons
(11–)

**Loses 1
electron**

10 electrons
(10–)

A positive ion is
smaller than the
atom that formed
it because it has
fewer electrons.

Sodium Atom (Na)

Sodium Ion (Na⁺)

Notice the size of the positive ion. Because there are fewer electrons, there is less of a repulsion among the remaining electrons. Therefore, the positive ion is smaller than the neutral atom.

Positive ions are represented by the symbol for the element with a raised plus sign to indicate the positive charge. In the above example, the sodium ion is represented as Na^+.

Some atoms form positive ions by losing more than one electron. In those cases, the symbol for the ion also indicates the number of positive charges on the ion. For example, calcium loses two electrons to form an ion Ca^{2+}, and aluminum loses three electrons to form Al^{3+}.

**CHECK YOUR
READING** What must happen to form a positive ion?

Formation of Negative Ions

The illustration below shows how a negative ion is formed. In this case the atom is chlorine (Cl). The nucleus of a chlorine atom contains 17 protons and some neutrons. The electron cloud has 17 electrons, so the atom has no overall charge. When an electron is added to the chlorine atom, a negatively charged ion is formed. Notice that a negative ion is larger than the neutral atom that formed it. The extra electron increases the repulsion within the cloud, causing it to expand.

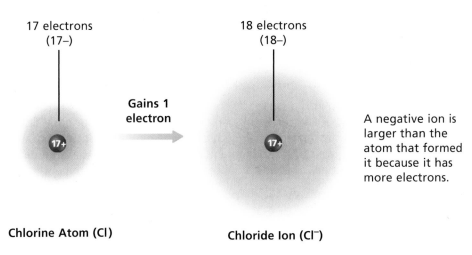

17 electrons
(17–)

Gains 1
electron

18 electrons
(18–)

17+

17+

A negative ion is larger than the atom that formed it because it has more electrons.

Chlorine Atom (Cl)

Chloride Ion (Cl⁻)

Negative ions are represented by placing a minus sign to the right and slightly above the element's symbol. The negative chloride ion in the example, therefore, would be written as Cl^-. If an ion has gained more than one electron, the number of added electrons is indicated by a number in front of the minus sign. Oxygen (O), for example, gains two electrons when it forms an ion. Its symbol is O^{2-}.

 **Review**

KEY CONCEPTS

1. Which two atoms are most common in Earth's crust? in the human body?

2. What are the particles that make up an atom?

3. What happens when an atom forms an ion?

CRITICAL THINKING

4. **Infer** Magnesium and sodium atoms are about the same size. How does the size of a magnesium ion with a 2+ charge compare with that of a sodium ion with a single + charge?

5. **Compare** The atomic number of potassium is 19. How does potassium-39 differ from potassium-41?

○ CHALLENGE

6. **Analyze** When determining the mass of an atom, the electrons are not considered. Why can scientists disregard the electrons?

Elements of Life

There are more than 25 different types of atoms in the cells of your body. The table below shows the amount of atoms of some of the elements in a 50-kilogram human. Atoms of the element oxygen account for about 61 percent of a person's mass. Atoms of carbon account for about 23 percent of a person's mass. Although the atoms of some elements are present only in very small amounts, they play an important role in the chemical processes that occur in your cells.

Blood and Other Fluids

Iron ions are part of the hemoglobin that gives your blood its red color and carries oxygen to cells throughout your body. Sodium and potassium ions help regulate the amount and location of the water in your body. Sodium and potassium ions also make up part of the sweat your body produces to regulate temperature.

Bones and Teeth

The sturdier structures of your body get their strength from calcium, magnesium, and phosphorus. You have less than a kilogram of calcium in your body, almost all of which is in your bones and teeth. Fluoride ions make up part of the hard coating on your teeth. This is why you'll often find fluoride ions added to toothpaste.

Elements to Avoid

In some way, the atoms of every element in the periodic table play a role in human lives. Many of them, however, can be hazardous if handled improperly. For example, arsenic and mercury are poisonous.

Mass of Elements in 50 kg Human	
Element	**Amount (kg)**
Oxygen (O)	30.5
Carbon (C)	11.5
Hydrogen (H)	5.0
Nitrogen (N)	1.3
Calcium (Ca)	0.7
Phosphorus (P)	0.6
Potassium (K)	0.1
Sodium (Na)	> 0.1
Chlorine (Cl)	> 0.1

Other elements are in the body in very small amounts.

SOURCE: *CRC Handbook of Chemistry and Physics*

EXPLORE

1. **CALCULATE** What percentage of your body is made up of oxygen, carbon, hydrogen, and nitrogen?

2. **CHALLENGE** Salt, made of sodium ions and chloride ions, is an essential part of your diet. However, too much salt can cause health problems. Use the Internet to find out about the problems caused by too much or too little salt in your diet.

RESOURCE CENTER
CLASSZONE.COM
Find out more about the elements important to life.

This photo shows a false color X-ray of the human skull. X-rays show the bones in the human body. Bones contain calcium.

Elements make up the periodic table.

 BEFORE, you learned

- Atoms have a structure
- Every element is made from a different type of atom

NOW, you will learn

- How the periodic table is organized
- How properties of elements are shown by the periodic table

VOCABULARY

atomic mass p. 17
periodic table p. 18
group p. 22
period p. 22

EXPLORE Similarities and Differences of Objects

How can different objects be organized?

PROCEDURE

1. With several classmates, organize the buttons into three or more groups.

2. Compare your team's organization of the buttons with another team's organization.

WHAT DO YOU THINK?

- What characteristics did you use to organize the buttons?
- In what other ways could you have organized the buttons?

MATERIALS
buttons

Elements can be organized by similarities.

One way of organizing elements is by the masses of their atoms. Finding the masses of atoms was a difficult task for the chemists of the past. They could not place an atom on a pan balance. All they could do was find the mass of a very large number of atoms of a certain element and then infer the mass of a single one of them.

Remember that not all the atoms of an element have the same atomic mass number. Elements have isotopes. When chemists attempt to measure the mass of an atom, therefore, they are actually finding the average mass of all its isotopes. The **atomic mass** of the atoms of an element is the average mass of all the element's isotopes. Even before chemists knew how the atoms of different elements could be different, they knew atoms had different atomic masses.

Mendeleev's Periodic Table

In the early 1800s several scientists proposed systems to organize the elements based on their properties. None of these suggested methods worked very well until a Russian chemist named Dmitri Mendeleev (MENH-duh-LAY-uhf) decided to work on the problem.

In the 1860s, Mendeleev began thinking about how he could organize the elements based on their physical and chemical properties. He made a set of element cards. Each card contained the atomic mass of an atom of an element as well as any information about the element's properties. Mendeleev spent hours arranging the cards in various ways, looking for a relationship between properties and atomic mass.

The exercise led Mendeleev to think of listing the elements in a chart. In the rows of the chart, he placed those elements showing similar chemical properties. He arranged the rows so the atomic masses increased as one moved down each vertical column. It took Mendeleev quite a bit of thinking and rethinking to get all the relationships correct, but in 1869 he produced the first **periodic table** of the elements. We call it the periodic table because it shows a periodic, or repeating, pattern of properties of the elements. In the reproduction of Mendeleev's first table shown below, notice how he placed carbon (C) and silicon (Si), two elements known for their similarities, in the same row.

CHECK YOUR READING   What organizing method did Mendeleev use?

Dmitri Mendeleev (1834–1907) first published a periodic table of the elements in 1869.

— 70 —

ъ ней, мнѣ кажется, уже ясно выражается примѣнимость вы лемаго мною. начала ко всей совокупности элементовъ, пай ыхъ извѣстенъ съ достовѣрностію. На этотъ разъ я и желалъ ущественно найдти общую систему элементовъ. Вотъ этотъ ъ:

			Ti = 50	Zr = 90	? = 180.
			V = 51	Nb = 94	Ta = 182.
			Cr = 52	Mo = 96	W = 186.
			Mn = 55	Rh = 104,4	Pt = 197,4
			Fe = 56	Ru = 104,4	Ir = 198.
		Ni = Co = 59		Pl = 106,6,	Os = 199.
H = 1			Cu = 63,4	Ag = 108	Hg = 200.
Be = 9,4	Mg = 24		Zn = 65,2	Cd = 112	
B = 11	Al = 27,4		? = 68	Ur = 116	Au = 197?
C = 12	Si = 28		? = 70	Sn = 118	
N = 14	P = 31		As = 75	Sb = 122	Bi = 210
O = 16	S = 32		Se = 79,4	Te = 128?	

Predicting New Elements

When Mendeleev constructed his table, he left some empty spaces where no known elements fit the pattern. He predicted that new elements that would complete the chart would eventually be discovered. He even described some of the properties of these unknown elements.

At the start, many chemists found it hard to accept Mendeleev's predictions of unknown elements. Only six years after he published the table, however, the first of these elements—represented by the question mark after aluminum (Al) on his table—was discovered. This element was given the name gallium, after the country France (Gaul) where it was discovered. In the next 20 years, two other elements Mendeleev predicted would be discovered.

The periodic table organizes the atoms of the elements by properties and atomic number.

The modern periodic table on pages 20 and 21 differs from Mendeleev's table in several ways. For one thing, elements with similar properties are found in columns, not rows. More important, the elements are not arranged by atomic mass but by atomic number.

MAIN IDEA WEB
Make a main idea web to summarize the information you can learn from the periodic table.

Reading the Periodic Table

Each square of the periodic table gives particular information about the atoms of an element.

1 The number at the top of the square is the atomic number, which is the number of protons in the nucleus of an atom of that element.

2 The chemical symbol is an abbreviation for the element's name. It contains one or two letters. Some elements that have not yet been named are designated by temporary three-letter symbols.

3 The name of the element is written below the symbol.

4 The number below the name indicates the average atomic mass of all the isotopes of the element.

The color of the element's symbol indicates the physical state of the element at room temperature. White letters—such as the *H* for hydrogen in the box to the right—indicate a gas. Blue letters indicate a liquid, and black letters indicate a solid. The background colors of the squares indicate whether the element is a metal, nonmetal, or metalloid. These terms will be explained in the next section.

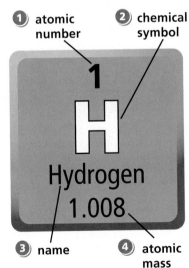

1 atomic number
2 chemical symbol
1
H
Hydrogen
1.008
3 name
4 atomic mass

The Periodic Table of the Elements

1

1								
1 **H** Hydrogen 1.008								

2

	2
2 **3** **Li** Lithium 6.941	**4** **Be** Beryllium 9.012
3 **11** **Na** Sodium 22.990	**12** **Mg** Magnesium 24.305

Period

Each row of the periodic table is called a **period**. As read from left to right, one proton and one electron are added from one element to the next.

		3	**4**	**5**	**6**	**7**	**8**	**9**
4	**19** **K** Potassium 39.098	**21** **Sc** Scandium 44.956	**22** **Ti** Titanium 47.87	**23** **V** Vanadium 50.942	**24** **Cr** Chromium 51.996	**25** **Mn** Manganese 54.938	**26** **Fe** Iron 55.845	**27** **Co** Cobalt 58.933

(Note: Period 4 begins with **20 Ca** Calcium 40.078 in group 2.)

20 **Ca** Calcium 40.078

5	**37** **Rb** Rubidium 85.468	**38** **Sr** Strontium 87.62	**39** **Y** Yttrium 88.906	**40** **Zr** Zirconium 91.224	**41** **Nb** Niobium 92.906	**42** **Mo** Molybdenum 95.94	**43** **Tc** Technetium (98)	**44** **Ru** Ruthenium 101.07	**45** **Rh** Rhodium 102.906

6	**55** **Cs** Cesium 132.905	**56** **Ba** Barium 137.327	**57** **La** Lanthanum 138.906	**72** **Hf** Hafnium 178.49	**73** **Ta** Tantalum 180.95	**74** **W** Tungsten 183.84	**75** **Re** Rhenium 186.207	**76** **Os** Osmium 190.23	**77** **Ir** Iridium 192.217

7	**87** **Fr** Francium (223)	**88** **Ra** Radium (226)	**89** **Ac** Actinium (227)	**104** **Rf** Rutherfordium (261)	**105** **Db** Dubnium (262)	**106** **Sg** Seaborgium (266)	**107** **Bh** Bohrium (264)	**108** **Hs** Hassium (269)	**109** **Mt** Meitnerium (268)

Group

Each column of the table is called a **group**. Elements in a group share similar properties. Groups are read from top to bottom.

58 **Ce** Cerium 140.116	**59** **Pr** Praseodymium 140.908	**60** **Nd** Neodymium 144.24	**61** **Pm** Promethium (145)	**62** **Sm** Samarium 150.36
90 **Th** Thorium 232.038	**91** **Pa** Protactinium 231.036	**92** **U** Uranium 238.029	**93** **Np** Neptunium (237)	**94** **Pu** Plutonium (244)

 Metal   Metalloid   Nonmetal   **Fe** Solid   Liquid   Gas

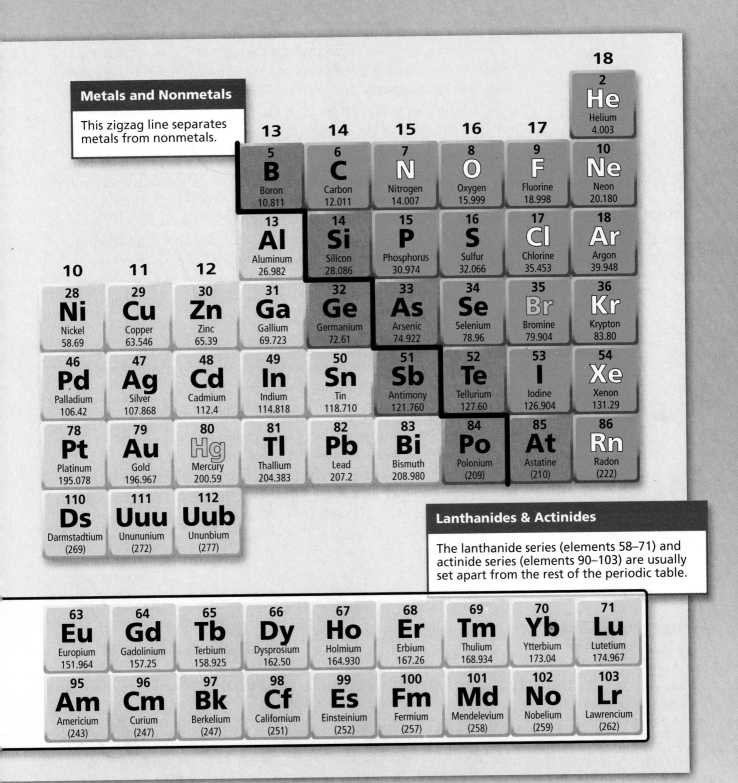

Metals and Nonmetals

This zigzag line separates metals from nonmetals.

			18
			2 **He** Helium 4.003

13	14	15	16	17	
5 **B** Boron 10.811	6 **C** Carbon 12.011	7 **N** Nitrogen 14.007	8 **O** Oxygen 15.999	9 **F** Fluorine 18.998	10 **Ne** Neon 20.180
13 **Al** Aluminum 26.982	14 **Si** Silicon 28.086	15 **P** Phosphorus 30.974	16 **S** Sulfur 32.066	17 **Cl** Chlorine 35.453	18 **Ar** Argon 39.948

10	11	12						
28 **Ni** Nickel 58.69	29 **Cu** Copper 63.546	30 **Zn** Zinc 65.39	31 **Ga** Gallium 69.723	32 **Ge** Germanium 72.61	33 **As** Arsenic 74.922	34 **Se** Selenium 78.96	35 **Br** Bromine 79.904	36 **Kr** Krypton 83.80
46 **Pd** Palladium 106.42	47 **Ag** Silver 107.868	48 **Cd** Cadmium 112.4	49 **In** Indium 114.818	50 **Sn** Tin 118.710	51 **Sb** Antimony 121.760	52 **Te** Tellurium 127.60	53 **I** Iodine 126.904	54 **Xe** Xenon 131.29
78 **Pt** Platinum 195.078	79 **Au** Gold 196.967	80 **Hg** Mercury 200.59	81 **Tl** Thallium 204.383	82 **Pb** Lead 207.2	83 **Bi** Bismuth 208.980	84 **Po** Polonium (209)	85 **At** Astatine (210)	86 **Rn** Radon (222)
110 **Ds** Darmstadtium (269)	111 **Uuu** Unununium (272)	112 **Uub** Ununbium (277)						

Lanthanides & Actinides

The lanthanide series (elements 58–71) and actinide series (elements 90–103) are usually set apart from the rest of the periodic table.

63 **Eu** Europium 151.964	64 **Gd** Gadolinium 157.25	65 **Tb** Terbium 158.925	66 **Dy** Dysprosium 162.50	67 **Ho** Holmium 164.930	68 **Er** Erbium 167.26	69 **Tm** Thulium 168.934	70 **Yb** Ytterbium 173.04	71 **Lu** Lutetium 174.967
95 **Am** Americium (243)	96 **Cm** Curium (247)	97 **Bk** Berkelium (247)	98 **Cf** Californium (251)	99 **Es** Einsteinium (252)	100 **Fm** Fermium (257)	101 **Md** Mendelevium (258)	102 **No** Nobelium (259)	103 **Lr** Lawrencium (262)

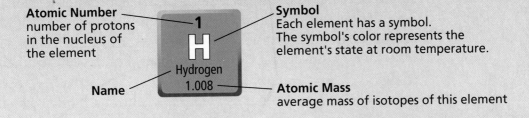

Atomic Number
number of protons in the nucleus of the element

1
H
Hydrogen
1.008

Symbol
Each element has a symbol. The symbol's color represents the element's state at room temperature.

Name

Atomic Mass
average mass of isotopes of this element

Groups and Periods

Elements in a vertical column of the periodic table show similarities in their chemical and physical properties. The elements in a column are known as a **group,** and they are labeled by a number at the top of the column. Sometimes a group is called a family of elements, because these elements seem to be related.

The illustration at the left shows Group 17, commonly referred to as the halogen group. Halogens tend to combine easily with many other elements and compounds, especially with the elements in Groups 1 and 2. Although the halogens have some similarities to one another, you can see from the periodic table that their physical properties are not the same. Fluorine and chlorine are gases, bromine is a liquid, and iodine and astatine are solids at room temperature. Remember that the members of a family of elements are related but not identical.

Metals like copper can be used to make containers for water. Some metals—such as lithium, sodium, and potassium—however, react violently if they come in contact with water. They are all in the same group, the vertical column labeled 1 on the table.

Each horizontal row in the periodic table is called a **period.** Properties of elements change in a predictable way from one end of a period to the other. In the illustration below, which shows Period 3, the elements on the far left are metals and the ones on the far right are nonmetals. The chemical properties of the elements show a progression; similar progressions appear in the periods above and below this one.

The elements in Group 17, the halogens, show many similarities.

Period 3 contains elements with a wide range of properties. Aluminum (Al) is used to make drink cans, while argon (Ar) is a gas used in light bulbs.

Trends in the Periodic Table

Because the periodic table organizes elements by properties, an element's position in the table can give information about the element. Remember that atoms form ions by gaining or losing electrons. Atoms of elements on the left side of the table form positive ions easily. For example, Group 1 atoms lose an electron to form ions with one positive charge (1+). Atoms of the elements in Group 2, likewise, can lose two electrons to form ions with a charge of 2+. At the other side of the table, the atoms of elements in Group 18 normally do not form ions at all. Atoms of elements in Group 17, however, often gain one electron to form a negative ion (1–). Similarly, the atoms of elements in Group 16 can gain two electrons to form a 2– ion. The atoms of the elements in Groups 3 to 12 all form positive ions, but the charge can vary.

Other information about atoms can be determined by their position in the table. The illustration to the right shows how the sizes of atoms vary across periods and within groups. An atom's size is important because it affects how the atom will react with another atom.

The densities of elements also follow a pattern. Density generally increases from the top of a group to the bottom. Within a period, however, the elements at the left and right sides of the table are the least dense, and the elements in the middle are the most dense. The element osmium (Os) has the highest known density, and it is located at the center of the table.

Chemists cannot predict the exact size or density of an atom of one element based on that of another. These trends, nonetheless, are a valuable tool in predicting the properties of different substances. The fact that the trends appeared after the periodic table was organized by atomic number was a victory for all of the scientists like Mendeleev who went looking for them all those years before.

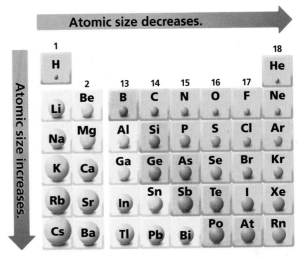

Atomic size is one property that changes in a predictable way across, up, and down the periodic table.

CHECK YOUR READING What are some properties that can be related to position on the periodic table?

1.2 Review

KEY CONCEPTS

1. How is the modern periodic table organized?

2. What information about an atom's properties can you read from the periodic table?

3. How are the relationships of elements in a group different from the relationships of elements in a period?

CRITICAL THINKING

4. **Infer** Would you expect strontium (Sr) to be more like potassium (K) or bromine (Br)? Why?

5. **Predict** Barium (Ba) is in Group 2. Recall that atoms in Group 1 lose one electron to form ions with a 1+ charge. What type of ion does barium form?

CHALLENGE

6. **Analyze** Explain how chemists can state with certainty that no one will discover an element between sulfur (S) and chlorine (Cl).

CHAPTER INVESTIGATION

Modeling Atomic Masses

OVERVIEW AND PURPOSE Atoms are extremely small. They are so small, in fact, that a single drop of water contains more atoms than you could count in a lifetime! Measuring the masses of atoms to discover the patterns in the periodic table was not an easy task for scientists in the past. This investigation will give you some sense of how scientists determined the mass of atoms. You will

- compare the masses of different film can "atoms"
- predict the number of washers in each film can "atom"

▶ Procedure

1 Create a data table similar to the one shown on the sample notebook page.

2 Find the mass of one empty film can. Record this mass in the second row of the table.

3 Collect the four film cans labeled A, B, C, and D in advance by your teacher. Each can contains a different number of washers and represents a different atom. The washers represent the protons and neutrons in an atom's nucleus.

4 Measure the mass of each of the four film cans. Record the masses of the film can atoms in the first row of your data table.

5 Subtract the mass of an empty film can from the mass of each film can atom. Record the differences in the correct spaces in your data table. These masses represent the masses of the washers in your film can atoms. Think of these masses as the masses of the nuclei.

6 Divide the mass of the washers in can B by the mass of the washers in can A. Record the value under the mass of the washers in can B.

MATERIALS
- empty film can
- balance
- 4 filled film cans

7 Repeat step 6 for film can atoms A, C, and D. Record the value under the masses of the washers in each can.

8 Round the values you obtained in steps 6 and 7 to the nearest whole number. Record the rounded figures in the next row of the table.

Observe and Analyze

1. **RECORD OBSERVATIONS** Be sure your data table and calculations are complete. Double-check your arithmetic.

2. **ANALYZE DATA** Examine your data table. Do you notice any patterns in how the masses increase? Given that all the washers in the film can atoms have identical masses, what might the ratio of the mass of the washers to the smallest mass tell you?

3. **PREDICT** Assume there is only one washer in can A. Estimate the number of washers in the other cans and record your estimates in the last row of the table.

4. **GRAPH DATA** On a sheet of graph paper, plot the masses (in grams) of the washers in the film can atoms on the *y*-axis and the number of washers in each can on the *x*-axis. Connect the points on the graph.

5. **INTERPRET DATA** Compare the masses of your film can atoms with the masses of the first four atoms on the periodic table. Which represents which?

Conclude

1. **IDENTIFY LIMITS** What can't this activity tell you about the identity of your film can atoms? (**Hint:** Protons and neutrons in real atoms have about the same mass.)

2. **INFER** Hydrogen has only a single proton in its nucleus. If your film can atoms represent the first four elements in the periodic table, what are the numbers of protons and neutrons in each atom?

3. **APPLY** Single atoms are far too small to place on a balance. How do you think scientists determine the masses of real atoms?

INVESTIGATE Further

CHALLENGE Use a periodic table to find the masses of the next two atoms (boron and carbon). How many washers would you need to make film can atom models for each?

Modeling Atomic Masses

Observe and Analyze

Table 1. Masses of Film Can Atoms

	A	B	C	D
Mass of film can atom (g)				
Mass of empty film can (g)				
Mass of washers (g)				
Mass of washers divided by can A				
Value rounded to nearest whole number				
Estimated number of washers in each can				

The periodic table is a map of the elements.

BEFORE, you learned

- The periodic table is organized into groups of elements with similar characteristics
- The periodic table organizes elements according to their properties

NOW, you will learn

- How elements are classified as metals, nonmetals, and metalloids
- About different groups of elements
- About radioactive elements

VOCABULARY

reactive p. 26
metal p. 27
nonmetal p. 29
metalloid p. 30
radioactivity p. 30
half-life p. 32

THINK ABOUT

How are elements different?

The photograph shows common uses of the elements copper, aluminum, and argon: copper in a penny, aluminum in a pie plate, and argon in a light bulb. Each element is located in a different part of the periodic table, and each has a very different use. Find these elements on the periodic table. What other elements are near these?

The periodic table has distinct regions.

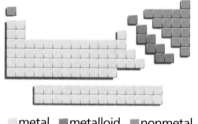

▢metal ▪metalloid ▪nonmetal

The periodic table is a kind of map of the elements. Just as a country's location on the globe gives you information about its climate, an atom's position on the periodic table indicates the properties of its element. The periodic table has three main regions—metals on the left, nonmetals (except hydrogen) on the right, and metalloids in between. The periodic table on pages 20 and 21 indicates these regions with different colors. A yellow box indicates a metal; green, a nonmetal; and purple, a metalloid.

An element's position in the table also indicates how reactive it is. The term **reactive** indicates how likely an element is to undergo a chemical change. Most elements are somewhat reactive and combine with other materials. The atoms of the elements in Groups 1 and 17 are the most reactive. The elements of Group 18 are the least reactive of all the elements.

CHECK YOUR READING How does the periodic table resemble a map?

B 26 Unit: Chemical Interactions

Most elements are metals.

When you look at the periodic table, it is obvious from the color that most of the elements are metals. In general, **metals** are elements that conduct electricity and heat well and have a shiny appearance. Metals can be shaped easily by pounding, bending, or being drawn into a long wire. Except for mercury, which is a liquid, metals are solids at room temperature.

Sodium is a metal that is so soft it can be cut with a knife at room temperature.

You probably can name many uses for the metal **copper**.

Aluminum is often used for devices that must be strong and light.

Reactive Metals

The metals in Group 1 of the periodic table, the alkali metals, are very reactive. Sodium and potassium are often stored in oil to keep them away from air. When exposed to air, these elements react rapidly with oxygen and water vapor. The ions of these metals, Na^+ and K^+, are important for life, and play an essential role in the functioning of living cells.

The metals in Group 2, the alkaline earth metals, are less reactive than the alkali metals. They are still more reactive than most other metals, however. Calcium ions are an essential part of your diet. Your bones and teeth contain calcium ions. Magnesium is a light, inexpensive metal that is often combined with other metals when a lightweight material is needed, such as for airplane frames.

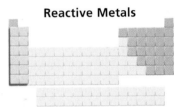

Reactive Metals

Transition Metals

The elements in Groups 3–12 are called the transition metals. Among these metals are some of the earliest known elements, such as copper, gold, silver, and iron. Transition metals are generally less reactive than most other metals. Because gold and silver are easily shaped and do not react easily, they have been used for thousands of years to make jewelry and coins. Ancient artifacts made from transition metals can be found in many museums and remain relatively unchanged since the time they were made. Today, dimes and quarters are made of copper and nickel, and pennies are made of zinc with a coating of copper. Transition metal ions even are found in the foods you eat.

Transition Metals

The properties of the transition metals make them particularly important to industry. Iron is the main part of steel, a material used for bridges and buildings. Most electric wires and many other electrical devices are made of copper. Copper is also used to make water pipes. Indeed, it would be hard to think of an industry that doesn't make use of transition metals.

Although other transition metals may be less familiar, many of them are important for modern technology. The tiny coil of wire inside incandescent light bulbs is made of tungsten. Platinum is in the catalytic converters that reduce pollution from automobile engines.

For many applications, two or more metals are combined to form an alloy. Alloys can be stronger, less likely to corrode, or easier to shape than pure metals. Steel, which is stronger than the pure iron it contains, often includes other transition metals, such as nickel, chromium, or manganese. Brass, an alloy of copper and zinc, is stronger than either metal alone. Jewelry is often made of an alloy of silver and copper, which is stronger than pure silver.

Rare Earth Elements

Rare Earth Elements

The rare earth elements are the elements in the top row of the two rows of metals that are usually shown outside the main body of the periodic table. Taking these elements out of the main body of the table makes the table more compact. The rare earth elements are often referred to as lanthanides because they follow the element lanthanum (La) on the table. They are called rare earth elements because scientists once thought that these elements were available only in tiny amounts in Earth's crust. As mining methods improved, scientists learned that the rare earths were actually not so rare at all—only hard to isolate in pure form.

More and more uses are being found for the rare earth elements. Europium (Eu), for example, is used as a coating for some television tubes. Praseodymium (Pr) provides a protective coating against harmful radiation in the welder's helmet in the photograph on the right.

Nonmetals and metalloids have a wide range of properties.

The elements to the right side of the periodic table are called **nonmetals.** As the name implies, the properties of nonmetals tend to be the opposite of those of metals. The properties of nonmetals also tend to vary more from element to element than the properties of the metals do. Many of them are gases at room temperature, and one—bromine—is a liquid. The solid nonmetals often have dull surfaces and cannot be shaped by hammering or drawing into wires. Nonmetals are generally poor conductors of heat and electric current.

The main components of the air that you breathe are the nonmetal elements nitrogen and oxygen. Nitrogen is a fairly unreactive element, but oxygen reacts easily to form compounds with many other elements. Burning and rusting are two familiar types of reactions involving oxygen. Compounds containing carbon are essential to living things. Two forms of the element carbon are graphite, which is a soft, slippery black material, and diamond, a hard crystal. Sulfur is a bright yellow powder that can be mined from deposits of the pure element.

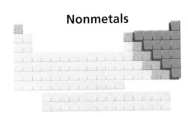

Nonmetals

Halogens

The elements in Group 17 are commonly known as halogens, from Greek words meaning "forming salts." Halogens are very reactive non-metals that easily form compounds called salts with many metals. Because they are so reactive, halogens are often used to kill harmful microorganisms. For example, the halogen chlorine is used to clean drinking water and to prevent the growth of algae in swimming pools. Solutions containing iodine are often used in hospitals and doctors' offices to kill germs on skin.

Halogens and Noble Gases

Noble Gases

Group 18 elements are called the noble, or inert, gases because they almost never react with other elements. Argon gas makes up about one percent of the atmosphere. The other noble gases are found in the atmosphere in smaller amounts. Colorful lights, such as those in the photograph on the right, are made by passing an electric current through tubes filled with neon, krypton, xenon, or argon gas. Argon gas also is placed in tungsten filament light bulbs, because it will not react with the hot filament.

Noble gases produce the light for many signs.

 CHECK YOUR READING Where on Earth can you find noble gases?

Metalloids

Metalloids

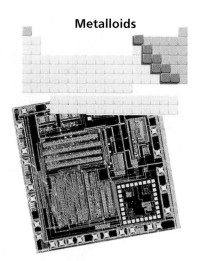

The metalloid silicon is found in sand and in computer microchips.

Metalloids are elements that have properties of both metals and nonmetals. In the periodic table, they lie on either side of a zigzag line separating metals from nonmetals. The most common metalloid is silicon. Silicon atoms are the second most common atoms in Earth's crust.

Metalloids often make up the semiconductors found in electronic devices. Semiconductors are special materials that conduct electricity under some conditions and not under others. Silicon, gallium, and germanium are three semiconductors used in computer chips.

Some atoms can change their identity.

Radioactive Elements

The identity of an element is determined by the number of protons in its nucleus. Chemical changes do not affect the nucleus, so chemical changes don't change one type of atom into another. There are, however, conditions under which the number of protons in a nucleus can change and so change the identity of an atom.

Recall that the nucleus of an atom contains protons and neutrons. Attractive forces between protons and neutrons hold the nucleus together even though protons repel one another. We say an atomic nucleus is stable when these attractive forces keep it together.

Each element has isotopes with different numbers of neutrons. The stability of a nucleus depends on the right balance of protons and neutrons. If there are too few or too many neutrons, the nucleus may become unstable. When this happens, particles are produced from the nucleus of the atom to restore the balance. This change is accompanied by a release of energy.

If the production of particles changes the number of protons, the atom is transformed into an atom of a different element. In the early 1900s, physicist Marie Curie named the process by which atoms produce energy and particles **radioactivity.** Curie was the first person to isolate polonium and radium, two radioactive elements.

An isotope is radioactive if the nucleus has too many or too few neutrons. Most elements have radioactive isotopes, although these isotopes are rare for small atoms. For the heaviest of elements—those beyond bismuth (Bi)—all of the isotopes are radioactive.

Scientists study radioactivity with a device called a Geiger counter. The Geiger counter detects the particles from the breakup of the atomic nucleus with audible clicks. More clicks indicate that more particles are being produced.

 CHECK YOUR READING How can an atom of one element change into an atom of a different element?

Uses of Radioactivity in Medicine

The radiation produced from unstable nuclei is used in hospitals to diagnose and treat patients. Some forms of radiation from nuclei are used to destroy harmful tumors inside a person's body without performing an operation. Another medical use of radiation is to monitor the activity of certain organs in the body. A patient is injected with a solution containing a radioactive isotope. Isotopes of a given atom move through the body in the same way whether or not they are radioactive. Doctors detect the particles produced by the radioactive isotopes to determine where and how the body is using the substance.

Although radiation has its benefits, in large doses it is harmful to living things and should be avoided. Radiation can damage or kill cells, and the energy from its particles can burn the skin. Prolonged exposure to radiation has been linked to cancer and other health problems.

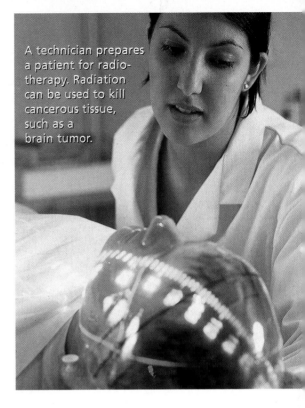

A technician prepares a patient for radio-therapy. Radiation can be used to kill cancerous tissue, such as a brain tumor.

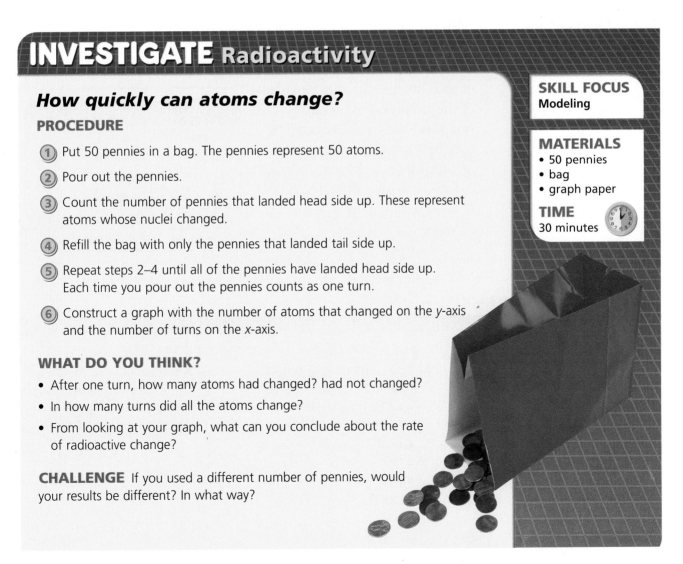

INVESTIGATE Radioactivity

How quickly can atoms change?

PROCEDURE

1. Put 50 pennies in a bag. The pennies represent 50 atoms.

2. Pour out the pennies.

3. Count the number of pennies that landed head side up. These represent atoms whose nuclei changed.

4. Refill the bag with only the pennies that landed tail side up.

5. Repeat steps 2–4 until all of the pennies have landed head side up. Each time you pour out the pennies counts as one turn.

6. Construct a graph with the number of atoms that changed on the y-axis and the number of turns on the x-axis.

WHAT DO YOU THINK?

- After one turn, how many atoms had changed? had not changed?
- In how many turns did all the atoms change?
- From looking at your graph, what can you conclude about the rate of radioactive change?

CHALLENGE If you used a different number of pennies, would your results be different? In what way?

SKILL FOCUS
Modeling

MATERIALS
- 50 pennies
- bag
- graph paper

TIME
30 minutes

Radioactive Decay

VISUALIZATION
CLASSZONE.COM

Watch how a radioactive element decays over time.

Radioactive atoms produce energy and particles from their nuclei. The identity of these atoms changes because the number of protons changes. This process is known as radioactive decay. Over time, all of the atoms of a radioactive isotope will change into atoms of another element.

Radioactive decay occurs at a steady rate that is characteristic of the particular isotope. The amount of time that it takes for one-half of the atoms in a particular sample to decay is called the **half-life** of the isotope. For example, if you had 1000 atoms of a radioactive isotope with a half-life of 1 year, 500 of the atoms would change into another element over the course of a year. In the next year, 250 more atoms would decay. The illustration to the right shows how the amount of the original isotope would decrease over time.

The half-life is a characteristic of each isotope and is independent of the amount of material. A half-life is also not affected by conditions such as temperature or pressure. Half-lives of isotopes can range from a small fraction of a second to many billions of years.

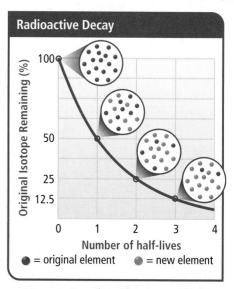

Radioactive Decay

Original Isotope Remaining (%)

100
50
25
12.5

0 1 2 3 4
Number of half-lives
● = original element   ● = new element

Half-Lives of Selected Elements

Isotope	Half-Life
Uranium-238	4,510,000,000 years
Carbon-14	5,730 years
Radon-222	3.82 days
Lead-214	27 minutes
Polonium-214	.00016 seconds

1.3 Review

KEY CONCEPTS

1. What are the three main classes of elements in the periodic table?

2. What are the major characteristics of metals?

3. How can an atom of one element change to an atom of another element?

CRITICAL THINKING

4. **Compare** Use the periodic table to determine whether a carbon or a fluorine atom would be more reactive.

5. **Calculate** What fraction of a radioactive sample remains after three half-lives?

● CHALLENGE

6. **Analyze** Why do you think the noble gases were among the last of the naturally occurring elements to be discovered?

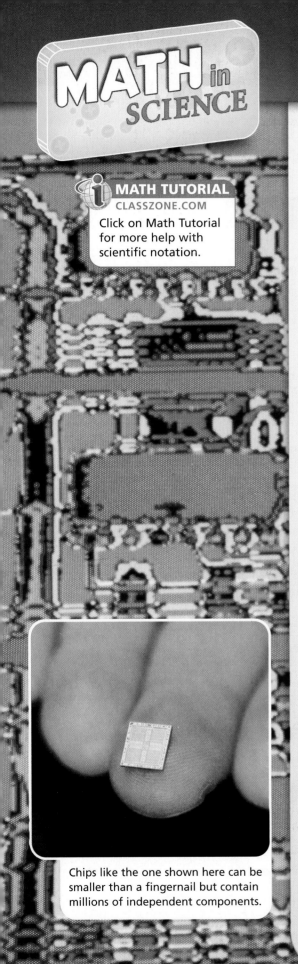

MATH TUTORIAL
CLASSZONE.COM

Click on Math Tutorial for more help with scientific notation.

Numbers with Many Zeros

Semiconductor devices are at the heart of the modern personal computer. Today tiny chips can contain more than 42,000,000 connections and perform about 3,000,000,000 calculations per second. Computers have little problem working with such large numbers. Scientists, however, use a scientific notation as a short-hand way to write large numbers. Scientific notation expresses a very large or very small number as the product of a number between 1 and 10 and a power of 10.

Example

Large Number How would you express the number 6,400,000,000—the approximate population of the world—in scientific notation?

(1) Look at the number and count how many spaces you would need to move the decimal point to get a number between 1 and 10.

$$6, \overset{9}{4} \overset{8}{0} \overset{7}{0}, \overset{6}{0} \overset{5}{0} \overset{4}{0}, \overset{3}{0} \overset{2}{0} \overset{1}{0}$$

(2) Place the decimal point in the space and multiply the number by the appropriate power of 10. The power of 10 will be equivalent to the number of spaces you moved the decimal point.

ANSWER 6.4×10^9

Small Number How would you express 0.0000023 in scientific notation?

(1) Count the number of places you need to move the decimal point to get a number between 1 and 10. This time you move the decimal point to the right, not the left.

$$0. \underset{1}{0} \underset{2}{0} \underset{3}{0} \underset{4}{0} \underset{5}{0} \underset{6}{2} 3$$

(2) The power of 10 you need to multiply this number by is still equal to the number of places you moved the decimal point. Place a negative sign in front of it to indicate that you moved the decimal point to the right.

ANSWER 2.3×10^{-6}

Answer the following questions.

1. Express the following numbers in scientific notation:
(a) 75,000   (b) 54,000,000,000   (c) 0.0000064

2. Express these numbers in decimal form:
(a) 6.0×10^{24} (b) 7.4×10^{22} (c) 5.7×10^{-10}

CHALLENGE What is 2.2×10^{22} subtracted from 4.6×10^{22}?

Chips like the one shown here can be smaller than a fingernail but contain millions of independent components.

the **BIG** idea

A substance's atomic structure determines its physical and chemical properties.

CONTENT REVIEW
CLASSZONE.COM

KEY CONCEPTS SUMMARY

1.1 **Atoms are the smallest form of elements.**

- All matter is made of the atoms of approximately 100 elements.
- Atoms are made of protons, neutrons, and electrons.
- Different elements are made of different atoms.
- Atoms form ions by gaining or losing electrons.

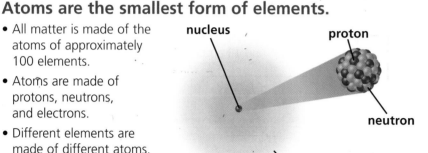

nucleus

proton

neutron

electron cloud

VOCABULARY
proton p. 11
neutron p. 11
nucleus p. 11
electron p. 11
atomic number p. 12
atomic mass number p. 12
isotope p. 12
ion p. 14

1.2 **Elements make up the periodic table.**

- Elements can be organized by similarities.
- The periodic table organizes the atoms of the elements by properties and atomic number.

Group 17

F
Cl
Br
I
At

Period 3 Na Mg   Al Si P S Cl Ar

Groups of elements have similar properties.
Elements in a period have varying properties.

VOCABULARY
atomic mass p. 17
periodic table p. 18
group p. 22
period p. 22

1.3 **The periodic table is a map of the elements.**

- The periodic table has distinct regions.
- Most elements are metals.
- Nonmetals and metalloids have a wide range of properties.
- Some atoms can change their identity through radioactive decay.

☐ metal ▧ metalloid ▨ nonmetal

VOCABULARY
reactive p. 26
metal p. 27
nonmetal p. 29
metalloid p. 30
radioactivity p. 30
half-life p. 32

Reviewing Vocabulary

Describe how the vocabulary terms in the following pairs are related to each other. Explain the relationship in a one- or two-sentence answer. Underline each vocabulary term in your answer.

1. isotope, nucleus

2. atomic mass, atomic number

3. electron, proton

4. atomic number, atomic mass number

5. group, period

6. metals, nonmetals

7. radioactivity, half-life

Reviewing Key Concepts

Multiple Choice *Choose the letter of the best answer.*

8. The central part of an atom is called the
  a. electron   **c.** proton
  b. nucleus   **d.** neutron

9. The electric charge on a proton is
  a. positive   **c.** neutral
  b. negative   **d.** changing

10. The number of protons in the nucleus is the
  a. atomic mass   **c.** atomic number
  b. isotope   **d.** half-life

11. Nitrogen has atomic number 7. An isotope of nitrogen containing seven neutrons would be
  a. nitrogen-13   **c.** nitrogen-15
  b. nitrogen-14   **d.** nitrogen-16

12. How does the size of a negative ion compare to the size of the atom that formed it?
  a. It's smaller.
  b. It's larger.
  c. It's the same size.
  d. It varies.

13. The modern periodic table is organized by
  a. size of atom
  b. atomic mass
  c. number of neutrons
  d. atomic number

14. Elements in a group have
  a. a wide range of chemical properties
  b. the same atomic radius
  c. similar chemical properties
  d. the same number of protons

15. Elements in a period have
  a. a wide range of chemical properties
  b. the same atomic radius
  c. similar chemical properties
  d. the same number of protons

16. From left to right in a period, the size of atoms
  a. increases   **c.** remains the same
  b. decreases   **d.** shows no pattern

17. The elements in Group 1 of the periodic table are commonly called the
  a. alkali metals   **c.** alkaline earth metals
  b. transition metals   **d.** rare earth metals

18. The isotope nitrogen-13 has a half-life of 10 minutes. If you start with 40 grams of this isotope, how many grams will you have left after 20 minutes?
  a. 10   **c.** 20
  b. 15   **d.** 30

Short Answer *Write a short answer to each question. You may need to consult a periodic table.*

19. Rubidium forms the positive ion Rb$^+$. Is this ion larger or smaller than the neutral atom? Explain.

20. How can you find the number of neutrons in the isotope nitrogen-16?

21. Explain how density varies across and up and down the periodic table.

22. Place these elements in order from least reactive to most reactive: nickel (Ni), xenon (Xe), lithium (Li). How did you determine the order?

Thinking Critically

The table below lists some properties of six elements. Use the information and your knowledge of the properties of elements to answer the next three questions.

Element	Appearance	Density (g/cm³)	Conducts Electricity
A	dark purple crystals	4.93	no
B	shiny silvery solid	0.97	yes
C	shiny silvery solid	22.65	yes
D	yellow powder	2.07	no
E	shiny gray solid	5.32	semiconductor
F	shiny bluish solid	8.91	yes

23. ANALYZE Based on the listed properties, identify each of the elements as a metal, nonmetal, or metalloid.

24. APPLY Which would weigh more: a cube of element A or a same-sized cube of element D?

25. HYPOTHESIZE Which element(s) do you think you might find in electronic devices? Why?

26. HYPOTHESIZE The thyroid gland, located in your throat, secretes hormones. In 1924 iodine was added to table salt. As more and more Americans used iodized salt, the number of cases of thyroid diseases decreased. Write a hypothesis that explains the observed decrease in thyroid-related diseases.

27. INFER How does the size of a beryllium (Be) atom compare with the size of an oxygen (O) atom?

28. PREDICT Although noble gases do not naturally react with other elements, xenon and krypton have been made to react with halogens such as chlorine in laboratories. Why are the halogens most likely to react with the noble gases?

Below is an element square from the periodic table. Use it to answer the next two questions.

29. CALCULATE One of the more common isotopes of mercury is mercury-200. How many protons and neutrons are in the nucleus of mercury-200?

30. INFER Cadmium occupies the square directly above mercury on the periodic table. Is a cadium atom larger or smaller than a mercury atom?

31. CALCULATE An isotope has a half-life of 40 minutes. How much of a 100-gram sample would remain unchanged after two hours?

32. APPLY When a uranium atom with 92 protons and 146 neutrons undergoes radioactive decay, it produces a particle that consists of two protons and two neutrons from its nucleus. Into which element is the uranium atom transformed?

the BIG idea

33. ANALYZE Look again at the photograph on pages 6–7. Answer the question again, using what you have learned in the chapter.

34. DRAW CONCLUSIONS Suppose you've been given the ability to take apart and assemble atoms. How could you turn lead into gold?

35. ANALYZE Explain how the structure of an atom determines its place in the periodic table.

UNIT PROJECTS

If you are doing a unit project, make a folder for your project. Include in your folder a list of the resources you will need, the date on which the project is due, and a schedule to track your progress. Begin gathering data.

Interpreting Tables

The table below shows part of the periodic table of elements.

			Group						
	1	2	13	14	15	16	17	18	

Period

	1 H	2							2 He
2	3 Li	4 Be	5 B	6 C	7 N	8 O	9 F	10 Ne	
3	11 Na	12 Mg	13 Al	14 Si	15 P	16 S	17 Cl	18 Ar	
4	19 K	20 Ca	31 Ga	32 Ge	33 As	34 Se	35 Br	36 Kr	

Answer the questions based on the information given in the table.

1. What does the number above the symbol for each element represent?

  a. Its number of isotopes

  b. Its atomic number

  c. Its number of neutrons

  d. Its atomic mass

2. The atom of what element is in Period 4, Group 13?

  a. Na   **c.** Al

  b. Ga   **d.** K

3. What do the elements on the far right of the table (He, Ne, Ar, and Kr) have in common?

  a. They do not generally react with other elements.

  b. They are in liquids under normal conditions.

  c. They are metals that rust easily.

  d. They are very reactive gases.

4. How many electrons does a neutral chlorine (Cl) atom contain?

  a. 16   **c.** 18

  b. 17   **d.** 19

5. If a sodium (Na) atom loses one electron to form a positive ion, how many electrons would lithium (Li) lose to form a positive ion?

  a. 0   **c.** 2

  b. 1   **d.** 3

6. If a fluorine (F) atom gains one electron to form a negative ion, how many electrons would bromine (Br) gain to form a negative ion?

  a. 0   **c.** 2

  b. 1   **d.** 3

Extended Response

Answer the following two questions in detail. Include some of the terms shown in the word box at right. Underline each term you use in your answer.

electron	nucleus	proton
isotope	neutron	radioactivity

7. Democritus was an ancient Greek philosopher who claimed that all matter was made of tiny particles he called atoms. Democritus said that all atoms were made of the same material. The objects of the world differed because each was made of atoms of different sizes and shapes. How does the modern view of atoms differ from this ancient view? How is it similar?

8. Half-life is a measure of the time it takes half of the radioactive atoms in a substance to decay into other atoms. If you know how much radioactive material an object had to begin with, how could you use half-life to determine its age now?

CHAPTER 2

Chemical Bonds and Compounds

the BIG idea

The properties of compounds depend on their atoms and chemical bonds.

Key Concepts

SECTION 2.1
Elements combine to form compounds.
Learn the difference between elements and compounds. Learn how to write and name chemical compounds.

SECTION 2.2
Chemical bonds hold compounds together.
Learn about the different types of chemical bonds.

SECTION 2.3
Substances' properties depend on their bonds.
Learn how bonds give compounds certain properties.

Internet Preview

CLASSZONE.COM

Chapter 2 online resources: Content Review, two Visualizations, two Resource Centers, Math Tutorial, Test Practice

How do these skydivers stay together? How is this similar to the way atoms stay together?

EXPLORE (the BIG idea)

Mixing It Up

Get some red and yellow modeling compound. Make three red and two yellow balls, each about the diameter of a nickel. Blend one red and one yellow ball together. Blend one yellow and two red balls together.

Observe and Think How different do your combinations look from the original? from each other?

The Shape of Things

Pour some salt onto dark paper. Look at the grains through a hand lens. Try to observe a single grain.

Observe and Think What do you notice about the salt grains? What do you think might affect the way the grains look?

Internet Activity: Bonding

Go to **ClassZone.com** and watch the animation showing ionic and covalent bonding. Observe the differences in the two types of bonding.

Observe and Think What's the difference between an ionic and a covalent bond? Explain how covalent bonding can have different characteristics.

NSTA scilinks.org
SCi LINKS

Compounds **Code: MDL023**

CHAPTER 2
Getting Ready to Learn

◀ CONCEPT REVIEW

- Electrons occupy a cloud around an atom's nucleus.
- Atoms form ions by losing or gaining electrons.

◀ VOCABULARY REVIEW

electron p. 11

element *See Glossary.*

CONTENT REVIEW
CLASSZONE.COM
Review concepts and vocabulary.

▶ TAKING NOTES

MAIN IDEA AND DETAIL NOTES

Make a two-column chart. Write the main ideas, such as those in the blue headings, in the column on the left. Write details about each of those main ideas in the column on the right.

VOCABULARY STRATEGY

Place each vocabulary term at the center of a **description wheel** diagram. Write some words describing it on the spokes.

See the Note-Taking Handbook on pages R45–R51.

SCIENCE NOTEBOOK

MAIN IDEAS	DETAIL NOTES
Atoms combine in predictable numbers.	• Each compound has a specific ratio of atoms. • A ratio is a comparison between two quantities.
Writing chemical formulas	• Find symbols on the periodic table. • Note ratio of atoms with subscripts.

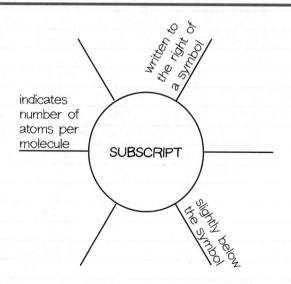

2.1

KEY CONCEPT

Elements combine to form compounds.

 BEFORE, you learned

- Atoms make up everything on Earth
- Atoms react with different atoms to form compounds

 NOW, you will learn

- How compounds differ from the elements that make them
- How a chemical formula represents the ratio of atoms in a compound
- How the same atoms can form different compounds

VOCABULARY

chemical formula p. 43
subscript p. 43

EXPLORE Compounds

How are compounds different from elements?

PROCEDURE

① Examine the lump of carbon, the beaker of water, and the sugar. Record your observations of each.

② Light the candle. Pour some sugar into a test tube and heat it over the candle for several minutes. Record your observations.

WHAT DO YOU THINK?

- The sugar is made up of atoms of the same elements that are in the carbon and water. How are sugar, carbon, and water different from one another?
- Does heating the sugar give you any clue that sugar contains more than one element?

MATERIALS

- carbon
- water
- sugar
- test tube
- test-tube holder
- candle
- matches

Compounds have different properties from the elements that make them.

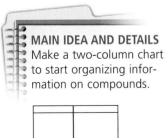

MAIN IDEA AND DETAILS
Make a two-column chart to start organizing information on compounds.

If you think about all of the different substances around you, it is clear that they cannot all be elements. In fact, while there are just over 100 elements, there are millions of different substances. Most substances are compounds. A compound is a substance made of atoms of two or more different elements. Just as the 26 letters in the alphabet can form thousands of words, the elements in the periodic table can form millions of compounds.

The atoms of different elements are held together in compounds by chemical bonds. Chemical bonds can hold atoms together in large networks or in small groups. Bonds help determine the properties of a compound.

Chapter 2: **Chemical Bonds and Compounds** 41 **B**

The properties of a compound depend not only on which atoms the compound contains, but also on how the atoms are arranged. Atoms of carbon and hydrogen, for example, can combine to form many thousands of different compounds. These compounds include natural gas, components of automobile gasoline, the hard waxes in candles, and many plastics. Each of these compounds has a certain number of carbon and hydrogen atoms arranged in a specific way.

The properties of compounds are often very different from the properties of the elements that make them. For example, water is made from two atoms of hydrogen bonded to one atom of oxygen. At room temperature, hydrogen and oxygen are both colorless, odorless gases, and they remain gases down to extremely low temperatures. Water, however, is a liquid at temperatures up to 100°C (212°F) and a solid below 0°C (32°F). Sugar is a compound composed of atoms of carbon, hydrogen, and oxygen. Its properties, however, are unlike those of carbon, hydrogen, or oxygen.

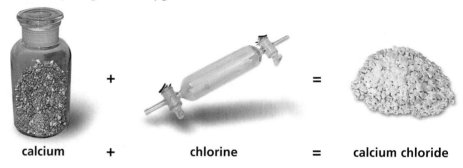

calcium   +   chlorine   =   calcium chloride

The picture above shows what happens when the elements calcium and chlorine combine to form the compound calcium chloride. Calcium is a soft, silvery metallic solid. Chlorine is a greenish-yellow gas that is extremely reactive and poisonous to humans. Calcium chloride, however, is a nonpoisonous white solid. People who live in cold climates often use calcium chloride to melt the ice that forms on streets in the wintertime.

CHECK YOUR READING How do the properties of a compound compare with the properties of the elements that make it?

Atoms combine in predictable numbers.

A given compound always contains atoms of elements in a specific ratio. For example, the compound ammonia always has three hydrogen atoms for every nitrogen atom—a 3 to 1 ratio of hydrogen to nitrogen. This same 3:1 ratio holds for every sample of ammonia, under all physical conditions. A substance with a different ratio of hydrogen to nitrogen atoms is not ammonia. For example, hydrazoic acid also contains atoms of hydrogen and nitrogen but in a ratio of one hydrogen atom to three nitrogen atoms, or 1:3.

INVESTIGATE Element Ratios

How can you model a compound?

PROCEDURE

1. Collect a number of nuts and bolts. The nuts represent hydrogen atoms. The bolts represent carbon atoms.

2. Connect the nuts to the bolts to model the compound methane. Methane contains four hydrogen atoms attached to one carbon atom. Make as many of these models as you can.

3. Count the nuts and bolts left over.

WHAT DO YOU THINK?

- What ratio of nuts to bolts did you use to make a model of a methane atom?
- How many methane models did you make? Why couldn't you make more?

CHALLENGE The compound ammonia has one nitrogen atom and three hydrogen atoms. How would you use the nuts and bolts to model this compound?

SKILL FOCUS
Modeling

MATERIAL
- nuts and bolts
- Modeling Compounds Datasheet

TIME
20 minutes

Chemical Formulas

Remember that atoms of elements can be represented by their chemical symbols, as given in the periodic table. A **chemical formula** uses these chemical symbols to represent the atoms of the elements and their ratios in a chemical compound.

Carbon dioxide is a compound consisting of one atom of carbon attached by chemical bonds to two atoms of oxygen. Here is how you would write the chemical formula for carbon dioxide:

- Find the symbols for carbon (C) and oxygen (O) on the periodic table. Write these symbols side by side.

- To indicate that there are two oxygen atoms for every carbon atom, place the subscript *2* to the right of the oxygen atom's symbol. A **subscript** is a number written to the right of a chemical symbol and slightly below it.

- Because there is only one atom of carbon in carbon dioxide, you need no subscript for carbon. The subscript 1 is never used. The chemical formula for carbon dioxide is, therefore,

$$CO_2$$

The chemical formula shows one carbon atom bonded to two oxygen atoms.

VOCABULARY
Remember to create a description wheel for *chemical formula* and other vocabulary words.

READING TiP

The word *subscript* comes from the prefix *sub-*, which means "under," and the Latin word *scriptum*, which means "written." A subscript is something written under something else.

Chemical Formulas

Chemical formulas show the ratios of atoms in a chemical compound.

Compound Name	Atoms	Atomic Ratio	Chemical Formula
Hydrogen chloride	H Cl	1:1	HCl
Water	H H O	2:1	H_2O
Ammonia	N H H H	1:3	NH_3
Methane	C H H H H	1:4	CH_4
Propane	C C C H H H H H H H H	3:8	C_3H_8

 How many more hydrogen atoms does propane have than methane?

 RESOURCE CENTER
CLASSZONE.COM

Find out more about chemical formulas.

The chart above shows the names, atoms, ratios, and chemical formulas for several chemical compounds. The subscripts for each compound indicate the number of atoms that combine to make that compound. Notice how hydrogen combines with different atoms in different ratios. Notice in particular that methane and propane are made of atoms of the same elements, carbon and hydrogen, only in different ratios. This example shows why it's important to pay attention to ratios when writing chemical formulas.

CHECK YOUR READING Why is the ratio of atoms in a chemical formula so important?

Same Elements, Different Compounds

Even before chemists devised a way to write chemical formulas, they realized that different compounds could be composed of atoms of the same elements. Nitrogen and oxygen, for example, form several compounds. One compound consists of one atom of nitrogen attached to one atom of oxygen. This compound's formula is NO. A second compound has one atom of nitrogen attached to two atoms of oxygen, so its formula is NO_2. A third compound has two nitrogen atoms attached to one oxygen atom; its formula is N_2O. The properties of these compounds are different, even though they are made of atoms of the same elements.

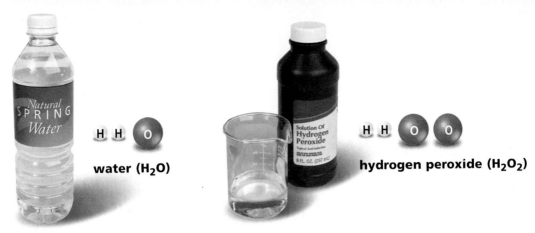

water (H_2O) hydrogen peroxide (H_2O_2)

There are many other examples of atoms of the same elements forming different compounds. The photographs above show two bottles filled with clear, colorless liquids. You might use the liquid in the first bottle to cool off after a soccer game. The bottle contains water, which is a compound made from two atoms of hydrogen and one atom of oxygen (H_2O). You could not survive for long without water.

You definitely would not want to drink the liquid in the second bottle, although this liquid resembles water. This bottle also contains a compound of hydrogen and oxygen, hydrogen peroxide, but hydrogen peroxide has two hydrogen and two oxygen atoms (H_2O_2). Hydrogen peroxide is commonly used to kill bacteria on skin. One way to tell these two compounds apart is to test them using a potato. A drop of hydrogen peroxide on a raw potato will bubble; a drop of water on the potato will not.

The difference between the two compounds is greater than the labels or their appearance would indicate. The hydrogen peroxide that you buy at a drugstore is a mixture of hydrogen peroxide and water. In its concentrated form, hydrogen peroxide is a thick, syrupy liquid that boils at 150°C (302°F). Hydrogen peroxide can even be used as a fuel.

 CHECK YOUR READING What are the chemical formulas for water and hydrogen peroxide?

2.1 Review

KEY CONCEPTS

1. How do the properties of compounds often compare with the properties of the elements that make them?

2. How many atoms are in the compound represented by the formula $C_{12}H_{22}O_{11}$?

3. How can millions of compounds be made from the atoms of about 100 elements?

CRITICAL THINKING

4. **Apply** If a chemical formula has no subscripts, what can you conclude about the ratio of the atoms in it?

5. **Infer** How might you distinguish between hydrogen peroxide and water?

◯ CHALLENGE

6. **Analyze** A chemist analyzes two compounds and finds that they both contain only carbon and oxygen. The two compounds, however, have different properties. How can two compounds made from the same elements be different?

MATH TUTORIAL
CLASSZONE.COM
Click on Math Tutorial for more help with ratios.

Regarding Ratios

No pitcher gets a batter out every time. Sometimes even the worst pitchers have spectacular games. If you're a fan of professional baseball, you've probably seen the quality of certain players rated by using a ratio. A ratio is a comparison of two quantities. For a major league baseball pitcher, for example, one ratio you might hear reported is the number of strikeouts to the number of walks during a season. Chemical formulas are also ratios—ratios that compare the numbers of atoms in a compound.

Example

Consider the chemical formula for the compound glucose:

$$C_6H_{12}O_6$$

From this formula you can write several ratios. To find the ratio of carbon atoms to hydrogen atoms, for instance, do the following:

(1) Find the number of each kind of atom by noting the subscripts.

6 carbon, 12 hydrogen

(2) Write the first number on the left and the second on the right, and place a colon between them.

6:12

(3) Reduce the ratio by dividing each side by the largest number that goes into each evenly, in this case 6.

1:2

ANSWER The ratio of carbon to hydrogen in glucose is 1:2.

Use the table below to answer the following questions.

Compounds and Formulas	
Compound Name	**Chemical Formula**
Carbon dioxide	CO_2
Methane	CH_4
Sulfuric acid	H_2SO_4
Glucose	$C_6H_{12}O_6$
Formic acid	CH_2O_2

1. In carbon dioxide, what is the ratio of carbon to oxygen?

2. What is the ratio of carbon to hydrogen in methane?

3. In sulfuric acid, what is the ratio of hydrogen to sulfur? the ratio of sulfur to oxygen?

CHALLENGE What two chemical compounds in the table have the same ratio of carbon atoms to oxygen atoms?

A good strikeout-to-walk ratio for a baseball pitcher is 2:1. This means that for every two strikeouts achieved, the pitcher only allows one walk.

2.2 Chemical bonds hold compounds together.

◀ **BEFORE, you learned**

- Elements combine to form compounds
- Electrons are located in a cloud around the nucleus
- Atoms can lose or gain electrons to form ions

▶ **NOW, you will learn**

- How electrons are involved in chemical bonding
- About the different types of chemical bonds
- How chemical bonds affect structure

VOCABULARY

ionic bond p. 48
covalent bond p. 50
molecule p. 51
polar covalent bond p. 51

THINK ABOUT

How do you keep things together?

Think about the different ways the workers at this construction site connect materials. They may use nails, screws, or even glue, depending on the materials they wish to keep together. Why would they choose the method they do? What factors do you consider when you join two objects?

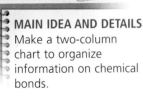

MAIN IDEA AND DETAILS
Make a two-column chart to organize information on chemical bonds.

Chemical bonds between atoms involve electrons.

Water is a compound of hydrogen and oxygen. The air you breathe, however, contains oxygen gas, a small amount of hydrogen gas, as well as some water vapor. How can hydrogen and oxygen be water sometimes and at other times not? The answer is by forming chemical bonds.

Chemical bonds are the "glue" that holds the atoms of elements together in compounds. Chemical bonds are what make compounds more than just mixtures of atoms.

Remember that an atom has a positively charged nucleus surrounded by a cloud of electrons. Chemical bonds form when the electrons in the electron clouds around two atoms interact. How the electron clouds interact determines the kind of chemical bond that is formed. Chemical bonds have a great effect on the chemical and physical properties of compounds. Chemical bonds also influence how different substances interact. You'll learn more about how substances interact in a later chapter.

Atoms can transfer electrons.

REMINDER

Remember that elements in columns show similar chemical properties.

Ions are formed when atoms gain or lose electrons. Gaining electrons changes an atom into a negative ion. Losing electrons changes an atom into a positive ion. Individual atoms do not form ions by themselves. Instead, ions typically form in pairs when one atom transfers one or more electrons to another atom.

An element's location on the periodic table can give a clue as to the type of ions the atoms of that element will form. The illustration to the left shows the characteristic ions formed by several groups. Notice that all metals lose electrons to form positive ions. Group 1 metals commonly lose only one electron to form ions with a single positive charge. Group 2 metals commonly lose two electrons to form ions with two positive charges. Other metals, like the transition metals, also always form positive ions, but the number of electrons they may lose varies.

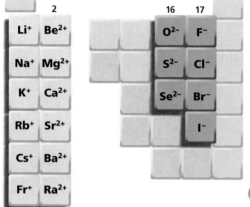

Nonmetals form ions by gaining electrons. Group 17 nonmetals, for example, gain one electron to form ions with a 1– charge. The nonmetals in Group 16 gain two electrons to form ions with a 2– charge. The noble gases do not normally gain or lose electrons and so do not normally form ions.

CHECK YOUR READING What type of ions do metals form?

Ionic Bonds

What happens when an atom of an element from Group 1, like sodium, meets an atom of an element from Group 17, like chlorine? Sodium is likely to lose an electron to form a positive ion. Chlorine is likely to gain an electron to form a negative ion. An electron, therefore, moves from the sodium atom to the chlorine atom.

sodium atom (Na)   chlorine atom (Cl)   sodium ion (Na⁺) chloride ion (Cl⁻)

Remember that particles with opposite electrical charges attract one another. When the ions are created, therefore, they are drawn toward one another by electrical attraction. This force of attraction between positive and negative ions is called an **ionic bond.**

Electrical forces act in all directions. Each ion, therefore, attracts all other nearby ions with the opposite charge. The next illustration shows how this all-around attraction produces a network of sodium and chloride ions known as a sodium chloride crystal.

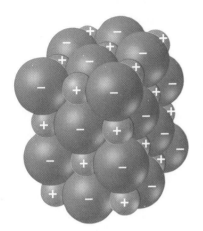

Notice how each positive ion is surrounded by six negative ions, and each negative ion is surrounded by six positive ions. This regular arrangement gives the sodium chloride crystal its characteristic cubic shape. You can see this distinctive crystal shape when you look at table salt crystals through a magnifying glass.

Ionic bonds form between all nearby ions of opposite charge. These interactions make ionic compounds very stable and their crystals very strong. Although sodium chloride crystals have a cubic shape, other ionic compounds form crystals with different regular patterns. The shape of the crystals of an ionic compound depends, in part, on the ratio of positive and negative ions and the sizes of the ions.

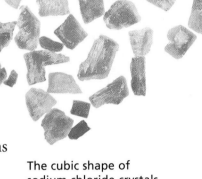

The cubic shape of sodium chloride crystals is a result of how the ions form crystals.

Names of Ionic Compounds

The name of an ionic compound is based on the names of the ions it is made of. The name for a positive ion is the same as the name of the atom from which it is formed. The name of a negative ion is formed by dropping the last part of the name of the atom and adding the suffix -ide. To name an ionic compound, the name of the positive ion is placed first, followed by the name of the negative ion. For example, the chemical name for table salt is sodium chloride. *Sodium* is the positive sodium ion and *chloride* is the negative ion formed from chlorine.

Therefore, to name the compound with the chemical formula BaI_2

- First, take the name of the positive metal element: barium.
- Second, take the name of the negative, nonmetal element, iodine, and give it the ending -ide: iodide.
- Third, combine the two names: barium iodide.

Similarly, the name for KBr is potassium bromide, and the name for MgF_2 is magnesium fluoride.

Atoms can share electrons.

In general, an ionic bond forms between atoms that lose electrons easily to form positive ions, such as metals, and atoms that gain electrons easily to form negative ions, such as nonmetals. Another way in which atoms can bond together is by sharing electrons. Nonmetal atoms usually form bonds with each other by sharing electrons.

Covalent Bonds

VOCABULARY
Make a description wheel for *covalent bond* and other vocabulary words.

A pair of shared electrons between two atoms is called a **covalent bond.** In forming a covalent bond, neither atom gains or loses an electron, so no ions are formed. The shared electrons are attracted to both positively charged nuclei. The illustrations below show a covalent bond between two iodine atoms. In the first illustration, notice how the electron clouds overlap. A covalent bond is also often represented as a line between the two atoms, as in the second illustration.

Iodine (I$_2$)

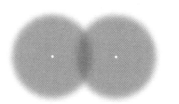
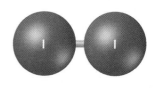

electron cloud model   ball-and-stick model

READING TIP
To help yourself remember that a covalent bond involves a sharing of electrons, remember that the prefix *co-* means "partner."

The number of covalent bonds that an atom can form depends on the number of electrons that it has available for sharing. For example, atoms of the halogen group and hydrogen can contribute only one electron to a covalent bond. These atoms, therefore, can form only one covalent bond. Atoms of Group 16 elements can form two covalent bonds. Atoms of the elements of Group 15 can form three bonds. Carbon and silicon in Group 14 can form four bonds. For example, in methane (CH$_4$), carbon forms four covalent bonds with four hydrogen atoms, as shown below.

Methane (CH$_4$)

ball-and-stick model   space-filling model

We don't always show the lines representing the covalent bonds between the atoms. The space-filling model still shows the general shape of the bonded atoms, but occupies far less space on the page.

Each carbon-hydrogen bond in methane is a single bond because one pair of electrons is shared between the atoms. Sometimes atoms may share more than one pair of electrons with another atom. For example, the carbon atom in carbon dioxide (CO_2) forms double bonds with each of the oxygen atoms. A double bond consists of four (two pairs of) shared electrons. Two nitrogen atoms form a triple bond, meaning that they share six (three pairs of) electrons.

Carbon Dioxide (CO₂)

Nitrogen (N₂)

READING TiP

Remember that each line in the model stands for a covalent bond—one shared pair of electrons.

A group of atoms held together by covalent bonds is called a **molecule.** A molecule can contain from two to many thousand atoms. Most molecules contain the atoms of two or more elements. For example, water (H_2O), ammonia (NH_3), and methane (CH_4) are all compounds made up of molecules. However, some molecules contain atoms of only one element. The following elements exist as two-atom molecules: H_2, N_2, O_2, F_2, Cl_2, Br_2, and I_2.

CHECK YOUR READING What is a molecule?

Polar Covalent Bonds

In an iodine molecule, both atoms are exactly the same. The shared electrons therefore are attracted equally to both nuclei. If the two atoms involved in a covalent bond are very different, however, the electrons have a stronger attraction to one nucleus than to the other and spend more time near that nucleus. A covalent bond in which the electrons are shared unequally is called a **polar covalent bond.** The word *polar* refers to anything that has two extremes, like a magnet with its two opposite poles.

READING TiP

To remind yourself that polar covalent bonds have opposite partial charges, remember that Earth has both a North Pole and a South Pole.

Water (H₂O)

ball-and-stick model

space-filling model

VISUALIZATION
CLASSZONE.COM

Examine how electrons move in a polar covalent molecule.

In a water molecule (H_2O), the oxygen atom attracts electrons far more strongly than the hydrogen atoms do. The oxygen nucleus has eight protons, and the hydrogen nucleus has only one proton. The oxygen atom pulls the shared electrons more strongly toward it. In a water molecule, therefore, the oxygen side has a slightly negative charge, and the hydrogen side has a slightly positive charge.

Comparing Bonds

In Salar de Uyuni, Bolivia, salt is mined in great quantities from salt water. The salt is harvested as the water evaporates into the air, leaving the salt behind. All types of chemical bonds are involved.

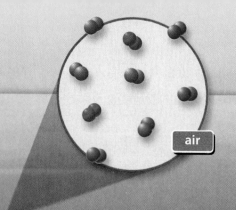
air

salt

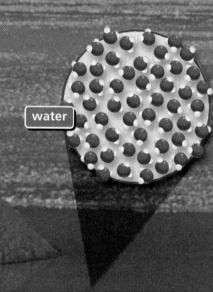
water

Ionic Bonds (salt)

Sodium Chloride (NaCl)
A complete transfer of electrons produces the ionic bonds that hold sodium chloride (table salt) crystals together.

Covalent Bonds (air)

Nitrogen (N_2) and Oxygen (O_2)
Some molecules in air contain multiple covalent bonds. Nitrogen has triple bonds. Oxygen has double bonds.

Polar Covalent Bonds (water)

Water (H_2O)
The covalent bonds in water are very polar because oxygen attracts electrons far more strongly than hydrogen does.

READING VISUALS Atoms of which element are shown both in the air and in the water?

Chemical bonds give all materials their structures.

The substances around you have many different properties. The structure of the crystals and molecules that make up these substances are responsible for many of these properties. For example, crystals bend rays of light, metals shine, and medications attack certain diseases in the body because their atoms are arranged in specific ways.

Ionic Compounds

Most ionic compounds have a regular crystal structure. Remember how the size, shape, and ratio of the sodium ions and chloride ions give the sodium chloride crystal its shape. Other ionic compounds, such as calcium chloride, have different but equally regular structures that depend upon the ratio and sizes of the ions. One consequence of such rigid structures is that, when enough force is applied to the crystal, it shatters rather than bends.

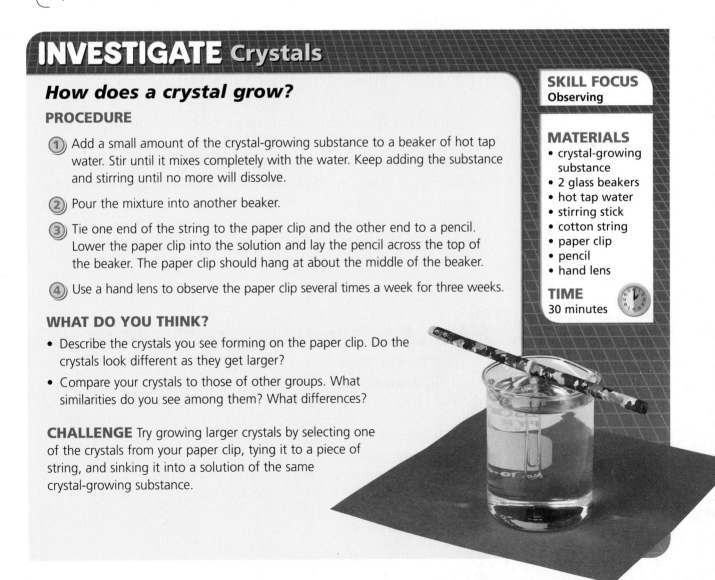

INVESTIGATE Crystals

How does a crystal grow?

SKILL FOCUS
Observing

PROCEDURE

1. Add a small amount of the crystal-growing substance to a beaker of hot tap water. Stir until it mixes completely with the water. Keep adding the substance and stirring until no more will dissolve.

2. Pour the mixture into another beaker.

3. Tie one end of the string to the paper clip and the other end to a pencil. Lower the paper clip into the solution and lay the pencil across the top of the beaker. The paper clip should hang at about the middle of the beaker.

4. Use a hand lens to observe the paper clip several times a week for three weeks.

WHAT DO YOU THINK?

- Describe the crystals you see forming on the paper clip. Do the crystals look different as they get larger?

- Compare your crystals to those of other groups. What similarities do you see among them? What differences?

CHALLENGE Try growing larger crystals by selecting one of the crystals from your paper clip, tying it to a piece of string, and sinking it into a solution of the same crystal-growing substance.

MATERIALS
- crystal-growing substance
- 2 glass beakers
- hot tap water
- stirring stick
- cotton string
- paper clip
- pencil
- hand lens

TIME
30 minutes

Covalent Compounds

Unlike ionic compounds, covalent compounds exist as individual molecules. Chemical bonds give each molecule a specific, three-dimensional shape called its molecular structure. Molecular structure can influence everything from how a specific substance feels to the touch to how well it interacts with other substances.

A few basic molecular structures are shown below. Molecules can have a simple linear shape, like iodine (I_2), or they can be bent, like a water molecule (H_2O). The atoms in an ammonia molecule (NH_3) form a pyramid, and methane (CH_4) molecules even have a slightly more complex shape. The shape of a molecule depends on the atoms it contains and the bonds holding it together.

READING TiP

To help yourself appreciate the differences among these structures, try making three-dimensional models of them.

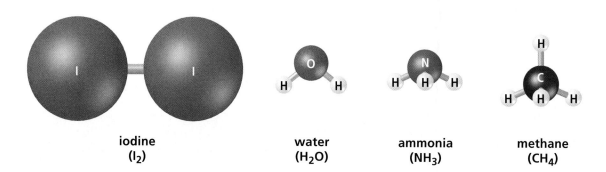

iodine
(I_2)

water
(H_2O)

ammonia
(NH_3)

methane
(CH_4)

Molecular shape can affect many properties of compounds. For example, there is some evidence to indicate that we detect scents because molecules with certain shapes fit into certain smell receptors in the nose. Molecules with similar shapes, therefore, should have similar smells. Molecular structure also plays an essential role in how our bodies respond to certain drugs. Some drugs work because molecules with certain shapes can fit into specific receptors in body cells.

2.2 Review

KEY CONCEPTS

1. What part of an atom is involved in chemical bonding?

2. How are ionic bonds and covalent bonds different?

3. Describe two ways that crystal and molecular structures affect the properties of ionic and covalent compounds.

CRITICAL THINKING

4. **Analyze** Would you expect the bonds in ammonia to be polar covalent? Why or why not?

5. **Infer** What kind of bond would you expect atoms of strontium and iodine to form? Why? Write the formula and name the compound.

⚠ CHALLENGE

6. **Conclude** Is the element silicon likely to form ionic or covalent bonds? Explain.

Stick to It

Glues join objects by forming something like chemical bonds between their surfaces. While glue manufacturers try to make glues as strong as possible, simply being strong does not mean that a glue will join all surfaces equally well. For example, a glue that will hold two pieces of wood together very well may not be able to form a lasting bond between two pieces of plastic piping or two metal sheets.

Variables

When testing a new glue, a scientist wants to know exactly how that glue will perform under all conditions. In any test, however, there are a number of variables that could affect the quality of the bonds formed by the glue. The scientist needs to discover exactly which of these variables most affects the glue's ability to form lasting bonds. Identifying these variables and the effects each has on the glue's strength and lifetime enables glue makers to recommend the best uses for the glue. Following are a few of the variables a glue maker may consider when testing a glue.

- What surfaces the glue is being used to join
- How much glue is used in a test
- How evenly the glue is applied to the surface
- How much force the glue can withstand
- Over how long a time the force is applied
- The environment the glue is used in (wet, dry, or dusty)

Variables to Test

On Your Own You are a scientist at a glue company. You have developed a new type of glue and need to know how specific conditions will affect its ability to hold surfaces together. First, select one variable you wish to test. Next, outline how you would ensure that only that variable will differ in each test. You might start out by listing all the variables you can think of and then put a check by each one and describe how you are controlling it.

As a Group Discuss the outlines of your tests with others. Are there any variables you haven't accounted for?

CHALLENGE Adhesive tapes come in many different types. Outline how you would test how well a certain tape holds in a wet environment and in a dry environment.

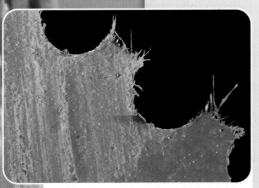

The glue on the back of a postage stamp must be activated somehow. This scanning electron microscope photo shows postage stamp glue before (green) and after (blue) it has been activated by moisture.

This highly magnified photograph shows the attachment formed by a colorless, waterproof wood glue.

Substances' properties depend on their bonds.

BEFORE, you learned

- Chemical bonds hold the atoms of compounds together
- Chemical bonds involve the transfer or sharing of electrons
- Molecules have a structure

NOW, you will learn

- How metal atoms form chemical bonds with one another
- How ionic and covalent bonds influence substances' properties

VOCABULARY

metallic bond p. 56

EXPLORE Bonds in Metals

What objects conduct electricity?

PROCEDURE

1. Tape one end of a copper wire to one terminal of the battery. Attach the other end of the copper wire to the light bulb holder. Attach a second wire to the holder. Tape a third wire to the other terminal of the battery.

2. Touch the ends of both wires to objects around the classroom. Notice if the bulb lights or not.

WHAT DO YOU THINK?

- Which objects make the bulb light?
- How are these objects similar?

MATERIALS

- masking tape
- 3 pieces of copper wire (15 cm)
- D cell (battery)
- light bulb and holder
- objects to test

Metals have unique bonds.

Metal atoms bond together by sharing their electrons with one another. The atoms share the electrons equally in all directions. The equal sharing allows the electrons to move easily among the atoms of the metal. This special type of bond is called a **metallic bond.**

The properties of metals are determined by metallic bonds. One common property of metals is that they are good conductors of electric current. The electrons in a metal flow through the material, carrying the electric current. The free movement of electrons among metal atoms also means that metals are good conductors of heat. Metals also typically have high melting points. Except for mercury, all metals are solids at room temperature.

> **REMINDER**
>
> Chemical bonds involve the sharing of or transfer of electrons.

Copper and other metals get their properties from metallic bonds.

The ability of electrons to move freely makes metals
• good conductors of electricity
• good conductors of heat
• easy to shape

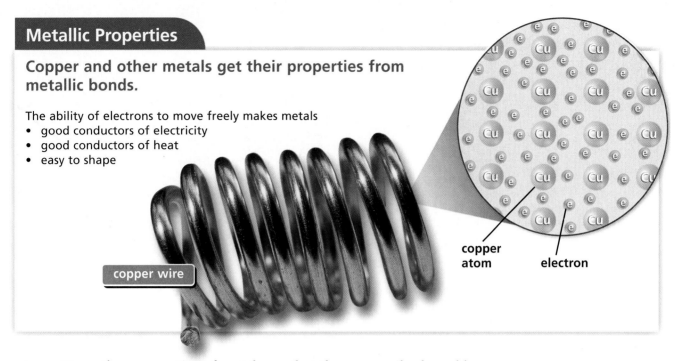

copper wire

copper atom

electron

Two other properties of metals are that they are easily shaped by pounding and can be drawn into a wire. These properties are also explained by the nature of the metallic bond. In metallic compounds, atoms can slide past one another. It is as if the atoms are swimming in a pool of surrounding electrons. Pounding the metal simply moves these atoms into other positions. This property makes metals ideal for making coins.

 CHECK YOUR READING What three properties do metals have because of metallic bonds?

Ionic and covalent bonds give compounds certain properties.

The properties of a compound depend on the chemical bonds that hold its atoms together. For example, you can be pretty certain an ionic compound will be a solid at room temperature. Ionic compounds, in fact, usually have extremely high melting and boiling points because it takes a lot of energy to break all the bonds among all the ions in the crystal. The rigid crystal network also makes ionic compounds hard, brittle, and poor conductors of electricity. No moving electrical charges means no current will flow.

Ionic compounds, however, often dissolve easily in water, separating into positive ions and negative ions. The separated ions can move freely, making solutions of ionic compounds good conductors of electricity. Your body, in fact, uses ionic solutions to help transmit impulses between nerve and muscle cells. Exercise can rapidly deplete these ionic solutions in the body, so sports drinks contain ionic compounds.

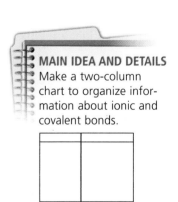

MAIN IDEA AND DETAILS
Make a two-column chart to organize information about ionic and covalent bonds.

A hot pool in Yellowstone Park's Upper Geyser Basin. These pools are often characterized by their striking colors.

RESOURCE CENTER
CLASSZONE.COM

Find out more about the properties of ionic and covalent compounds.

These compounds, such as potassium chloride, replace the ions lost during physical activity.

Mineral hot springs, like those found in Yellowstone National Park, are another example of ionic solutions. Many of the ionic compounds dissolved in these hot springs contain the element sulfur, which can have an unpleasant odor. Evidence of these ionic compounds can be seen in the white deposits around the pool's rim.

Covalent compounds have almost the exact opposite properties of ionic compounds. Since the atoms are organized as individual molecules, melting or boiling a covalent compound does not require breaking chemical bonds. Therefore, covalent compounds often melt and boil at lower temperatures than ionic compounds. Unlike ionic compounds, molecules stay together when dissolved in water, which means covalent compounds are poor conductors of electricity. Table sugar, for example, does not conduct an electric current when in solution.

Bonds can make the same element look different.

Covalent bonds do not always form small individual molecules. This explains how the element carbon can exist in three very different forms—diamond, graphite, and fullerene. The properties of each form depend on how the carbon atoms are bonded to each other.

Diamond is the hardest natural substance. This property makes diamond useful for cutting other substances. Diamonds are made entirely of carbon. Each carbon atom forms covalent bonds with four other carbon atoms. The pattern of linked atoms extends throughout the entire volume of a diamond crystal. This three-dimensional structure of carbon atoms gives diamonds their strength—diamond bonds do not break easily.

Another form of carbon is graphite. Graphite is the dark, slippery component of pencil "lead." Graphite has a different structure from diamond, although both are networks of interconnected atoms. Each carbon atom in graphite forms covalent bonds with three other atoms to form two-dimensional layers. These layers stack on top of one another like sheets of paper. The layers can slide past one another easily. Graphite feels slippery and is used as a lubricant to reduce friction between metal parts of machines.

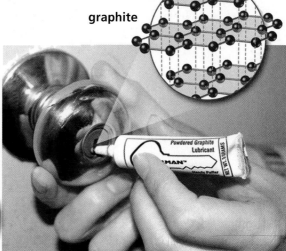

graphite

diamond

A third form of carbon, fullerene, contains large molecules. One type of fullerene, called buckminsterfullerene, has molecules shaped like a soccer ball. In 1985 chemists made a fullerene molecule consisting of 60 carbon atoms. Since then, many similar molecules have been made, ranging from 20 to more than 100 atoms per molecule.

buckminsterfullerene

2.3 Review

KEY CONCEPTS

1. How do metal atoms bond together?

2. Why do ionic compounds have high melting points?

3. What are three forms of the element carbon?

CRITICAL THINKING

4. **Apply** A compound known as cubic boron nitride has a structure similar to that of a diamond. What properties would you expect it to have?

5. **Infer** Sterling silver is a combination of silver and copper. How are the silver and copper atoms held together?

⬥ CHALLENGE

6. **Infer** Why might the water in mineral springs be a better conductor of electricity than drinking water?

CHAPTER INVESTIGATION

Chemical Bonds

OVERVIEW AND PURPOSE Chemists can identify the type of bonds in a substance by examining its properties. In this investigation you will examine the properties of different substances and use what you have learned about chemical bonds to identify the type of bond each substance contains. You will

- observe the structure of substances with a hand lens
- test the conductivity of substances
- determine the melting point of substances

Problem

How can you determine the type of chemical bond a substance has?

Hypothesize

Write three hypotheses in "if . . . , then . . . , because . . ." form to answer the problem question for each bond type—ionic, covalent, and metallic.

Procedure

1. Create a data table similar to the one shown on the sample notebook page.

2. To build the conductivity tester, connect the first wire to one terminal of the battery and to one of the metal strips. Attach the second wire to the other terminal and to the lamp socket. Finally, connect the lamp socket to the third wire, and connect the other end of this wire to the second metal strip.

3. To make sure your tester works properly, touch the tips of the metal strips together. If the bulb lights, the tester is working properly. If not, check the connections carefully.

4. Get the following test compounds from your teacher: Epsom salts (MgSO$_4$), sugar (C$_{12}$H$_{22}$O$_{11}$), and iron filings (Fe). For each substance, put about 20 grams in a cup and label it.

MATERIALS

- 3 wire leads with alligator clips
- battery
- zinc and copper strips
- light bulb and socket
- test compounds
- 3 plastic cups
- distilled water
- beaker
- construction paper
- hand lens
- plastic spoon
- 3 test tubes
- test-tube rack
- candle
- wire test-tube holder

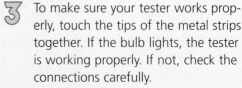

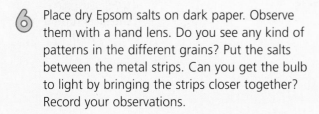

5 Test the conductivity of distilled water. Fill the beaker with 30 mL of water. Place the two metal strips into the water. Does the bulb light? Record your observations. Dry the strips completely.

6 Place dry Epsom salts on dark paper. Observe them with a hand lens. Do you see any kind of patterns in the different grains? Put the salts between the metal strips. Can you get the bulb to light by bringing the strips closer together? Record your observations.

7 Add all but a small amount of the Epsom salts to the beaker of water. Stir well. Repeat the conductivity test. What happens when you put the metal strips into the solution? Record your results.

8 Rinse and dry the beaker. Repeat steps 6–7 with other test substances. Record your results.

9 Put the remainder of each test substance into its own clean, dry test tube. Label the tubes. Light the candle. Use a test tube holder to hold each compound over the candle flame for 2 minutes. Do you notice any signs of melting? Record your observations.

Observe and Analyze   Write It Up

1. **RECORD OBSERVATIONS** Be sure you have entered all your observations in your data table.

2. **CLASSIFY** Using the periodic table, find the elements these compounds contain. How might consulting the periodic table help you determine what type of bond exists in the compound?

Conclude   Write It Up

1. **INTERPRET** Review your recorded observations. Classify the compounds as having ionic, covalent, or metallic bonds. Fill in the last row of the data table with your conclusions.

2. **INFER** Compare your results with your hypotheses. Did your results support your hypotheses?

3. **EVALUATE** Describe possible limitations, errors, or places where errors might have occurred.

4. **APPLY** Electrocardiograms are graphs that show the electrical activity of the heart. When an electrocardiogram is made, a paste of sodium chloride is used to hold small metal discs on the patient's skin. What property of ionic compounds does this medical test make use of?

▶ INVESTIGATE Further

CHALLENGE To grow crystals, put about 60 grams of Epsom salts into a baby-food jar that is half full of hot water. Do the same using a second jar containing about 60 grams of sugar. Cover and shake the jars for a count of 60. Line two clean jar lids with dark paper. Brush or spoon a thin coating of each liquid over the paper. Let them stand in a warm place. After several days, observe the crystals that form, using a hand lens.

Chemical Bonds
Problem How can you determine the type of chemical bond a substance has?

Hypothesize

Observe and Analyze
Table 1: Properties of Bonds

Property	Epsom Salts (MgSO4)	Sugar (C12H22O11)	Iron Filings (Fe)
Crystal structure			
Conductivity of solid			
Conductivity in water			
Melting			
Bond type			

Conclude

Chapter Review

the **BIG** idea

The properties of compounds depend on their atoms and chemical bonds.

◀ KEY CONCEPTS SUMMARY

2.1 **Elements combine to form compounds.**
- Compounds have different properties from the elements that made them.
- Atoms combine in predictable numbers.

calcium (Ca)   +   chlorine (Cl₂)   =   calcium chloride (CaCl₂)

VOCABULARY
chemical formula p. 43
subscript p. 43

2.2 **Chemical bonds hold compounds together.**
- Chemical bonds between atoms involve electrons.
- Atoms can transfer electrons.
- Atoms can share electrons.
- Chemical bonds give all materials their structure.

ionic bond   covalent bond

VOCABULARY
ionic bond p. 48
covalent bond p. 50
molecule p. 51
polar covalent bond p. 51

2.3 **Substances' properties depend on their bonds.**
- Metals have unique bonds.
- Ionic and covalent bonds give compounds certain properties.
- Bonds can make the same element look different.

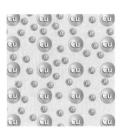  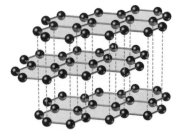

copper   diamond fragment   graphite fragment

VOCABULARY
metallic bond p. 56

Copy and complete the table below. Under each bond type, describe
• how electrons are distributed
• how the compound is structured
• one of the properties of the compound containing this type of bond

Some of the table has been filled out for you.

Ionic Bonds	Covalent Bonds	Metallic Bonds
1.	shared electron pair	2.
3.	4.	close-packed atoms in sea of electrons
have high melting points	5.	6.

Reviewing Key Concepts

Multiple Choice *Choose the letter of the best answer.*

7. Most substances are
   a. elements
   c. metals
   b. compounds
   d. nonmetals

8. All compounds are made of
   a. atoms of two or more elements
   b. two or more atoms of the same element
   c. atoms arranged in a crystal
   d. atoms joined by covalent bonds

9. The chemical formula for a compound having one barium (Ba) ion and two chloride (Cl) ions is
   a. BCl
   c. $BaCl_2$
   b. BaCl
   d. Ba_2Cl_2

10. The 4 in the chemical formula CH_4 means there are
   a. four carbon atoms to one hydrogen atom
   b. four carbon and four hydrogen atoms
   c. four hydrogen atoms to one carbon atom
   d. four total carbon CH combinations

11. The compound KBr has the name
   a. potassium bromide
   b. potassium bromine
   c. bromide potassium
   d. bromine potassium

12. An atom becomes a positive ion when it
   a. is attracted to all nearby atoms
   b. gains an electron from another atom
   c. loses an electron to another atom
   d. shares an electron with another atom

13. A polar covalent bond forms when two atoms
   a. share one electron equally
   b. share two electrons equally
   c. share one electron unequally
   d. share two electrons unequally

14. Metallic bonds make many metals
   a. poor conductors of heat
   b. liquid at room temperature
   c. difficult to shape
   d. good conductors of electricity

15. Three forms of carbon are
   a. diamond, graphite, and salt
   b. diamond, graphite, and fullerene
   c. graphite, salt, and carbonate
   d. diamond, salt, and fullerene

Short Answer *Write a short answer to each question.*

16. Why does a mixture of sodium chloride and water conduct electricity but a sodium chloride crystal does not?

17. Describe what makes diamond and graphite, two forms of the element carbon, so different.

Thinking Critically

Use the illustration above to answer the next two questions.

18. IDENTIFY Write the chemical formula for the molecule pictured above.

19. ANALYZE The nitrogen atom has a far greater attraction for electrons than hydrogen atoms. Copy the molecule pictured above and indicate which parts of the molecule have a slightly positive charge and which parts have a slightly negative charge.

20. PREDICT The chemical formula for calcium chloride is $CaCl_2$. What would you predict the formula for magnesium chloride to be? [**Hint:** Find magnesium on the periodic table.]

21. INFER When scientists make artificial diamonds, they sometimes subject graphite to very high temperatures and pressures. What do you think happens to change the graphite into diamond?

22. SYNTHESIZE Why would seawater be a better conductor of electricity than river water?

23. ANALYZE How does the nature of the metallic bond explain the observation that most metals can be drawn into a wire?

24. EVALUATE Do you think the types of bonds you've studied occur on the planet Mars? Explain.

25. INFER Why don't we use the term *ionic molecule?*

Use the chemical formulas below and a periodic table to answer the next three questions.

Compound
I. K_2SO_4
II. CF_4
III. C_4H_{10}
IV. KCl

26. APPLY Name compound IV. Does this compound have ionic or covalent bonds?

27. ANALYZE Name the elements in each compound. Tell how many atoms are in each compound.

28. CALCULATE Express the ratio of atoms in compounds II, III, and IV. For compound I, express all three ratios.

29. APPLY By 1800 Alessandro Volta had made the first electric battery. He placed pieces of cardboard soaked in saltwater in between alternating zinc and silver discs. What properties of the metals and the saltwater made them good materials for a battery?

30. PREDICT What is the maximum number of covalent bonds that a hydrogen atom can form? Explain your answer.

the BIG idea

31. DRAW CONCLUSIONS Look at the photograph on pages 38–39 again. Can you now recognize any similarities between how the skydivers stay together and how atoms stay together?

32. APPLY Phosphorus can be a strange element. Pure phosphorus is sometimes white, black, or red. What can account for the differences in appearance?

UNIT PROJECTS

If you need to create graphs or other visuals for your project, be sure you have graph paper, poster board, markers, or other supplies.

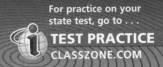
Interpreting Tables

The table below lists some of the characteristics of substances that contain different types of bonds. Use the table to answer the questions.

Bond Type	Usually Forms Between	Electrons	Properties	Examples
Ionic	an atom of a metal and an atom of a nonmetal	transferred between atoms	• high melting points • conducts electricity when in water	BaS, $BaBr_2$, Ca_3N_2, $LiCl$, ZnO
Covalent	atoms of nonmetallic elements	shared between atoms but often not equally	• low melting points • does not conduct electricity	C_2H_6, C, Cl_2, H_2, $AsCl_3$
Metallic	atoms of metallic elements	freely moving about the atoms	• high melting points • conducts electricity at all times • easily shaped	Ca, Fe, Na, Cu, Zn

1. Which of these compounds would you expect to have the highest melting point?

 a. C_2H_6 **c.** $AsCl_3$

 b. Cl_2 **d.** $BaBr_2$

2. Which substance is likely to be easily shaped?

 a. $BaBr_2$ **c.** Na

 b. $LiCl$ **d.** C

3. In the compound $LiCl$, electrons are

 a. shared equally

 b. shared but not equally

 c. transferred between atoms to form ions

 d. freely moving among the atoms

4. Which of the following is an ionic compound?

 a. C_2H_6 **c.** $AsCl_3$

 b. Cl_2 **d.** ZnO

5. Which of the following compounds has a low melting point?

 a. Cl_2 **c.** Cu

 b. ZnO **d.** $BaBr_2$

6. A solid mass of which substance would conduct electricity?

 a. Ca_3N_2 **c.** Cu

 b. $LiCl$ **d.** $AsCl_3$

Extended Response

Answer the next two questions in detail.
Include some of the terms from the list in the box.
Underline each term you use in your answer.

share electron	transfer electron
freely moving electrons	charge
compound	chemical formula

7. Compare how electrons are involved in making the three main types of bonds: ionic, covalent, and metallic.

8. Just about 100 elements occur naturally. There are, however, millions of different materials. How can so few basic substances make so many different materials?

CHAPTER 3

Chemical Reactions

the BIG idea

Chemical reactions form new substances by breaking and making chemical bonds.

Key Concepts

Internet Preview

CLASSZONE.COM

Chapter 3 online resources: Content Review, two Visualizations, two Resource Centers, Math Tutorial, Test Practice

What changes are happening in this chemical reaction?

Changing Steel Wool

Place a small lump of steel wool in a cup. Pour in enough vinegar to cover the steel wool. After five minutes, take the steel wool out of the vinegar. Shake the steel wool to remove any excess vinegar. Place the steel wool in a small plastic bottle, and cover the mouth of the bottle with a balloon. Observe the steel wool and balloon after one hour.

Observe and Think What happened to the steel wool and balloon? What might have caused this to occur?

A Different Rate

Half fill one cup with hot tap water and a second cup with cold tap water. Drop a seltzer tablet into each cup at the same time. Time how long it takes for each tablet to stop fizzing.

Observe and Think Which tablet fizzed for a longer period of time? How might you explain any differences?

Internet Activity: Reactions

Go to **ClassZone.com** to explore chemical reactions and chemical equations. Learn how a chemical equation can be balanced.

Observe and Think How do chemical equations show what happens during a chemical reaction?

NSTA
scilinks.org
SCiLINKS

Chemical Reactions **Code: MDL024**

Getting Ready to Learn

◀ CONCEPT REVIEW

- Atoms combine to form compounds.
- Atoms gain or lose electrons when they form ionic bonds.
- Atoms share electrons in covalent bonds.

◀ VOCABULARY REVIEW

electron p. 11
ionic bond p. 48
covalent bond p. 50
See Glossary for definitions.
atom, chemical change

CONTENT REVIEW
CLASSZONE.COM
Review concepts and vocabulary.

▶ TAKING NOTES

COMBINATION NOTES

To take notes about a new concept, first make an informal outline of the information. Then make a sketch of the concept and label it so you can study it later.

VOCABULARY STRATEGY

Write each new vocabulary term in the center of a **four square** diagram. Write notes in the squares around each term. Include a definition, some characteristics, and some examples of the term. If possible, write some things that are not examples of the term.

See the Note-Taking Handbook on pages R45–R51.

SCIENCE NOTEBOOK

NOTES

Chemical reactions
- cause chemical changes
- make new substances
- change reactants into products

Evidence of Chemical Reactions

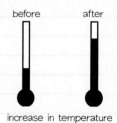

before   after

increase in temperature

Definition	Characteristics
substance present before a chemical reaction occurs	its bonds are broken during a reaction
REACTANT	
Examples	Nonexample
oxygen in a combustion reaction	carbon dioxide in a combustion reaction

Chemical reactions alter arrangements of atoms.

BEFORE, you learned

- Atoms of one element differ from atoms of all other elements
- Chemical bonds hold compounds together
- Chemical bonds may be ionic or covalent

NOW, you will learn

- About chemical changes and how they occur
- About three types of chemical reactions
- How the rate of a chemical reaction can be changed

VOCABULARY

chemical reaction p. 69
reactant p. 71
product p. 71
precipitate p. 72
catalyst p. 76

EXPLORE Chemical Changes

How can you identify a chemical change?

PROCEDURE

1. Pour about 3 cm (1 in.) of vinegar into the bowl. Add a spoonful of salt. Stir until the salt dissolves.

2. Put the pennies into the bowl. Wait two minutes, and then put the nail into the bowl.

3. Observe the nail after five minutes and record your observations.

WHAT DO YOU THINK?

- What did you see on the nail? Where do you think it came from?
- Did a new substance form? What evidence supports your conclusion?

MATERIALS
- vinegar
- clear bowl
- plastic spoon
- table salt
- 20 pennies
- large iron nail

Atoms interact in chemical reactions.

You see substances change every day. Some changes are physical, such as when liquid water changes to water vapor during boiling. Other changes are chemical, such as when wood burns to form smoke and ash, or when rust forms on iron. During a chemical change, substances change into one or more different substances.

A **chemical reaction** produces new substances by changing the way in which atoms are arranged. In a chemical reaction, bonds between atoms are broken and new bonds form between different atoms. This breaking and forming of bonds takes place when particles of the original materials collide with one another. After a chemical reaction, the new arrangements of atoms form different substances.

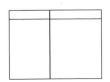

COMBINATION NOTES
Use combination notes to organize information about how atoms interact during chemical reactions.

Physical Changes

A change in the state of a substance is an example of a physical change. The substance may have some different properties after a physical change, but it is still the same substance. For example, you know that water can exist in three different physical states: the solid state (ice), the liquid state (water), and the gas state (water vapor). However, regardless of what state water is in, it still remains water, that is, H_2O molecules. As ice melts, the molecules of water move around more quickly, but the molecules do not change. As water vapor condenses, the molecules of water move more slowly, but they are still the same molecules.

Substances can undergo different kinds of physical changes. For example, sugar dissolves in water but still tastes sweet because the molecules that make up sugar do not change when it dissolves. The pressure of helium changes when it is pumped from a high-pressure tank into a balloon, but the gas still remains helium.

CHECK YOUR READING | What happens to a substance when it undergoes a physical change?

When water changes from a liquid to a solid, it undergoes a physical change.

Ice is composed of water molecules that are locked together.

Liquid water is composed of molecules that move freely past each other.

Chemical Changes

Water can also undergo a chemical change. Water molecules can be broken down into hydrogen and oxygen molecules by a chemical reaction called electrolysis. When an electric current is passed through liquid water (H_2O), it changes the water into two gases—hydrogen and oxygen. The molecules of water break apart into individual atoms, which then recombine into hydrogen molecules (H_2) and oxygen molecules (O_2). The original material (water) changes into different substances through a chemical reaction.

Hydrogen and oxygen are used as rocket fuel for the space shuttle. During liftoff, liquid hydrogen and liquid oxygen are combined in a reaction that is the opposite of electrolysis. This reaction produces water and a large amount of energy that helps push the shuttle into orbit.

 How does a chemical change differ from a physical change?

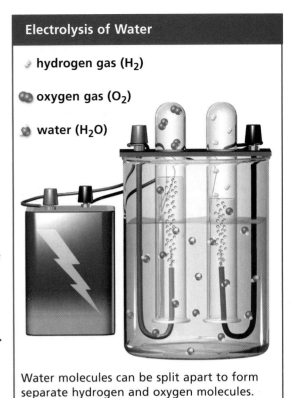

Electrolysis of Water

- hydrogen gas (H_2)
- oxygen gas (O_2)
- water (H_2O)

Water molecules can be split apart to form separate hydrogen and oxygen molecules.

Reactants and Products

Reactants are the substances present at the beginning of a chemical reaction. In the burning of natural gas, for example, methane (CH_4) and oxygen (O_2) are the reactants in the chemical reaction. **Products** are the substances formed by a chemical reaction. In the burning of natural gas, carbon dioxide (CO_2) and water (H_2O) are the products formed by the reaction. Reactants and products can be elements or compounds, depending on the reaction taking place.

During a chemical reaction, bonds between atoms in the reactants are broken and new bonds are formed in the products. When natural gas is burned, bonds between the carbon and hydrogen atoms in methane are broken, as are the bonds between the oxygen atoms in oxygen molecules. New bonds are formed between carbon and oxygen in carbon dioxide gas and between hydrogen and oxygen in water vapor.

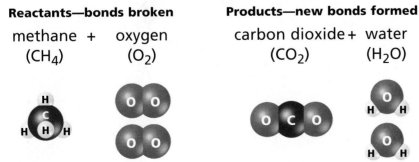

Reactants—bonds broken

methane + oxygen
(CH₄)   (O₂)

Products—new bonds formed

carbon dioxide + water
(CO₂)   (H₂O)

 What must happen for reactants to be changed into products?

Evidence of Chemical Reactions

Some chemical changes are easy to observe—the products formed by the rearrangement of atoms look different than the reactants. Other changes are not easy to see but can be detected in other ways.

Color Change Substances often change color during a chemical reaction. For example, when gray iron rusts, the product that forms is brown, as shown in the photograph below.

Formation of a Precipitate Many chemical reactions form products that exist in a different physical state from the reactants. A solid product called a **precipitate** may form when chemicals in two liquids react, as shown in the photograph below. Seashells are often formed this way when a sea creature releases a liquid that reacts with seawater.

VOCABULARY
Remember to use a four square diagram for *precipitate* and other vocabulary terms.

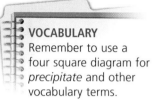

Color Change

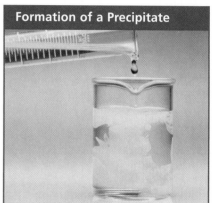

Formation of a Precipitate

Formation of a Gas Chemical reactions may produce a gas, like that often formed when antacid pills are mixed with excess stomach acid. The photograph below shows an example in which carbon dioxide gas is produced by a chemical reaction.

Temperature Change Most chemical reactions involve a temperature change. Sometimes this change can be inferred from the observation of a flame, as in the burning of the metal magnesium in the photograph below. Other temperature changes are not immediately obvious. If you have touched concrete before it hardens, you may have noticed that it felt warm. This warmth is due to a chemical reaction.

Formation of a Gas

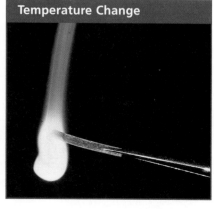

Temperature Change

Chemical reactions can be classified.

Scientists classify chemical reactions in several ways to help make the different types of reactions easier to understand. All reactions form new products, but the ways in which products are made can differ.

Synthesis In a synthesis reaction, a new compound is formed by the combination of simpler reactants. For example, nitrogen dioxide (NO_2), a component of smog, forms when nitrogen and oxygen combine in the air.

READING TiP

Synthesis means "making a substance from simpler substances."

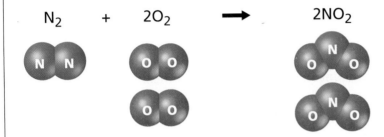

$$N_2 \quad + \quad 2O_2 \quad \longrightarrow \quad 2NO_2$$

Decomposition In a decomposition reaction, a reactant breaks down into simpler products, which could be elements or other compounds. Decomposition reactions can be thought of as being the reverse of synthesis reactions. For example, water can be decomposed into its elements—hydrogen and oxygen.

READING TiP

Decomposition means "separation into parts."

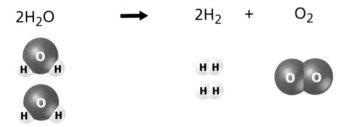

$$2H_2O \quad \longrightarrow \quad 2H_2 \quad + \quad O_2$$

Combustion In a combustion reaction, one reactant is always oxygen and another reactant often contains carbon and hydrogen. The carbon and hydrogen atoms combine with oxygen, producing carbon dioxide and water. The burning of methane is a combustion reaction.

READING TiP

Combustion is the process of burning with oxygen.

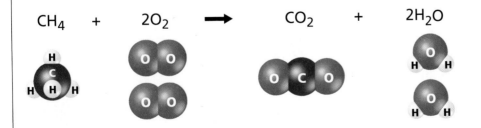

$$CH_4 \quad + \quad 2O_2 \quad \longrightarrow \quad CO_2 \quad + \quad 2H_2O$$

CHECK YOUR READING How are synthesis reactions different from decomposition reactions?

The rates of chemical reactions can vary.

Most chemical reactions take place when particles of reactants collide with enough force to react. Chemical reactions can occur at different rates. Striking a match causes a very quick chemical reaction, while the rusting of an iron nail may take months. However, the rate of a reaction can be changed. For instance, a nail can be made to rust more quickly. Three physical factors—concentration, surface area, and temperature—and a chemical factor—a catalyst—can greatly affect the rate of a chemical reaction.

Concentration

Observe how changing the concentration of a reactant can change the rate of a reaction.

Concentration measures the number of particles present in a certain volume. A high concentration of reactants means that there is a large number of particles that can collide and react. Turning the valve on a gas stove to increase the flow of gas increases the concentration of methane molecules that can combine with oxygen in the air. The result is a bigger flame and a faster combustion reaction.

Surface Area

Suppose one of the reactants in a chemical reaction is present as a single large piece of material. Particles of the second reactant cannot get inside the large piece, so they can react only with particles on the surface. To make the reaction go faster, the large piece of material could be broken into smaller pieces before the reaction starts.

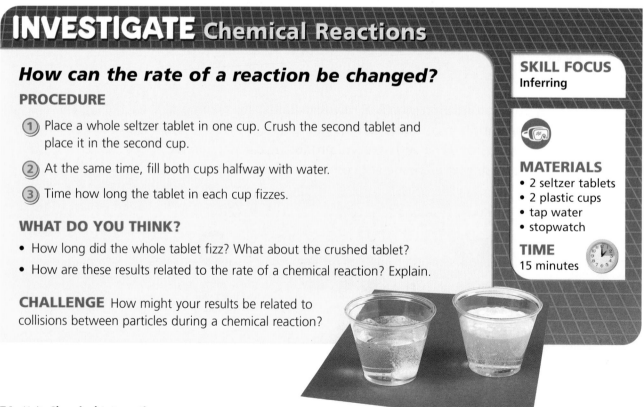

INVESTIGATE Chemical Reactions

How can the rate of a reaction be changed?

PROCEDURE

1. Place a whole seltzer tablet in one cup. Crush the second tablet and place it in the second cup.
2. At the same time, fill both cups halfway with water.
3. Time how long the tablet in each cup fizzes.

WHAT DO YOU THINK?

- How long did the whole tablet fizz? What about the crushed tablet?
- How are these results related to the rate of a chemical reaction? Explain.

CHALLENGE How might your results be related to collisions between particles during a chemical reaction?

SKILL FOCUS
Inferring

MATERIALS
- 2 seltzer tablets
- 2 plastic cups
- tap water
- stopwatch

TIME
15 minutes

Breaking a large piece of material into smaller parts increases the surface area of the material. All of the inner material has no surface when it is inside a larger piece. Each time the large piece is broken, however, more surfaces are exposed. The amount of material does not change, but breaking it into smaller parts increases its surface area. Increasing the surface area increases the rate of the reaction.

 CHECK YOUR READING Why does a reaction proceed faster when the reactants have greater surface areas?

Temperature

The rate of a reaction can be increased by making the particles move faster. The result is that more collisions take place per second and occur with greater force. The most common way to make the particles move faster is to add energy to the reactants, which will raise their temperature.

Many chemical reactions during cooking go very slowly, or do not take place at all, unless energy is added to the reactants. Too much heat can make a reaction go too fast, and food ends up burned. Chemical reactions can also be slowed or stopped by decreasing the temperature of the reactants. Again, think about cooking. The reactions that take place during cooking can be stopped by removing the food from the heat source.

REMINDER

Temperature is the average amount of kinetic energy of the particles in a substance.

Particles and Reaction Rates		
Changes in Reactants	**Normal Reaction Rate**	**Increased Reaction Rate**
Concentration An increase in concentration of the reactants increases the number of particles that can interact.		
Surface area An increase in the surface area of the reactants increases the number of particles that can interact.		
Temperature Adding energy makes particles move faster and increases temperature. The increase in motion allows reactants to collide and react more frequently.		

Catalysts

RESOURCE CENTER
CLASSZONE.COM

Learn more about catalysts and how they work in living things.

The rate of a reaction can be changed chemically by adding a catalyst. A **catalyst** is a substance that increases the rate of a chemical reaction but is not itself consumed in the reaction. This means that after the reaction is complete, the catalyst remains unchanged. Catalysts are very important for many industrial and biological reactions. In fact, many chemical reactions would proceed slowly or not take place at all without catalysts.

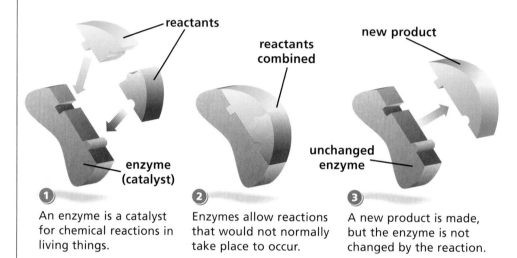

reactants

reactants combined

new product

enzyme (catalyst)

unchanged enzyme

1 An enzyme is a catalyst for chemical reactions in living things.

2 Enzymes allow reactions that would not normally take place to occur.

3 A new product is made, but the enzyme is not changed by the reaction.

In living things, catalysts called enzymes are absolutely necessary for life. Without them, many important reactions could not take place under the conditions within your body. In fact, in 2003, scientists reported that they had discovered the slowest known chemical reaction in living things. This reaction would normally take one trillion years. Enzymes, though, allow the reaction to occur in 0.01 seconds.

 CHECK YOUR READING Why are catalysts important in chemical reactions?

3.1 Review

KEY CONCEPTS

1. How do physical changes differ from chemical changes? Explain.

2. Describe four types of evidence of a chemical reaction.

3. Describe the ways in which the rate of a chemical reaction can be changed.

CRITICAL THINKING

4. **Synthesize** What evidence shows that the burning of methane is a chemical reaction?

5. **Compare** What about combustion reactions makes them different from either synthesis or decomposition reactions?

○ CHALLENGE

6. **Apply** How might the chewing of food be related to the rate of a chemical reaction—digestion—that occurs in your body? Explain.

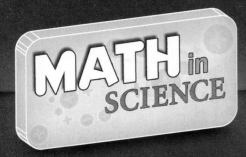

The Iodine Clock

Can a chemical reaction be timed? In the iodine clock reaction, a sudden color change indicates that the reaction has occurred. The length of time that passes before the color changes depends on the concentration ratios of the reactants. As shown in the graph below, the greater the concentration of the reactants, the faster the reaction.

 MATH TUTORIAL
CLASSZONE.COM

Click on Math Tutorial for more help with interpreting line graphs.

The reactants in the iodine clock reaction produce a sudden color change several seconds after the reactants are mixed.

Example

Suppose you are given an unknown iodine concentration to test in the iodine clock reaction. What is the concentration ratio of the iodine if it takes 40 seconds for the color change to occur?

(1) Find 40 seconds on the *x*-axis of the graph below and follow the vertical line up to the plotted data.

(2) Draw a horizontal line from that point on the curve to the *y*-axis to find the iodine concentration ratio in your sample.

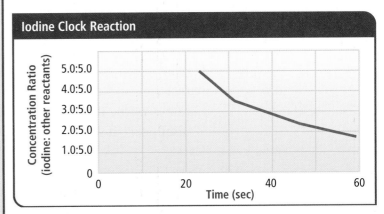

Iodine Clock Reaction

ANSWER The unknown concentration ratio is approximately 3.0:5.0.

Answer the following questions using the information in the graph above.

1. Approximately how long will it take for the reaction to occur if the concentration ratio is 4.0:5.0? 2.0:5.0?

2. Suppose you could extend the curve on the graph. If the reaction took 70 seconds to occur, what would be the approximate iodine concentration ratio?

CHALLENGE Using the following concentration ratios and times for another reactant, draw a reaction rate graph similar to the one shown above.

Concentration Ratios = 5.0:5.0, 4.0:5.0, 3.0:5.0, 2.0:5.0

Times = 24 sec, 25 sec, 43 sec, 68 sec

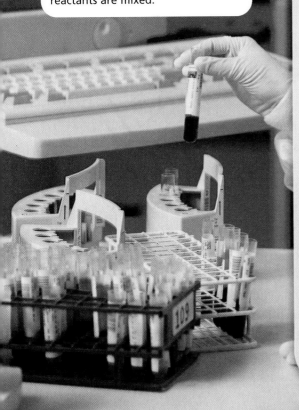

KEY CONCEPT

3.2 The masses of reactants and products are equal.

◁ **BEFORE,** you learned

- Chemical reactions turn reactants into products by rearranging atoms
- Chemical reactions can be observed and identified
- The rate of chemical reactions can be changed

▷ **NOW,** you will learn

- About the law of conservation of mass
- How a chemical equation represents a chemical reaction
- How to balance a simple chemical equation

VOCABULARY

law of conservation of mass p. 79
coefficient p. 82

THiNK ABOUT

What happens to burning matter?

You have probably watched a fire burn in a fireplace, a campfire, or a candle flame. It looks as if the wood or candle disappears over time, leaving a small pile of ashes or wax when the fire has finished burning. But does matter really disappear? Combustion is a chemical reaction, and chemical reactions involve rearrangements of atoms. The atoms do not disappear, so where do they go?

Careful observations led to the discovery of the conservation of mass.

COMBINATION NOTES
Take notes on the conservation of mass using combination notes.

The ashes left over from a wood fire contain less mass than the wood. In many other chemical reactions, mass also appears to decrease. That is, the mass of the products appears to be less than the mass of the reactants. In other reactions, the products appear to gain mass. For example, plants grow through a complex series of reactions, but where does their extra mass come from? At one time, scientists thought that chemical reactions could create or destroy matter.

During the 1780s the French chemist Antoine Lavoisier (luh-VWAH-zee-ay) showed that matter can never be created or destroyed in a chemical reaction. Lavoisier emphasized the importance of making very careful measurements in his experiments. Because of his methods, he was able to show that reactions that seem to gain mass or lose mass actually involve reactions with gases in the air. These gases could not be seen, but their masses could be measured.

An example of Lavoisier's work is his study of the reaction of the metal mercury when heated in air. In this reaction, the reddish-orange product formed has more mass than the original metal. Lavoisier placed some mercury in a jar, sealed the jar, and recorded the total mass of the setup. After the mercury had been heated in the jar, the total mass of the jar and its contents had not changed.

Lavoisier showed that the air left in the jar would no longer support burning—a candle flame was snuffed out by this air. He concluded that a gas in the air, which he called oxygen, had combined with the mercury to form the new product.

Lavoisier conducted many experiments of this type and found in all cases that the mass of the reactants is equal to the mass of the products. This conclusion, called the **law of conservation of mass,** states that in a chemical reaction atoms are neither created nor destroyed. All atoms present in the reactants are also present in the products.

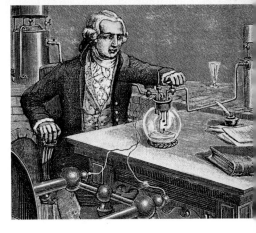

Lavoisier carefully measured both the reactants and the products of chemical reactions.

 How did Lavoisier investigate the conservation of mass?

INVESTIGATE Conservation of Mass

Why is it important to measure the masses of reactants and products?

PROCEDURE

1. Measure 2 tsp of baking soda. Use a funnel to put the baking soda in a balloon.

2. Pour 2 tsp of vinegar into the plastic bottle.

3. Secure the balloon over the mouth of the bottle with the balloon hanging to the side of the bottle. Find and record the mass of the experimental setup.

4. Lift the balloon so that the baking soda drops into the bottle. Observe for five minutes, and then find and record the mass of the setup again.

WHAT DO YOU THINK?

- Did the mass of the experimental setup change?
- How do your observations demonstrate the conservation of mass?

CHALLENGE What do you think you would have observed if you had not used the balloon? Explain.

SKILL FOCUS
Measuring

MATERIALS
- teaspoon
- baking soda
- funnel
- balloon
- vinegar
- plastic bottle
- balance

TIME
35 minutes

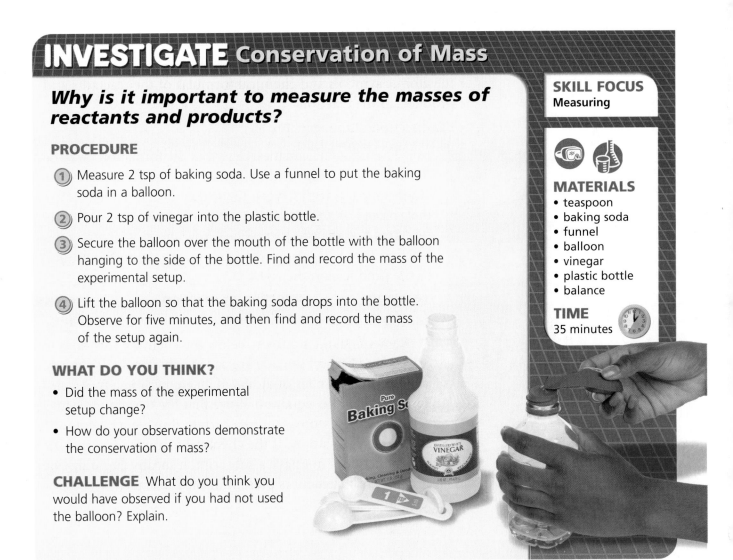

Chemical reactions can be described by chemical equations.

The law of conservation of mass states that in a chemical reaction, the total mass of reactants is equal to the total mass of products. For example, the mass of sodium plus the mass of chlorine that reacts with the sodium equals the mass of the product sodium chloride. Because atoms are rearranged in a chemical reaction, there must be the same number of sodium atoms and chlorine atoms in both the reactants and products.

Chemical equations represent how atoms are rearranged in a chemical reaction. The atoms in the reactants are shown on the left side of the equation. The atoms in the products are shown on the right side of the equation. Because atoms are rearranged and not created or destroyed, the number of atoms of each different element must be the same on each side of the equation.

 CHECK YOUR READING How does a chemical equation show the conservation of mass?

In order to write a chemical equation, the information that you need to know is

- the reactants and products in the reaction
- the atomic symbols and chemical formulas of the reactants and products in the reaction
- the direction of the reaction

Carbon dioxide is a gas that animals exhale.

The following equation describes the formation of carbon dioxide from carbon and oxygen. In words, this equation says "Carbon reacts with oxygen to yield carbon dioxide." Notice that instead of an equal sign, an arrow appears between the reactants and the products. The arrow shows which way the reaction proceeds—from reactants on the left to the product or the products on the right.

reactants	**direction of reaction**	**product**
$C + O_2$	$\longrightarrow$	CO_2

Remember, the numbers below the chemical formulas for oxygen and carbon dioxide are called subscripts. A subscript indicates the number of atoms of an element in a molecule. You can see in the equation above that the oxygen molecule has two oxygen atoms, and the carbon dioxide molecule also has two oxygen atoms. If the chemical formula of a reactant or product does not have a subscript, it means that only one atom of each element is present in the molecule.

Chemical equations must be balanced.

Remember, chemical reactions follow the law of conservation of mass. Chemical equations show this conservation, or equality, in terms of atoms. The same number of atoms of each element must appear on both sides of a chemical equation. However, simply writing down the chemical formulas of reactants and products does not always result in equal numbers of atoms. You have to balance the equation to make the number of atoms equal on each side of an equation.

Balancing Chemical Equations

To learn how to balance an equation, look at the example of the combustion of natural gas, which is mostly methane (CH_4). The reactants are methane and oxygen. The products are carbon dioxide and water. You can write this reaction as the following equation.

REMINDER

Oxygen is always a reactant in a combustion reaction.

Unbalanced Equation

This equation is not balanced. There is one C on each side of the equation, so C is balanced. However, on the left side, H has a subscript of 4, which means there are four hydrogen atoms. On the right side, H has a subscript of 2, which means there are two hydrogen atoms. Also, there are two oxygen atoms on the left and three oxygen atoms on the right. Because of the conservation of mass, you know that hydrogen atoms do not disappear and oxygen atoms do not suddenly appear.

You can balance a chemical equation by changing the amounts of reactants or products represented.

READING TiP

As you read how to balance the equation, look at the illustrations and count the atoms. The number of each type of atom is shown below the formula.

- To balance H first, add another H_2O molecule on the right. Now, both C and H are balanced.
- There are now two oxygen atoms on the left side and four oxygen atoms on the right side. To balance O, add another O_2 molecule on the left.

Balanced Equation

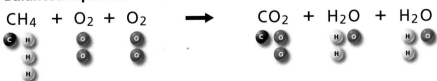

Using Coefficients to Balance Equations

The balanced equation for the combustion of methane shows that one molecule of methane reacts with two molecules of oxygen to produce one molecule of carbon dioxide and two molecules of water. The equation can be simplified by writing $2O_2$ instead of $O_2 + O_2$, and $2H_2O$ instead of $H_2O + H_2O$.

The numbers in front of the chemical formulas are called coefficients. **Coefficients** indicate how many molecules take part in the reaction. If there is no coefficient, then only one molecule of that type takes part in the reaction. The balanced equation, with coefficients, for the combustion of methane is shown below.

Balanced Equation with Coefficients

$$CH_4 \quad + \quad \underset{\text{coefficient}}{2O_2} \quad \longrightarrow \quad \underset{\text{subscript}}{CO_2} \quad + \quad 2H_2O$$

Chemical formulas can have both coefficients and subscripts. In these cases, multiply the two numbers together to find the number of atoms involved in the reaction. For example, two water molecules ($2H_2O$) contain $2 \cdot 2 = 4$ hydrogen atoms and $2 \cdot 1 = 2$ oxygen atoms. Remember, coefficients in a chemical equation indicate how many molecules of each type take part in the reaction.

Only coefficients can be changed in order to balance a chemical equation. Subscripts are part of the chemical formula for reactants or products and cannot be changed to balance an equation. Changing a subscript changes the substance represented by the formula.

For example, the equation for the combustion of methane cannot be balanced by changing the formula CO_2 to CO. The formula CO_2 represents carbon dioxide gas, which animals exhale when they breathe. The formula CO represents carbon monoxide gas, which is a very different compound from CO_2. Carbon monoxide gas is poisonous, and breathing too much of it can be fatal.

○ **CHECK YOUR READING** Why are coefficients used to balance equations?

The combustion of methane (CH_4) is used to melt glass.

Balancing Equations with Coefficients

The steps below show how to balance the equation for the synthesis reaction between nitrogen (N_2) and hydrogen (H_2), which produces ammonia (NH_3).

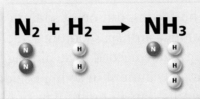

$$N_2 + H_2 \rightarrow NH_3$$

1 **Count the atoms.** Neither N nor H is balanced. The reactants contain two atoms each of N and H, but the product contains one N atom and three H atoms.

$N_2 + H_2 \rightarrow NH_3$

N = 2	N = 1
H = 2	H = 3

Tip: Listing the number of atoms of each element makes it easy to see which elements must be balanced.

2 **Use a coefficient to add atoms to one side of the equation.** A coefficient of 2 on NH_3 balances the number of N atoms.

$N_2 + H_2 \rightarrow 2\ NH_3$

N = 2	N = 2
H = 2	H = 6

Tip: When adding coefficients, start with the reactant or product that contains the greatest number of different elements.

3 **Add a coefficient to another reactant or product.** Adding a coefficient of 3 to H_2 on the left side of the equation balances the number of H atoms on both sides. Now the equation is balanced.

$N_2 + 3\ H_2 \rightarrow 2NH_3$

N = 2	N = 2
H = 6	H = 6

Tip: Make sure that the coefficients in your balanced equation are the smallest whole numbers possible—that is, they have no common factor other than 1.

$$N_2 + 3H_2 \rightarrow 2NH_3$$

APPLY

Balance the following equations.
1. $Hg + O_2 \rightarrow HgO$
2. $Zn + HCl \rightarrow ZnCl_2 + H_2$

Chapter 3: **Chemical Reactions** 83 **B**

The decomposition of sodium azide is used to inflate air bags in automobiles.

Using the Conservation of Mass

A balanced chemical equation shows that no matter how atoms are rearranged during a chemical reaction, the same number of atoms must be present before and after the reaction. The following example demonstrates the usefulness of chemical equations and the conservation of mass.

The decomposition of sodium azide (NaN_3) is used to inflate automobile air bags. Sodium azide is a solid, and the amount of sodium azide needed in an air bag fills only a small amount of space. In fact, the amount of sodium azide used in air bags is only about 130 grams—an amount that would fit in a large spoon. An inflated air bag, though, takes up much more space even though it contains the same number of atoms that entered the reaction. The reason is illustrated by the chemical equation for this reaction.

Balanced Equation

$$2NaN_3 \longrightarrow 2Na + 3N_2$$

According to the balanced equation shown above, three molecules of nitrogen gas are formed for every two molecules of sodium azide that decompose. Because the nitrogen is a gas, it fills a much greater volume than the original sodium azide. In fact, 67 liters of nitrogen gas are produced by the 130 grams of sodium azide in the reaction. This amount of nitrogen is enough to quickly inflate the air bag during a collision—the decomposition of sodium azide to sodium and nitrogen takes 0.03 seconds.

 CHECK YOUR READING Why must chemical equations be balanced?

3.2 Review

KEY CONCEPTS

1. State the law of conservation of mass.

2. Write the chemical equation that shows sodium (Na) and chlorine (Cl_2) combining to form table salt (NaCl).

3. Is the following equation balanced? Why or why not?

$$CO \longrightarrow C + O_2$$

CRITICAL THINKING

4. **Communicate** Describe Lavoisier's experiment with mercury. How does this experiment show the law of conservation of mass?

5. **Synthesize** Suppose a log's mass is 5 kg. After burning, the mass of the ash is 1 kg. Explain what may have happened to the other 4 kg of mass.

CHALLENGE

6. **Synthesize** Suppose a container holds 1000 hydrogen molecules (H_2) and 1000 oxygen molecules (O_2) that react to form water. How many water molecules will be in the container? Will anything else be in the container? If so, what?

Chemistry in Firefighting

A firefighter's job may seem simple: to put out fires. However, a firefighter needs to know about chemicals and chemical reactions. A fire is a combustion reaction that requires oxygen as a reactant. Without oxygen, a fire will normally burn itself out, so firefighters try to prevent oxygen from reaching the burning substances. Firefighters often use water or carbon dioxide for this purpose, but these materials make some types of fires more dangerous.

Grease Fires

Some fires can be extinguished by a chemical reaction. In kitchen grease fires, the chemicals that are used to fight the fire react with the grease. The reaction produces a foam that puts out the fire.

Metal Fires

Some fires involve metals such as magnesium. This metal burns at a very high temperature and reacts violently with water. Firefighters try to smother metal fires with a material such as sand.

Hazardous Reactions

Chemicals may react with water to form poisonous gases or acids. Firefighters might use a foam that extinguishes the fire, cools the area around the fire, and traps gases released by the fire. The symbols shown on the left are among several that show firefighters what chemical dangers may be present.

The fire shown above is a magnesium fire in Chicago in 1998. Firefighters used water to protect surrounding buildings, but dumped road salt on the burning magnesium.

EXPLORE

Build a carbon dioxide fire extinguisher.

1. Put 3 tsp of baking soda on a tissue and roll it into a tube. Tie the ends and middle of the tube with thread. Leave extra thread at one end of the tube.
2. Mold clay tightly around a straw.
3. Pour some vinegar into a bottle.
4. Hold the thread to suspend the tissue tube above the vinegar. Place the straw inside the bottle. Use the clay molded around the straw to hold the thread in place. Be sure that the straw is not touching the vinegar.
5. Shake and observe the fire extinguisher.

3.3
Chemical reactions involve energy changes.

BEFORE, you learned

- Bonds are broken and made during chemical reactions
- Mass is conserved in all chemical reactions
- Chemical reactions are represented by balanced chemical equations

NOW, you will learn

- About the energy in chemical bonds between atoms
- Why some chemical reactions release energy
- Why some chemical reactions absorb energy

VOCABULARY

bond energy p. 86
exothermic reaction p. 87
endothermic reaction p. 87
photosynthesis p. 90

EXPLORE Energy Changes

How can you identify a transfer of energy?

PROCEDURE

1. Pour 50 mL of hot tap water into the cup and place the thermometer in the cup.

2. Wait 30 seconds, then record the temperature of the water.

3. Measure 5 tsp of Epsom salts. Add the Epsom salts to the cup and immediately record the temperature while stirring the contents of the cup.

4. Continue to record the temperature every 30 seconds for 2 minutes.

WHAT DO YOU THINK?

- What happened to the temperature after you added the Epsom salts?
- What do you think caused this change to occur?

MATERIALS

- graduated cylinder
- hot tap water
- plastic cup
- thermometer
- stopwatch
- plastic spoon
- Epsom salts

WATER

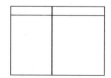

COMBINATION NOTES
Use combination notes to organize information on how chemical reactions absorb or release energy.

Chemical reactions release or absorb energy.

Chemical reactions involve breaking bonds in reactants and forming new bonds in products. Breaking bonds requires energy, and forming bonds releases energy. The energy associated with bonds is called **bond energy.** What happens to this energy during a chemical reaction?

Chemists have determined the bond energy for bonds between atoms. Breaking a bond between carbon and hydrogen requires a certain amount of energy. This amount of energy is different from the amount of energy needed to break a bond between carbon and oxygen, or between hydrogen and oxygen.

Energy is needed to break bonds in reactant molecules. Energy is released when bonds are formed in product molecules. By adding up the bond energies in the reactants and products, you can determine whether energy will be released or absorbed.

If more energy is released when the products form than is needed to break the bonds in the reactants, then energy is released during the reaction. A reaction in which energy is released is called an **exothermic reaction.**

If more energy is required to break the bonds in the reactants than is released when the products form, then energy must be added to the reaction. That is, the reaction absorbs energy. A reaction in which energy is absorbed is called an **endothermic reaction.**

These types of energy changes can also be observed in different physical changes such as dissolving or changing state. The state change from a liquid to a solid, or freezing, releases energy—this is an exothermic process. The state change from a solid to a liquid, or melting, absorbs energy—this is an endothermic process.

 How are exothermic and endothermic reactions different?

The white clouds of water vapor are formed by the exothermic reaction between hydrogen and oxygen.

$$2H_2 + O_2 \longrightarrow 2H_2O$$

Exothermic reactions release energy.

Exothermic chemical reactions often produce an increase in temperature. In exothermic reactions, the bond energies of the reactants are less than the bond energies of the products. As a result, less energy is needed to break the bonds in the reactants than is released during the formation of the products. This energy difference between reactants and products is often released as heat. The release of heat causes a change in the temperature of the reaction mixture.

Even though energy is released by exothermic reactions, some energy must first be added to break bonds in the reactants. In exothermic reactions, the formation of bonds in the products releases more energy. Overall, more energy is released than is added.

Some reactions are highly exothermic. These reactions produce a great deal of heat and significantly raise the temperature of their surroundings. One example is the reaction of powdered aluminum metal with a type of iron oxide, a reaction known as the thermite reaction. The equation for this reaction is

$$2Al + Fe_2O_3 \longrightarrow Al_2O_3 + 2Fe$$

This reaction releases enough heat to melt the iron that is produced. In fact, this reaction is used to weld iron rails together.

The thermite reaction releases enough heat to weld pieces of iron together.

 What is evidence for an exothermic chemical reaction?

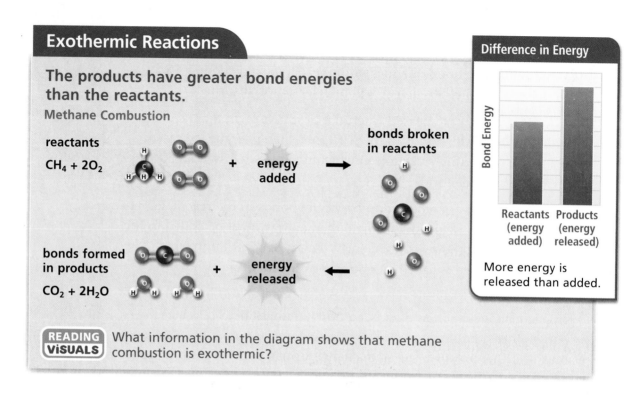

Exothermic Reactions

The products have greater bond energies than the reactants.

Methane Combustion

reactants

$CH_4 + 2O_2$ + energy added → bonds broken in reactants

bonds formed in products

$CO_2 + 2H_2O$ + energy released ←

Difference in Energy

Bond Energy

Reactants (energy added) Products (energy released)

More energy is released than added.

READING VISUALS What information in the diagram shows that methane combustion is exothermic?

All common combustion reactions, such as the combustion of methane, are exothermic. To determine how energy changes in this reaction, the bond energies in the reactants—oxygen and methane—and in the products—carbon dioxide and water—can be added and compared. This process is illustrated by the diagram shown above. The difference in energy is released to the surrounding air as heat.

Some chemical reactions release excess energy as light instead of heat. For example, glow sticks work by a chemical reaction that releases energy as light. One of the reactants, a solution of hydrogen peroxide, is contained in a thin glass tube within the plastic stick. The rest of the stick is filled with a second chemical and a brightly colored dye. When you bend the stick, the glass tube inside it breaks and the two solutions mix. The result is a bright glow of light.

These cup coral polyps glow because of exothermic chemical reactions.

Exothermic chemical reactions also occur in living things. Some of these reactions release energy as heat, and others release energy as light. Fireflies light up due to a reaction that takes place between oxygen and a chemical called luciferin. This type of exothermic reaction is not unique to fireflies. In fact, similar reactions are found in several different species of fish, squid, jellyfish, and shrimp.

CHECK YOUR READING In which ways might an exothermic reaction release energy?

The bombardier beetle, shown in the photograph on the right, uses natural exothermic reactions to defend itself. Although several chemical reactions are involved, the end result is the production of a hot, toxic spray. The most important reaction in the process is the decomposition of hydrogen peroxide into water and oxygen.

$$2H_2O_2 \longrightarrow 2H_2O + O_2$$

When the hydrogen peroxide rapidly breaks down, the hot, toxic mixture made by the series of reactions is pressurized by the oxygen gas from the reaction in the equation above. After enough pressure builds up, the beetle can spray the mixture.

Endothermic reactions absorb energy.

Endothermic reactions often produce a decrease in temperature. In endothermic reactions, the bond energies of the reactants are greater than the bond energies of the products. As a result, more energy is needed to break the bonds in the reactants than is released during the formation of the products. The difference in energy is usually absorbed from the surroundings as heat. This often causes a decrease in the temperature of the reaction mixture.

All endothermic reactions absorb energy. However, they do not all absorb energy as heat. One example of an endothermic reaction of this type is the decomposition of water by electrolysis. In this case, the energy that is absorbed is in the form of electrical energy. When the electric current is turned off, the reaction stops. The change in energy that occurs in this reaction is shown below.

READING **TiP**

The prefix *endo-* means "inside."

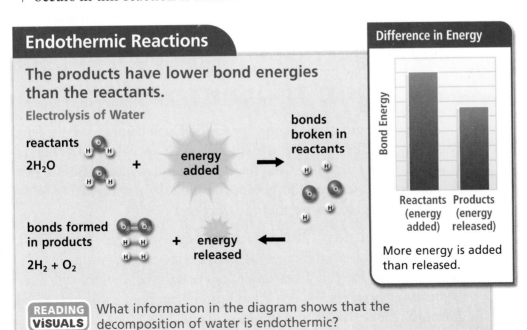

Endothermic Reactions

The products have lower bond energies than the reactants.

Electrolysis of Water

reactants

$2H_2O$ + energy added → bonds broken in reactants

bonds formed in products $2H_2 + O_2$ + energy released ←

Difference in Energy

Bond Energy

Reactants (energy added)   Products (energy released)

More energy is added than released.

READING VISUALS What information in the diagram shows that the decomposition of water is endothermic?

Probably the most important series of endothermic reactions on Earth is photosynthesis. Many steps occur in the process, but the overall chemical reaction is

$$6CO_2 + 6H_2O \longrightarrow C_6H_{12}O_6 + 6O_2$$

Unlike many other endothermic reactions, photosynthesis does not absorb energy as heat. Instead, during **photosynthesis,** plants absorb energy from sunlight to turn carbon dioxide and water into oxygen and glucose, which is a type of sugar molecule. The energy is stored in the glucose molecules, ready to be used when needed.

 How can you determine if a reaction is endothermic?

Exothermic and endothermic reactions work together to supply energy.

When thinking about exothermic and endothermic reactions, it is often useful to consider energy as part of the reaction. An exothermic reaction releases energy, so energy is on the product side of the chemical equation. An endothermic reaction absorbs energy, so energy is on the reactant side of the chemical equation.

Exothermic Reaction
Reactants ➡ Products + Energy

Endothermic Reaction
Reactants + Energy ➡ Products

As you can see in the general reactions above, exothermic and endothermic reactions have opposite energy changes. This means that if an exothermic chemical reaction proceeds in the opposite direction, it becomes an endothermic reaction that absorbs energy. Similarly, if an endothermic reaction proceeds in the opposite direction, it becomes an exothermic reaction that releases energy.

 What happens when an exothermic reaction is reversed?

A large amount of the energy we use on Earth comes from the Sun. This energy includes energy in fossil fuels such as coal and petroleum, as well as energy obtained from food. In all of these cases, the energy in sunlight is stored by endothermic reactions. When the energy is needed, it is released by exothermic reactions.

This combination of reactions forms a cycle of energy storage and use. For example, examine the photosynthesis equation at the top of the page. If you look at this equation in reverse—that is, if the direction of the arrow is reversed—it is a combustion reaction, with oxygen and glucose as the reactants, and it is exothermic.

View examples of endothermic and exothermic reactions.

Plants store energy through the endothermic reactions of photosynthesis. Living things can release this energy through a series of exothermic reactions that will be described in the next section.

The energy stored in plants through photosynthesis can also be released in other ways. Consider energy from fossil fuels. Fossil fuels include petroleum, natural gas, and coal. These substances formed from fossilized materials, mainly plants, that had been under high pressures and temperatures for millions of years. When these plants were alive, they used photosynthesis to produce glucose and other molecules from carbon dioxide and water.

The energy stored in the bonds of these molecules remains, even though the molecules have changed over time. The burning of gasoline in a car releases this energy, enabling the car's engine to work. Similarly, the burning of coal in a power plant, or the burning of natural gas in a stove, releases the energy originally stored by the endothermic series of photosynthesis reactions.

Plants such as trees store energy through photosynthesis. Cars and trucks release this energy through combustion.

CHECK YOUR READING How can endothermic and exothermic reactions work together?

3.3 Review

KEY CONCEPTS

1. What are the differences between exothermic and endothermic reactions?

2. Is the combustion of methane an exothermic or endothermic reaction? Explain.

3. Is photosynthesis an exothermic or endothermic reaction? Explain.

CRITICAL THINKING

4. **Synthesize** Describe the connections between the processes of photosynthesis and combustion.

5. **Communicate** Explain how most energy used on Earth can be traced back to the Sun.

◯ CHALLENGE

6. **Synthesize** Electrolysis of water is endothermic. What does this indicate about the bond energy in the reactants and products? What happens when this reaction is reversed?

CHAPTER INVESTIGATION

Exothermic or Endothermic?

OVERVIEW AND PURPOSE A clue that a chemical reaction has taken place is a transfer of energy, often in the form of heat or light. The chemical reaction used to demolish an old building, as shown in the photograph to the left, is a dramatic example of energy release by a reaction. In this investigation, you will use what you have learned about chemical reactions to
- measure and record temperature changes in two processes
- compare temperature changes during the processes in order to classify them as exothermic or endothermic

▶ Procedure

1. Make a data table like the one shown on the sample notebook page.

2. Work with a partner. One should keep track of time. The other should observe the thermometer and report the temperature.

PART 1

3. Pour 30 mL of hydrogen peroxide into a beaker. Put a thermometer into the beaker. Wait 2 minutes to allow the thermometer to reach the temperature of the hydrogen peroxide. During the time you are waiting, measure 1 g of yeast with the balance.

4. Record the starting temperature. Add the yeast to the beaker and immediately record the temperature while gently stirring the contents of the beaker. Continue to record the temperature every 30 seconds as you observe the process for 5 minutes.

step 4

MATERIALS
- graduated cylinder
- hydrogen peroxide
- 2 beakers
- 2 thermometers
- stopwatch
- measuring spoons
- yeast
- balance
- plastic spoon
- large plastic cup
- hot tap water
- vinegar
- baking soda

PART 2

5 Make a hot water bath by filling a large plastic cup halfway with hot tap water.

6 Measure and pour 30 mL of vinegar into a small beaker. Set this beaker in the hot water bath and place a thermometer in the vinegar. Wait until the temperature of the vinegar rises to between 32 and 38°C (90 to 100°F). While waiting for the vinegar's temperature to increase, measure 1 g of baking soda.

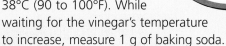

7 Remove the beaker from the hot water bath. Record the starting temperature.

8 Add the baking soda to the vinegar and immediately record the temperature as you swirl the contents of the beaker. Continue to record the temperature every 30 seconds as you observe the reaction for 5 minutes.

▶ Observe and Analyze
Write It Up

1. **RECORD OBSERVATIONS** Remember to complete your data table.

2. **GRAPH** Use the information from your data table to graph your results. Make a double-line graph, plotting your data in a different color for each part of the investigation. Plot temperature in degrees Celsius on the vertical, or y-axis. Plot the time in minutes on the horizontal, or x-axis.

3. **ANALYZE DATA** Examine the graph. When did the temperature change the most in each part of the investigation? When did it change the least? Compare the temperature at the start of each process with the temperature after 5 minutes. How do the temperature changes compare?

▶ Conclude

Write It Up

1. **CLASSIFY** Is the mixture of hydrogen peroxide and yeast endothermic or exothermic? Is the reaction between vinegar and baking soda endothermic or exothermic? Provide evidence for your answers.

2. **EVALUATE** Did you have any difficulties obtaining accurate measurements? Describe possible limitations or sources of error.

3. **APPLY** What does the reaction between baking soda and vinegar tell you about their bond energies?

▶ INVESTIGATE Further

CHALLENGE Repeat Part 2, but instead of using the hot water bath, add the hot water directly to the vinegar before pouring in the baking soda. Does this change in procedure change the results of the experiment? Why might your observations have changed? Explain your answers.

Exothermic or Endothermic?

Observe and Analyze

Table 1. Temperature Measurements

Time (min)	Hydrogen Peroxide and Yeast Temperature (°C)	Vinegar and Baking Soda Temperature (°C)
0		
0.5		
1.0		
....		
5.0		

Conclude

KEY CONCEPT

3.4 Life and industry depend on chemical reactions.

◀ BEFORE, you learned	▶ NOW, you will learn
• Chemical reactions turn reactants into products by rearranging atoms	• About the importance of chemical reactions in living things
• Mass is conserved during chemical reactions	• How chemistry has helped the development of new technology
• Chemical reactions involve energy changes	

VOCABULARY

respiration p. 94

THINK ABOUT

How is a glow stick like a firefly?

When a firefly glows in the dark, a chemical reaction that emits light is taking place. Similarly, when you activate a glow stick, a chemical reaction that causes the glow stick to emit light occurs. Many reactions in modern life and technology adapt chemical reactions found in nature. Can you think of other examples?

Living things require chemical reactions.

In section 3, you saw that photosynthesis stores energy from the Sun in forms that can be used later. These forms of stored energy include fossil fuels and the sugar glucose. The glucose molecules produced by photosynthesis make up the basic food used for energy by almost all living things. For example, animals obtain glucose molecules by eating plants or eating other animals that have eaten plants.

Living cells obtain energy from glucose molecules through the process of **respiration,** which is the "combustion" of glucose to obtain energy. This series of chemical reactions is, in general, the reverse of photosynthesis. It produces carbon dioxide and water from oxygen and glucose. The overall reactions for both photosynthesis and respiration are shown on the top of page 95. From a chemical point of view, respiration is the same as any other combustion reaction.

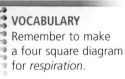

VOCABULARY
Remember to make a four square diagram for *respiration*.

Photosynthesis

$$6CO_2 + 6H_2O + energy \longrightarrow C_6H_{12}O_6 + 6O_2$$

Respiration

$$C_6H_{12}O_6 + 6O_2 \longrightarrow 6CO_2 + 6H_2O + energy$$

The energy released by respiration can be used for growth of new cells, movement, or any other life function. Suppose that you are late for school and have to run to get to class on time. Your body needs to activate nerves and muscles right away, without waiting for you to first eat some food as a source of energy. The glucose molecules in food are stored in your body until you need energy. Then, respiration consumes them in a process that includes several steps.

To make these steps go quickly, the body uses catalysts—enzymes— for each step. Some enzymes break the glucose molecules into smaller pieces, while other enzymes break bonds within each piece. Still other enzymes help form the reaction products—carbon dioxide and water. With the help of enzymes, these reactions take place quickly and automatically. You do not have to think about breaking down glucose when you run—you just start to run and the energy is there.

 CHECK YOUR READING How are photosynthesis and respiration opposites?

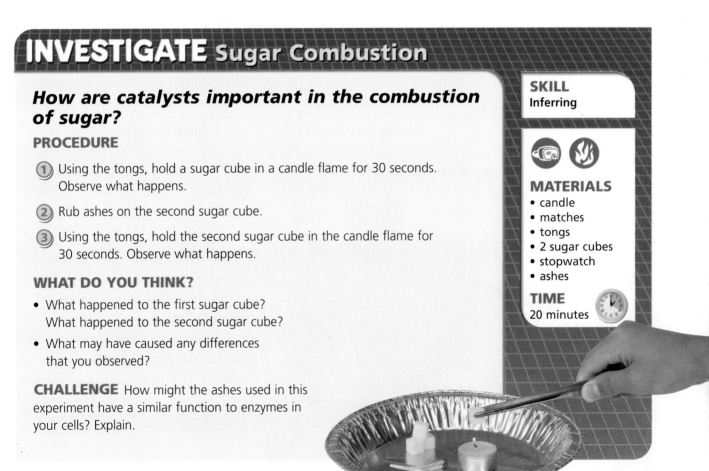

INVESTIGATE Sugar Combustion

How are catalysts important in the combustion of sugar?

PROCEDURE

1. Using the tongs, hold a sugar cube in a candle flame for 30 seconds. Observe what happens.

2. Rub ashes on the second sugar cube.

3. Using the tongs, hold the second sugar cube in the candle flame for 30 seconds. Observe what happens.

WHAT DO YOU THINK?

- What happened to the first sugar cube? What happened to the second sugar cube?

- What may have caused any differences that you observed?

CHALLENGE How might the ashes used in this experiment have a similar function to enzymes in your cells? Explain.

SKILL
Inferring

MATERIALS
- candle
- matches
- tongs
- 2 sugar cubes
- stopwatch
- ashes

TIME
20 minutes

Chemical reactions are used in technology.

Every time your cells need energy, they essentially complete respiration—the "combustion" of glucose. The series of chemical reactions in respiration involves enzymes, which are catalysts. Every time someone drives a car, another combustion reaction occurs—the combustion of gasoline. While the combustion of gasoline does not require a catalyst, the chemical reactions that change a car's exhaust gases do use a catalyst.

No chemical reaction is ever completely efficient. It does not matter what the reaction is or how the reaction conditions are set up. There are always some reactants that do not change completely into products. Sometimes a chemical reaction makes unwanted waste products.

In the case of gasoline combustion, some of the original carbon compounds, called hydrocarbons, do not burn completely, and carbon monoxide gas (CO) is produced. Also, nitrogen in the air reacts with oxygen in a car's engine to produce compounds of nitrogen and oxygen, including nitric oxide (NO). The production of these gases lowers the overall efficiency of combustion. More importantly, these gases can react with water vapor in the air to form smog and acid rain.

Sometimes, as you can see with gasoline combustion, chemical technology causes a problem. Then, new chemical technology is designed to treat the problem. For example, it was necessary to reduce carbon monoxide and nitric oxide emissions from car exhaust. As a result, engineers in the 1970s developed a device called a catalytic converter. This device causes chemical reactions that remove the unwanted waste products from the combustion of gasoline.

Catalytic converters contain metal catalysts such as platinum, palladium, and rhodium. The products of the reactions in the catalytic converter are nitrogen (N_2), oxygen (O_2), water (H_2O), and carbon dioxide (CO_2), which are all ordinary parts of Earth's atmosphere.

Even though catalytic converters have been used for many years, scientists and engineers are still trying to improve them. One goal of this research is to use less expensive metals, such as magnesium and zinc, inside catalytic converters, while forming the same exhaust products.

Many states inspect vehicles to test the pollutants in their exhaust gases.

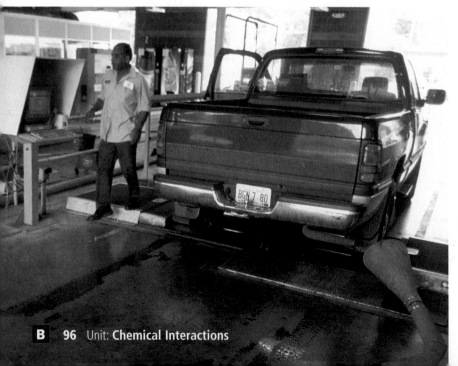

CHECK YOUR READING Why were catalytic converters developed?

Chemical Reactions in Catalytic Converters

The combustion of gasoline makes harmful waste products. Chemical reactions in catalytic converters make these waste products less harmful.

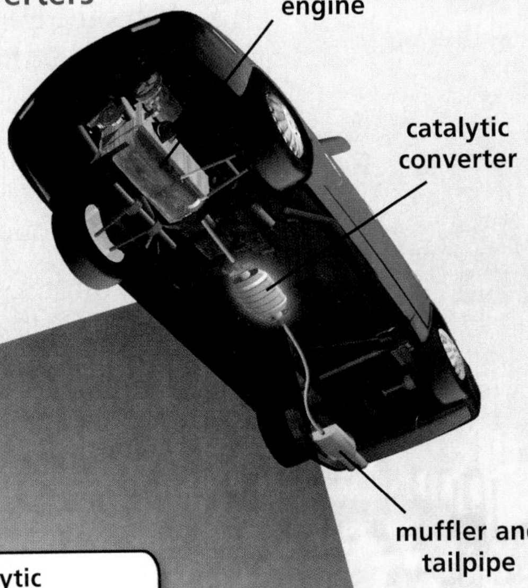

engine

catalytic converter

muffler and tailpipe

1 Into the Catalytic Converter
When gasoline is mixed with air and burned in a car's engine, the reaction produces some unwanted waste products, such as
- carbon monoxide (CO)
- nitric oxide (NO)
- unburned hydrocarbons

2 Inside the Catalytic Converter Catalysts in a car's catalytic converter help change these unwanted products into other gases. The catalysts are metals that are bonded to a ceramic structure.

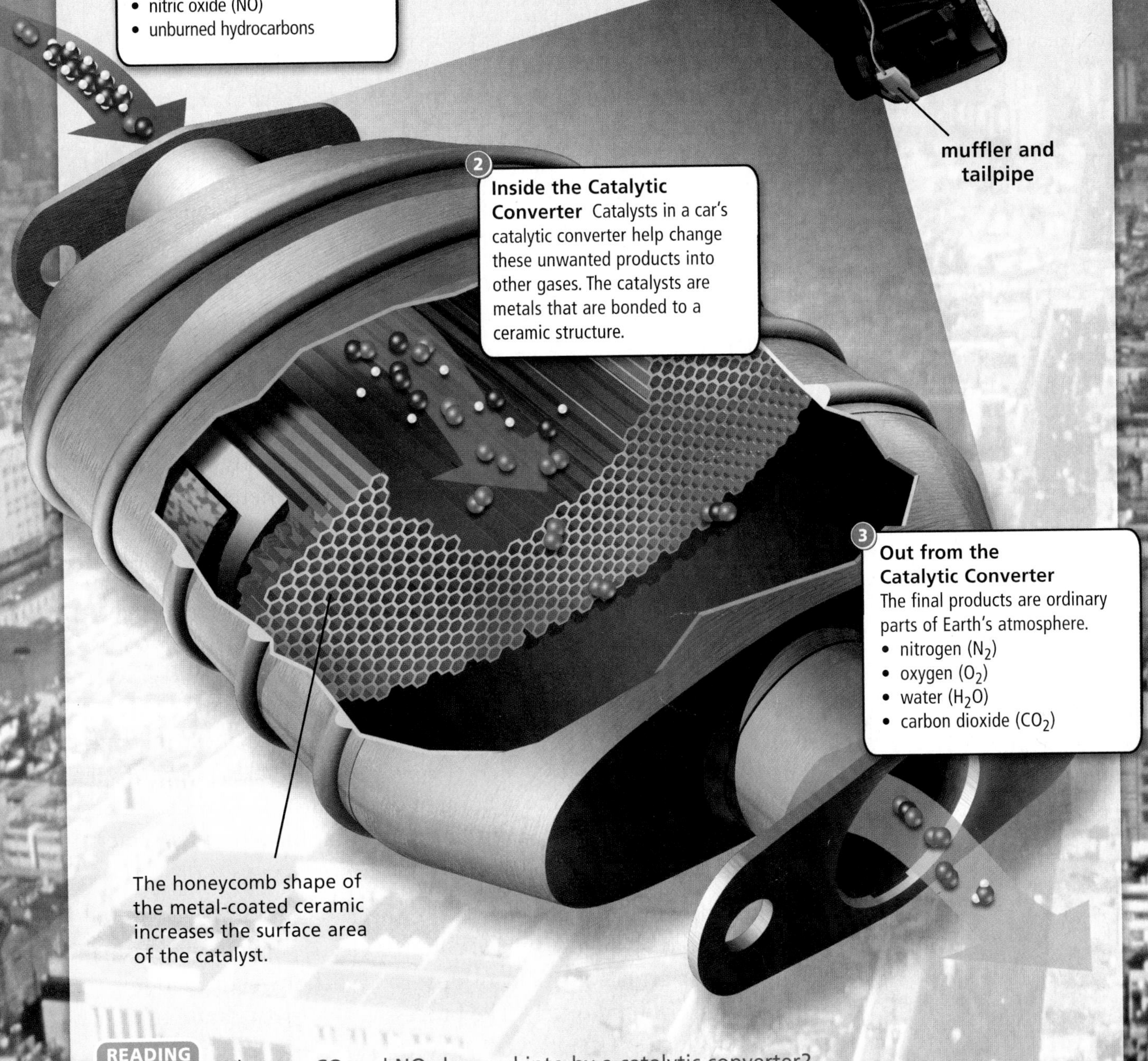

3 Out from the Catalytic Converter
The final products are ordinary parts of Earth's atmosphere.
- nitrogen (N_2)
- oxygen (O_2)
- water (H_2O)
- carbon dioxide (CO_2)

The honeycomb shape of the metal-coated ceramic increases the surface area of the catalyst.

READING VISUALS What are CO and NO changed into by a catalytic converter?

Industry uses chemical reactions to make useful products.

No area of science and technology has changed today's society as much as the electronics industry has. Just think about all the common electronic products that did not even exist as recently as 30 years ago—from personal computers to CD players to cellular phones. All of these devices are based on the electrical properties of materials called semiconductors. A semiconductor is a material that can precisely control the conduction of electrical signals.

READING TiP

The prefix *semi-* means "partial," so a semiconductor partially conducts electricity.

The most common semiconductor material is the element silicon (Si). Silicon is the second most common element in Earth's crust after oxygen, and it is found in most rocks and sand. Pure silicon is obtained from quartz (SiO_2). The quartz is heated with carbon in an electric furnace at 3000°C. The chemical reaction that takes place is

$$SiO_2 + 2C \longrightarrow Si + 2CO$$

This reaction produces silicon that is about 98 percent pure. However, this silicon is still not pure enough to be used in electronics. Several other refining steps must be used to make silicon that is more than 99.999999999 percent pure.

CHECK YOUR READING What property makes silicon useful in electronic devices?

Quartz (SiO_2) is the source of silicon for chips.

Early electronic devices had to be large enough to fit various types of glass tubes and connecting wires inside. In the 1950s, however, engineers figured out how to replace all of these different tubes and wires with thin layers of material placed on a piece of silicon. The resulting circuits are often called microchips, or simply chips.

In order to make these chips, another reaction is used. This reaction involves a material called photoresist (FOH-toh-rih-ZIST), whose properties change when it is exposed to ultraviolet light. Silicon wafers are first coated with photoresist. A stencil is placed over the surface, which allows some areas of the wafer to be exposed to ultraviolet light while other areas are protected. A chemical reaction takes place between the ultraviolet light and the coating of photoresist. The exposed areas of photoresist remain on the silicon surface after the rest of the material is washed away.

The entire process is carried out in special clean rooms to prevent contamination by dust. A typical chip has electrical pathways so small that a single particle of smoke or dust can block the path, stopping the chip from working properly. The process is automated, and no human hand ever touches a chip.

From Quartz to Microchips

A chemical reaction makes the tiny circuits that are used to run electronic devices such as cellular phones.

1 After silicon is sliced into very thin wafers, it is coated with photoresist. The silicon is covered with a stencil and exposed to ultraviolet light, which reacts with the photoresist.

2 The entire process takes place in clean rooms, where workers wear special clothing to prevent dust from reaching the chips.

3 The areas of the chip that were exposed to ultraviolet light form tiny circuits used in electronic devices.

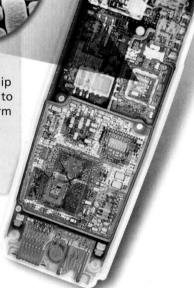

The reaction of photoresist with ultraviolet light is an important chemical reaction. The same type of material is used in the printing of books and newspapers. A similar reaction occurs in photocopiers and laser printers. This is an example of how one type of chemical reaction has helped change industry and society in important ways.

One of the many uses of silicon chips is in cellular phones.

 CHECK YOUR READING Describe how chemical reactions are important in industry.

3.4 Review

KEY CONCEPTS

1. Explain how respiration and photosynthesis are chemically opposite from each other.

2. Provide an example of how catalysts are used in technology.

3. Describe two chemical reactions used in making silicon chips.

CRITICAL THINKING

4. **Compare and Contrast** How are respiration and the combustion of gasoline similar? How are they different?

5. **Analyze** In microchip manufacture, what would happen if the clean rooms had outside windows? Explain.

▲ CHALLENGE

6. **Infer** The gases released from a catalytic converter include N_2, O_2, H_2O, and CO_2. The original reactants must contain atoms of which elements?

Chapter Review

the **BIG** idea

Chemical reactions form new substances by breaking and making chemical bonds.

CONTENT REVIEW
CLASSZONE.COM

KEY CONCEPTS SUMMARY

3.1 Chemical reactions alter arrangements of atoms.

- Chemical changes occur through chemical reactions.
- Evidence of a chemical reaction includes a color change, the formation of a precipitate, the formation of a gas, and a change in temperature.
- Chemical reactions change reactants into products.

VOCABULARY
chemical reaction p. 69
reactant p. 71
product p. 71
precipitate p. 72
catalyst p. 76

3.2 The masses of reactants and products are equal.

- Mass is conserved in chemical reactions.
- Chemical equations summarize chemical reactions.
- Balanced chemical equations show the conservation of mass.

$$CH_4 + O_2 + O_2 \longrightarrow CO_2 + H_2O + H_2O$$

$$CH_4 + 2O_2 \longrightarrow CO_2 + 2H_2O$$

VOCABULARY
law of conservation of mass p. 79
coefficient p. 82

3.3 Chemical reactions involve energy changes.

- Different bonds contain different amounts of energy.
- In an exothermic reaction, more energy is released than added.
- In an endothermic reaction, more energy is added than released.

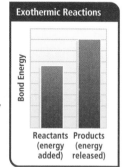

Exothermic Reactions

Bond Energy

Reactants (energy added)   Products (energy released)

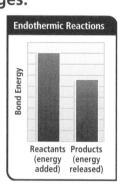

Endothermic Reactions

Bond Energy

Reactants (energy added)   Products (energy released)

VOCABULARY
bond energy p. 86
exothermic reaction p. 87
endothermic reaction p. 87
photosynthesis p. 90

3.4 Life and industry depend on chemical reactions.

- Living things rely on chemical reactions that release energy from molecules.
- Different parts of modern society rely on chemical reactions.

VOCABULARY
respiration p. 94

Reviewing Vocabulary

Describe how the vocabulary terms in the following pairs are related to each other. Explain the relationship in a one- or two-sentence answer.

1. reactant, product

2. law of conservation of mass, chemical reaction

3. endothermic, exothermic

4. respiration, photosynthesis

Reviewing Key Concepts

Multiple Choice *Choose the letter of the best answer.*

5. During a chemical reaction, reactants always
  a. become more complex
  b. require catalysts
  c. lose mass
  d. form products

6. The splitting of water molecules into hydrogen and oxygen molecules is an example of a
  a. combination reaction
  b. chemical change
  c. synthesis reaction
  d. physical change

7. Combustion reactions
  a. destroy atoms
  c. form precipitates
  b. require glucose
  d. require oxygen

8. Which of the following will increase the rate of a reaction?
  a. breaking solid reactants into smaller pieces
  b. removing a catalyst
  c. decreasing the temperature
  d. decreasing the concentration

9. What does a catalyst do in a chemical reaction?
  a. It slows the reaction down.
  b. It speeds the reaction up.
  c. It becomes a product.
  d. It is a reactant.

10. During a chemical reaction, the total amount of mass present
  a. increases
  b. decreases
  c. may increase or decrease
  d. does not change

11. Chemical equations show summaries of
  a. physical changes
  b. changes of state
  c. chemical reactions
  d. changes in temperature

12. A chemical equation must
  a. show energy
  c. use subscripts
  b. be balanced
  d. use coefficients

13. What type of reaction occurs if the reactants have a greater total bond energy than the products?
  a. an endothermic reaction
  b. a synthesis reaction
  c. an exothermic reaction
  d. a decomposition reaction

14. Endothermic reactions always
  a. absorb energy
  b. make more complex products
  c. release energy
  d. make less complex products

Short Answer *Write a short answer to each question.*

15. Describe the differences between physical and chemical changes. How can each be identified?

16. Compare and contrast the overall chemical reactions of photosynthesis and respiration. How can these reactions be described in terms of bond energy in the reactants and products?

17. Describe an example of an advance in technology that makes use of a chemical reaction.

18. When you balance a chemical equation, why can you change coefficients of reactants or products, but not subscripts?

Thinking Critically

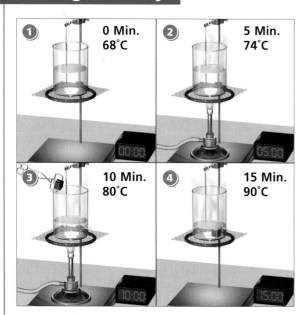

① 0 Min. 68°C	② 5 Min. 74°C
③ 10 Min. 80°C	④ 15 Min. 90°C

The series of illustrations above shows a chemical reaction at five-minute intervals. Use the information in the illustrations to answer the following six questions.

19. OBSERVE What happened to the temperature of the substance in the beaker from the beginning to the end of each five-minute interval?

20. ANALYZE Does the reaction appear to continue in step 4? What evidence tells you?

21. CLASSIFY Is this an endothermic or exothermic reaction? Explain.

22. INFER Suppose the metal cube placed in the beaker in step 3 is a catalyst. What effect did the metal have on the reaction? Why?

23. PREDICT If the metal cube is a catalyst, how much of the metal cube will be left in the beaker when the reaction is completed? Explain.

24. SYNTHESIZE Assume that the reaction shown is a decomposition reaction. Describe what happens to the reactants.

Using Math Skills in Science

Answer the following ten questions based on the equations below.

$$\text{Equation 1—HgO} \longrightarrow \text{Hg} + \text{O}_2$$

$$\text{Equation 2—Al} + \text{O}_2 \longrightarrow \text{Al}_2\text{O}_3$$

$$\text{Equation 3—S}_8 + \text{O}_2 \longrightarrow \text{SO}_3$$

25. Copy and balance equation 1.

26. What coefficients, if any, did you add to equation 1 to balance it?

27. How many Hg atoms take part in the reaction represented by equation 1 when it is balanced?

28. Copy and balance equation 2.

29. What coefficients, if any, did you add to equation 2 to balance it?

30. How many O atoms take part in the reaction represented by equation 2 when it is balanced?

31. Copy and balance equation 3.

32. What coefficients, if any, did you add to equation 3 to balance it?

33. How many S atoms take part in the reaction represented by equation 3 when it is balanced?

34. How many O atoms take part in the reaction represented by equation 3 when it is balanced?

the BIG idea

35. DRAW CONCLUSIONS Describe three ways in which chemical reactions are important in your life.

36. ANALYZE Look back at the photograph and question on pages 66 and 67. Answer the question in terms of the chapter's Big Idea.

UNIT PROJECTS

Check your schedule for your unit project. How are you doing? Be sure that you have placed data or notes from your research in your project folder.

Analyzing Theories

Answer the questions based on the information in the following passage.

During the 1700s, scientists thought that matter contained a substance called phlogiston. According to this theory, wood was made of phlogiston and ash. When wood burned, the phlogiston was released and the ash was left behind.

The ash that remained had less mass than the original wood. This decrease in mass was explained by the release of phlogiston. However, when substances such as phosphorus and mercury burned, the material that remained had more mass than the original substances. This increase in mass did not make sense to some scientists.

The scientists who supported the phlogiston theory said that the phlogiston in some substances had negative mass. So, when the substances burned, they released phlogiston and gained mass. Other scientists disagreed, and their research led to the discovery of a scientific law. Antoine Lavoisier carried out several experiments by burning metals in sealed containers. He showed that mass is never lost or gained in a chemical reaction.

1. What did the phlogiston theory successfully explain?
   a. the presence of ash in unburned wood
   b. the apparent gain of mass in some reactions
   c. the chemical makeup of the air
   d. the apparent decrease in mass in some situations

2. Why did some scientists disagree with the phlogiston theory?
   a. Burning a substance always produced an increase in mass.
   b. Burning a substance always produced a decrease in mass.
   c. Burning could produce either an increase or decrease in mass.
   d. Burning wood produced ash and phlogiston.

3. What law did Lavoisier's work establish?
   a. conservation of energy
   b. conservation of mass
   c. conservation of momentum
   d. conservation of resources

4. To carry out his experiments, what kind of equipment did Lavoisier need?
   a. devices to separate the different elements in the air
   b. machines that could separate wood from ash
   c. microscopes that could be used to study rust and ash
   d. balances that could measure mass very accurately

Extended Response

Answer the following questions in detail.
Include some of the terms from the list on the right.
Underline each term you use in your answers.

catalyst	coefficient	concentration
temperature	reaction	subscript
surface area		

5. Suppose you wanted to change the rate of a chemical reaction. What might you change in the reaction? Explain each factor.

6. Is the chemical equation shown below balanced? Why or why not? How are balanced chemical equations related to conservation of mass?

$$6CO_2 + 6H_2O \longrightarrow C_6H_{12}O_6 + O_2$$

TIMELINES in Science

THE STORY OF
ATOMIC STRUCTURE

About 2500 years ago, certain Greek thinkers proposed that all matter consisted of extremely tiny particles called atoms. The sizes and shapes of different atoms, they reasoned, was what determined the properties of a substance. This early atomic theory, however, was not widely accepted. Many at the time found these tiny, invisible particles difficult to accept.

What everyone could observe was that all substances were liquid, solid, or gas, light or heavy, hot or cold. Everything, they thought, must then be made of only a few basic substances or elements. They reasoned these elements must be water, air, fire, and earth. Different substances contained different amounts of each of these four substances.

The timeline shows a few of the major events that led scientists to accept the idea that matter is made of atoms and agree on the basic structure of atoms. With the revised atomic theory, scientists were able to explain how elements could be basic but different.

1661

Boyle Challenges Concept of the Four Elements

British chemist Robert Boyle proposes that more than four basic substances exist. Boyle also concludes that all matter is made of very tiny particles he calls corpuscles.

EVENTS

| 1600 | 1620 | 1640 | 1660 |

APPLICATIONS AND TECHNOLOGY

TECHNOLOGY

Collecting and Studying Gases

Throughout the 1600s, scientists tried to study gases but had difficulty collecting them. English biologist Stephen Hales designed an apparatus to collect gases. The "pneumatic trough" was a breakthrough in chemistry because it allowed scientists to collect and study gases for the first time. The pneumatic trough was later used by such chemists as Joseph Black, Henry Cavendish, and Joseph Priestley to study the gases that make up the air we breathe. The work of these scientists showed that air was made of more than a single gas.

1808

John Dalton Says: "Bring Back the Atom"

English chemist John Dalton revives the ancient Greek idea that all matter is made of atoms. Dalton claims that each element has its own type of atom and that the atoms combine in fixed and predictable ratios with one another in different substances.

1897

It's Smaller Than the Atom!

English physicist Joseph John Thomson discovers the electron—the first subatomic particle to be identified. Thomson concludes that these tiny particles have a negative charge. Thomson will later propose that atoms are made of a great many of these negative particles floating in a sea of positive charge. Thomson suggests that each atom resembles a dish of pudding with raisins in it. The electrons are the raisins and the pudding the positive charge in which they float.

1808

Humphrey Davy Shocks Chemistry

English chemist Humphrey Davy applies an electric current to different materials. He discovers that many materials once thought to be elements break apart into even simpler materials. Davy succeeds in isolating the elements sodium, calcium, strontium, and barium.

| 1800 | 1820 | 1840 | 1860 | 1880 |

TECHNOLOGY

Chemistry and Electric Charge

In 1800 Italian physicist Alessandro Volta announced that he had produced an electric current from a pile, or battery, of alternating zinc and silver discs. Volta's invention was important for the study of atoms and elements in two ways. First, the fact that the contact of two different metals could produce an electric current suggested that electric charge must be part of matter. Second, the powerful electric current produced by the batteries enabled chemists to break apart many other substances, showing that there were more elements than previously thought.

1903
Atoms Release Energy

Polish-born French physicist Marie Curie and her husband, Pierre, have won the Nobel Prize for their isolation of the elements polonium and radium. These elements are unique because they release energy. Marie Curie names this trait "radioactivity." They share the award with Henri Becquerel, who previously observed this trait with the element uranium.

1911
Atoms Have a Center

By aiming a stream of particles at a piece of gold foil, New Zealand-born physicist Ernest Rutherford finds that atoms are not like a dish of pudding filled with raisins, as J. J. Thomson had suggested. Atoms must have a positive center because many of the particles bounce back. He calls the atom's center its nucleus.

1913
Bohr Puts Electrons into Orbit

Building on the work of Rutherford, Danish physicist Niels Bohr claims that electrons move about the nucleus only in certain, well-defined orbits. Bohr also says that electrons can jump to different orbits and emit or absorb energy when doing so.

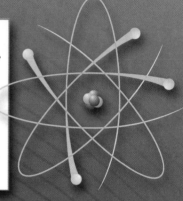

1919
Atoms Share a Common Bond

U.S. chemists G.N. Lewis and Irving Langmuir suggest that atoms of many elements form bonds by sharing pairs of electrons. The idea that atoms could share electrons leads to a greater understanding of how molecules are structured.

1900   1905   1910   1915   1920   1940

APPLICATION

The Chemistry of Communication

The discovery of the electron resulted in more than a greater understanding of the atom. It also opened new ways of communicating. In 1906, U.S. inventor Lee De Forest invented a device for detecting and amplifying radio signals that he called the audion. The audion worked by producing a beam of electrons inside a vacuum tube. The beam was then made to respond to radio signals that it received from an antenna. The audion helped pave the way for later devices such as the transistor.

1960s

Smaller Particles Discovered

By smashing atoms into one another, scientists discover that protons and neutrons are themselves composed of even smaller particles. In a bit of scientific humor, these smaller particles are named "quarks," a nonsense word taken from a novel. Scientists detect these particles by observing the tracks they make in special detectors.

1980s

Tunneling to the Atomic Level

Scanning tunneling microscopes (STMs) allow scientists to interact with matter at the atomic level. Electrons on the tiny tip of an STM "tunnel" through the gap between the tip and target surface. By recording changes in the tunneling current, researchers get an accurate picture.

 RESOURCE CENTER
CLASSZONE.COM

Explore advances in atomic research.

1960   **1980**   **2000**

TECHNOLOGY

Particle Accelerators

Particle accelerators speed up charged particles by passing them through an electric field. By smashing subatomic particles into one another, scientists are able to learn what these particles are made of as well as the forces holding them together. The H1 particle detector in Hamburg, Germany, can accelerate protons to 800 billion volts and is used to study the quarks that make up protons.

INTO THE **FUTURE**

Humans have gone from hypothesizing atoms exist to being able to see and move them. People once considered only four substances to be true elements; today we understand how there are more than a hundred simple substances. Not only have scientists learned atoms contain electric charges, they have also learned how to use these charges.

As scientists learn more and more about the atom, it is difficult to say what they will find next. Is there something smaller than a quark? Is there one type of particle from which all other particles are made? Will we one day be able to move and connect atoms in any way we want? Are there other kinds of atoms to discover? Maybe one day we will find answers to these questions.

ACTIVITIES

Explore a Model Atom

The discovery of the nucleus was one of the most important discoveries in human history. Rutherford's experiment, however, was a simple one that you can model. Take an aluminum pie plate and place a table tennis ball-sized piece of clay at its center. The clay represents a nucleus. Place the end of a grooved ruler at the edge of the plate. Hold the other end up to form a ramp. Roll a marble down the groove toward the clay. Move the ruler to different angles with each roll. Roll the marble 20 times. How many rolls out of 20 hit the clay ball? How do you think the results would be different if the atoms looked like pudding with raisins in it, as Thomson suggested?

Writing About Science

Suppose you are an atom. Choose one of the events on the timeline and describe it from the atom's point of view.

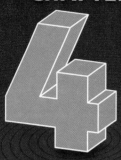
Solutions

the **BIG** idea

When substances dissolve to form a solution, the properties of the mixture change.

Why might some substances dissolve in the seawater in this photograph, but others do not?

Key Concepts

SECTION

(4.1) A solution is a type of mixture.
Learn how solutions differ from other types of mixtures.

SECTION

(4.2) The amount of solute that dissolves can vary.
Learn how solutions can contain different amounts of dissolved substances.

SECTION

(4.3) Solutions can be acidic, basic, or neutral.
Learn about acids and bases and where they are found.

SECTION

(4.4) Metal alloys are solid mixtures.
Learn about alloys and how they are used.

Internet Preview

CLASSZONE.COM

Chapter 4 online resources: Content Review, Simulation, Visualization, three Resource Centers, Math Tutorial, Test Practice

EXPLORE (the BIG idea)

Does It Dissolve?

Pour water into four small clear cups. Add a teaspoon of each of the following: in cup 1, powdered drink mix; in cup 2, vinegar; in cup 3, milk; in cup 4, sand. Stir briefly. Observe the contents of all four cups for five minutes.

Observe and Think Do all of the substances dissolve in water? How can you tell?

Acid Test

Rub a radish on three blank index cards until the marks on the cards become dark pink. Use cotton swabs to wipe lemon juice onto the mark on the first card, tap water onto the mark on the second card, and soda water onto the mark on the third card. Observe the color of the radish mark on each index card.

Observe and Think What happened to the color on each index card? How might the three liquids that you tested differ?

Internet Activity: Alloys

Go to **ClassZone.com** to investigate alloys. Explore the production of different varieties of an alloy by changing the percentages of the metals used to make them. Find out how different alloys have different properties.

Observe and Think How does changing the composition of an alloy change its properties? Why?

NSTA
scilinks.org

SCiLINKS

Solutions **Code:** MDL025

Getting Ready to Learn

◀ CONCEPT REVIEW

- Matter can change from one physical state to another.
- A mixture is a blend of substances that do not react chemically.
- Particles can have electrical charges.

◀ VOCABULARY REVIEW

proton p. 11

ion p. 14

molecule p. 51

chemical reaction p. 69

mixture *See Glossary.*

 **CONTENT REVIEW**
CLASSZONE.COM
Review concepts and vocabulary.

▶ TAKING NOTES

MIND MAP

Write each main idea, or blue heading, in an oval; then write details that relate to each other and to the main idea. Organize the details so that each line of the map has a note about one part of the main idea.

CHOOSE YOUR OWN STRATEGY

For each new vocabulary term, take notes by choosing one of the strategies from earlier chapters—**frame game**, **description wheel**, or **four square** diagram. You can also use other vocabulary strategies that you might already know.

See the Note-Taking Handbook on pages R45–R51.

SCIENCE NOTEBOOK

parts not easily separated or differentiated
substances dissolved in a solvent

A solution is a type of mixture.

can be solid, liquid, or gas
physical properties differ from solvent

Frame Game
example
example — TERM — example
example

Description Wheel
feature
feature — TERM — feature
feature

Four Square
definition	characteristics
TERM	
examples	nonexamples

A solution is a type of mixture.

BEFORE, you learned

- Ionic or covalent bonds hold a compound together
- Chemical reactions produce chemical changes
- Chemical reactions alter the arrangements of atoms

NOW, you will learn

- How a solution differs from other types of mixtures
- About the parts of a solution
- How properties of solutions differ from properties of their separate components

VOCABULARY

solution p. 111
solute p. 112
solvent p. 112
suspension p. 113

EXPLORE Mixtures

Which substances dissolve in water?

PROCEDURE

1. Pour equal amounts of water into each cup.
2. Pour one spoonful of table salt into one of the cups. Stir.
3. Pour one spoonful of flour into the other cup. Stir.
4. Record your observations.

WHAT DO YOU THINK?

- Did the salt dissolve? Did the flour dissolve?
- How can you tell?

MATERIALS

- tap water
- 2 clear plastic cups
- plastic spoon
- table salt
- flour

VOCABULARY
Remember to use the strategy of your choice. You might use a four square diagram for *solution*.

The parts of a solution are mixed evenly.

A mixture is a combination of substances, such as a fruit salad. The ingredients of any mixture can be physically separated from each other because they are not chemically changed—they are still the same substances. Sometimes, however, a mixture is so completely blended that its ingredients cannot be identified as different substances. A **solution** is a type of mixture, called a homogeneous mixture, that is the same throughout. A solution can be physically separated, but all portions of a solution have the same properties.

If you stir sand into a glass of water, you can identify the sand as a separate substance that falls to the bottom of the glass. Sand in water is a mixture that is not a solution. If you stir sugar into a glass of water, you cannot identify the sugar as a separate substance. Sugar in water is a common solution, as are examples such as seawater, gasoline, and the liquid part of your blood.

Solutes and Solvents

READING TIP

The words *solute* and *solvent* are both related to the Latin word *solvere,* which means "to loosen."

Like other mixtures, a solution has definite components. A **solute** (SAHL-yoot) is a substance that is dissolved to make a solution. When a solute dissolves, it separates into individual particles. A **solvent** is a substance that dissolves a solute. Because a solute dissolves into individual particles in a solvent, it is not possible to identify the solute and solvent as different substances when they form a solution.

In a solution of table salt and water, the salt is the solute and the water is the solvent. In the cells of your body, substances such as calcium ions and sugar are solutes, and water is the solvent. Water is the most common and important solvent, but other substances can also be solvents. For example, if you have ever used an oil-based paint you know that water will not clean the paintbrushes. Instead, a solvent like turpentine must be used.

CHECK YOUR READING What is the difference between a solute and a solvent?

Types of Solutions

Many solutions are made of solids dissolved in liquids. However, solutes, solvents, and solutions can be gases, liquids, or solids. For example, oxygen, a gas, is dissolved in seawater. The bubbles in carbonated drinks come from the release of carbon dioxide gas that was dissolved in the drink.

In some solutions, both the solute and the solvent are in the same physical state. Vinegar, for example, is a solution of acetic acid in water. In a solution of different liquids, it may be difficult to say which substance is the solute and which is the solvent. In general, the substance present in the greater amount is the solvent. Since there is more water than acetic acid in vinegar, water is the solvent and acetic acid is the solute.

Although you may usually think of a solution as a liquid, solid solutions also exist. For example, bronze is a solid solution in which tin is the solute and copper is the solvent. Solid solutions are not formed as solids. Instead, the solvent metal is heated until it melts and becomes a liquid. Then the solute is added, and the substances are thoroughly mixed together. When the mixture cools, it is a solid solution.

Solutions made of combinations of gases are also common. The air you breathe is a solution. Because nitrogen makes up the largest portion of air, it is the solvent. Other gases present, such as oxygen and carbon dioxide, are solutes.

Gas Solution
Air is oxygen and other gases dissolved in nitrogen.

Solid Solution
Bronze consists of tin dissolved in copper.

Liquid Solution
Water often contains many dissolved substances.

CHECK YOUR READING When substances in a solution are in the same physical state, which is the solvent?

INVESTIGATE Solutions

How can you separate the parts of a solution?

PROCEDURE

1. Draw a solid black circular region 6 cm in diameter around the point of the filter.
2. Place the filter, point up, over the top of the bottle.
3. Squeeze several drops of water onto the point of the filter.
4. Observe the filter once every minute for 10 minutes. Record your observations.

WHAT DO YOU THINK?

- What happened to the ink on the filter?
- Identify, in general, the solutes and the solution in this investigation.

CHALLENGE Relate your observations of the ink and water on the coffee filter to the properties of solutions.

SKILL FOCUS
Observing

MATERIALS
- black marker
- coffee filter
- plastic bottle
- eyedropper
- tap water
- stopwatch

TIME

15 minutes

Suspensions

When you add flour to water, the mixture turns cloudy, and you cannot see through it. This mixture is not a solution but a suspension. In a **suspension**, the particles are larger than those found in a solution. Instead of dissolving, these larger particles turn the liquid cloudy. Sometimes you can separate the components of a suspension by filtering the mixture.

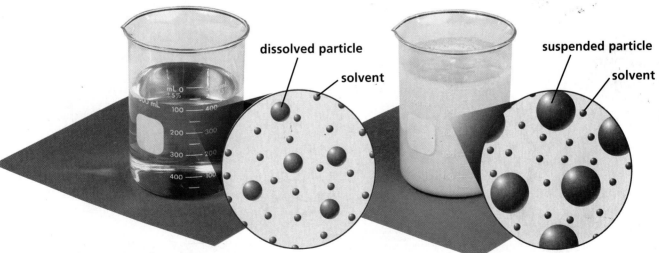

Solution Dissolved particles cannot be identified as a substance different from the solvent.

Suspension Particles that do not dissolve make a suspension look cloudy.

Solvent and solute particles interact.

The parts of a solution—that is, the solute and the solvent—can be physically separated because they are not changed into new substances. However, individual particles of solute and solvent do interact. When a solid dissolves in a liquid, the particles of the solute are surrounded by particles of the liquid. The solute particles become evenly distributed throughout the solvent.

The way in which a solid compound dissolves in a liquid depends on the type of bonds in the compound. Ionic compounds, such as table salt (NaCl), split apart into individual ions. When table salt dissolves in water, the sodium and chloride ions separate, and each ion is surrounded by water molecules. When a covalent compound, such as table sugar ($C_{12}H_{22}O_{11}$), dissolves, each molecule stays together and is surrounded by solvent molecules. The general processes that take place when ionic compounds dissolve and when covalent compounds dissolve are shown below.

How Solutes Dissolve

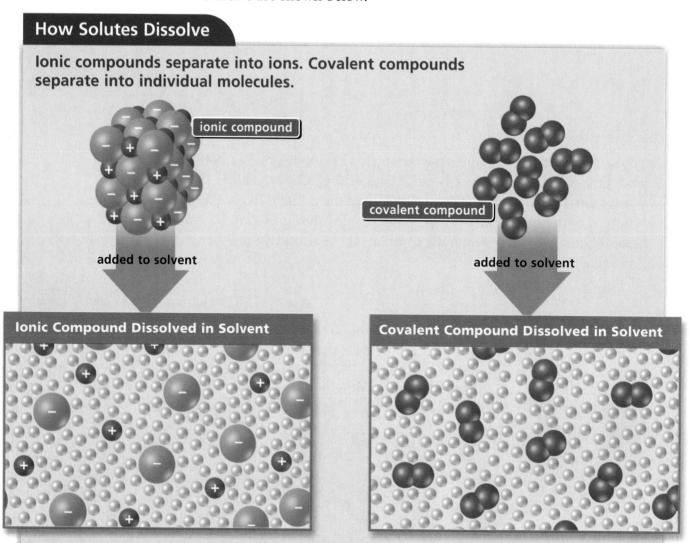

Ionic compounds separate into ions. Covalent compounds separate into individual molecules.

ionic compound

covalent compound

added to solvent

added to solvent

Ionic Compound Dissolved in Solvent

Covalent Compound Dissolved in Solvent

READING VISUALS   What difference between the two illustrations tells you whether a compound is ionic or covalent?

Properties of solvents change in solutions.

In every solution—solid, liquid, and gas—solutes change the physical properties of a solvent. Therefore, a solution's physical properties differ from the physical properties of the pure solvent. The amount of solute in the solution determines how much the physical properties of the solvent are changed.

Lowering the Freezing Point

Recall that the freezing point is the temperature at which a liquid becomes a solid. The freezing point of a liquid solvent decreases—becomes lower—when a solute is dissolved in it. For example, pure water freezes at 0°C (32°F) under normal conditions. When a solute is dissolved in water, the resulting solution has a freezing point below 0°C.

Lowering the freezing point of water can be very useful in winter. Road crews spread salt on streets and highways during snowstorms because salt lowers the freezing point of water. When snow mixes with salt on the roads, a saltwater solution that does not freeze at 0°C is formed. The more salt that is used, the lower the freezing point of the solution.

Since salt dissolves in the small amount of water usually present on the surface of ice, it helps to melt any ice already present on the roads. However, there is a limit to salt's effectiveness because there is a limit to how much will dissolve. No matter how much salt is used, once the temperature goes below −21°C (−6°F), the melted ice will freeze again.

> **REMINDER**
>
> In temperature measurements, *C* stands for "Celsius" and *F* stands for "Fahrenheit."

CHECK YOUR READING How does the freezing point of a solvent change when a solute is dissolved in it?

Making ice cream also depends on lowering the freezing point of a solvent. Most hand-cranked ice cream makers hold the liquid ice cream ingredients in a canister surrounded by a mixture of salt and ice. The salt added to the ice lowers the freezing point of this mixture. This causes the ice to melt—absorbing heat from its surroundings, including the ice cream ingredients. The ice cream mix is chilled while its ingredients are constantly stirred. As a result, tiny ice crystals form all at once in the ice cream mixture instead of a few crystals forming and growing larger as the mix freezes. This whole process helps to make ice cream that is smooth and creamy.

Adding salt to lower the freezing point of ice helps to make ice cream.

Raising the Boiling Point

The boiling point of a liquid is the temperature at which the liquid forms bubbles in its interior and becomes a gas. Under normal conditions, a substance cannot exist as a liquid at a temperature greater than its boiling point. However, the boiling point of a solution is higher than the boiling point of the pure solvent. Therefore, a solution can remain a liquid at a higher temperature than its pure solvent.

For example, the boiling point of pure water is 100°C (212°F) under normal conditions. Saltwater, however, can be a liquid at temperatures above 100°C because salt raises the boiling point of water. The amount of salt in the water determines how much the boiling point is increased. The more solute that is dissolved in a solution, the greater the increase in boiling point.

APPLY Why might the addition of antifreeze to the water in this car's radiator have prevented the car from overheating?

CHECK YOUR READING How does the boiling point of a solution depend on the amount of solute in it?

A solute lowers the freezing point and raises the boiling point of the solvent in the solution. The result is that the solute extends the temperature range in which the solvent remains a liquid. One way in which both a decrease in freezing point and an increase in boiling point can be useful in the same solution involves a car's radiator. Antifreeze, which is mostly a chemical called ethylene glycol, is often added to the water in the radiator. This solution prevents the water from freezing in the winter and also keeps it from boiling in the summer.

4.1 Review

KEY CONCEPTS

1. How is a solution different from other mixtures?

2. Describe the two parts of a solution. How can you tell them apart?

3. How does the boiling point of a solvent change when a solute is dissolved in it? How does the freezing point change?

CRITICAL THINKING

4. **Contrast** Contrast the way in which an ionic compound, such as table salt, dissolves with the way in which a covalent compound, such as sugar, dissolves.

5. **Infer** Pure water freezes at 0°C and boils at 100°C. Would tap water likely freeze and boil at those exact temperatures? Why or why not?

CHALLENGE

6. **Synthesize** People often sprinkle salt on icy driveways and sidewalks. Would a substance like flour have a similar effect on the ice? Explain.

The amount of solute that dissolves can vary.

BEFORE, you learned

- Solutions are a type of mixture
- A solution is made when a solute is dissolved in a solvent
- Solutes change the properties of solvents

NOW, you will learn

- About the concentration of a solution
- How a solute's solubility can be changed
- How solubility depends on molecular structure

VOCABULARY

concentration p. 117
dilute p. 118
saturated p. 118
solubility p. 119

EXPLORE Solutions and Temperature

How does temperature affect a solution?

PROCEDURE

1. Pour cold soda water into one cup and warm soda water into another cup. Record your observations.

2. After 5 minutes, observe both cups of soda water. Record your observations.

WHAT DO YOU THINK?

- Which solution bubbled more at first?
- Which solution bubbled for a longer period of time?

MATERIALS
- soda water
- 2 clear plastic cups

A solution with a high concentration contains a large amount of solute.

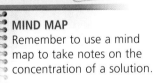

MIND MAP
Remember to use a mind map to take notes on the concentration of a solution.

Think of water from the ocean and drinking water from a well. Water from the ocean tastes salty, but water from a well does not. The well water does contain salt, but in a concentration so low that you cannot taste it. A solution's **concentration** depends on the amount of solute dissolved in a solvent at a particular temperature. A solution with only a small amount of dissolved solute, such as the salt dissolved in well water, is said to have a low concentration. As more solute is dissolved, the concentration gets higher.

If you have ever used a powdered mix to make lemonade, you probably know that you can change the concentration of the drink by varying the amount of mix you put into a certain amount of water. Two scoops of mix in a pitcher of water makes the lemonade stronger than just one scoop. The lemonade with two scoops of mix has a higher concentration of the mix than the lemonade made with one scoop.

Degrees of Concentration

READING **TiP**

The word *dilute* can be used as either an adjective or a verb. A dilute solution has a low concentration of solute. To dilute a solution is to add more solvent to it, thus lowering the concentration of the solution.

A solution that has a low concentration of solute is called a **dilute** solution. Salt dissolved in the drinking water from a well is a dilute solution. The concentration of a solution can be even further reduced, or diluted, by adding more solvent. On the other hand, as more solute is added to a solution, the solution becomes more concentrated. A concentrated solution has a large amount of solute.

Less solute is dissolved in a dilute solution.

More solute is dissolved in a concentrated solution.

Have you ever wondered how much sugar can be dissolved in a glass of iced tea? If you keep adding sugar to the tea, eventually no more sugar will dissolve. The tea will contain as much dissolved sugar as it can hold at that temperature. Such a solution is called a **saturated** solution because it contains the maximum amount of solute that can be dissolved in the solvent at a given temperature. If a solution contains less solute than this maximum amount, it is an unsaturated solution.

 CHECK YOUR READING How are the terms *dilute* and *saturated* related to the concept of concentration?

Supersaturated Solutions

VISUALIZATION
CLASSZONE.COM
Explore supersaturated solutions and precipitation.

Sometimes, a solution contains more dissolved solute than is normally possible. This type of solution is said to be supersaturated. A saturated solution can become supersaturated if more solute is added while the temperature is raised. Then if this solution is slowly cooled, the solute can remain dissolved. This type of solution is very unstable, though. If the solution is disturbed, or more solute is added in the form of a crystal, the excess solute will quickly solidify and form a precipitate. This process is shown in the photographs on the top of page 119.

solute crystal

1

A supersaturated solution contains more dissolved solute than is normally possible.

2

After a crystal of solute is added, or the solution is disturbed, a precipitate forms.

REMINDER

A precipitate is a solid substance that comes out of a solution.

One example of a supersaturated solution is a chemical heat pack that contains sodium acetate and water. The pack contains more sodium acetate than can normally dissolve at room temperature, but when the pack is heated in a microwave oven, all of the sodium acetate dissolves. The solution inside the pack is supersaturated. The heat pack is activated by bending it. This disturbs the solution, solidifying the sodium acetate and releasing a large amount of heat over a long period of time.

Solubility

The **solubility** (SAHL-yuh-BIHL-ih-tee) of a substance is the amount of that substance that will dissolve in a certain amount of solvent at a given temperature. For example, consider household ammonia used for cleaning. This ammonia is not pure ammonia—it is a solution of ammonia in water.

Because a large amount of ammonia can dissolve in water, ammonia is said to have a high solubility in water. However, other substances do not dissolve in such large amounts in water. Only a small amount of carbon dioxide will dissolve in water, so carbon dioxide has a low solubility in water. Oils do not dissolve at all in water, so oils are said to be insoluble in water.

The amount of solute needed to make a saturated solution depends on the solubility of a solute in a particular solvent.

- If the solute is highly soluble, a saturated solution will be very concentrated.
- If the solute has a low solubility, the saturated solution will be dilute.

In other words, a saturated solution can be either dilute or concentrated, depending on the solubility of a solute in a particular solvent.

READING TiP

The word *solubility* is related to the words *solute* and *solvent*, and means "ability to be dissolved." A substance that is insoluble will not dissolve.

CHECK YOUR READING   How does solubility affect a solution?

The solubility of a solute can be changed.

The solubility of a solute can be changed in two ways. Raising the temperature is one way to change the solubility of the solute, because most solids are more soluble at higher temperatures. Another way to change solubility when the solute is a gas is to change the pressure. The solubility of gases in a liquid solvent increases at high pressure.

Temperature and Solubility

An increase in temperature has two effects on most solid solutes—they dissolve more quickly, and a greater amount of the solid dissolves in a given amount of solvent. In general, solids are more soluble at higher temperatures, and they dissolve faster.

The opposite is true of all gases—an increase in temperature makes a gas less soluble in water. You can see this by warming tap water in a pan. As the water approaches its boiling point, any air that is dissolved in the water comes out of solution. The air forms tiny bubbles that rise to the surface.

CHECK YOUR READING What effect does temperature have on most solid solutes? on gaseous solutes?

INVESTIGATE Solubility

How can you change solubility?

Use what you know about solubility to design an experiment that shows how a change in temperature can change the amount of table salt that will dissolve in water.

DESIGN — YOUR OWN — EXPERIMENT

PROCEDURE

1. Use the materials in the list to identify the relationship between temperature and solubility.

2. Write your procedure, identifying the constants and variables.

3. Perform your experiment and record your results.

WHAT DO YOU THINK?

- Which variable did you change? What were your constants? Why?

- How do your results demonstrate the effect of temperature on solubility?

SKILL FOCUS
Designing experiments

MATERIALS
- clear plastic cups
- thermometer
- tap water
- table salt
- balance
- plastic spoon
- hot-water bath
- cold-water bath

TIME
20 minutes

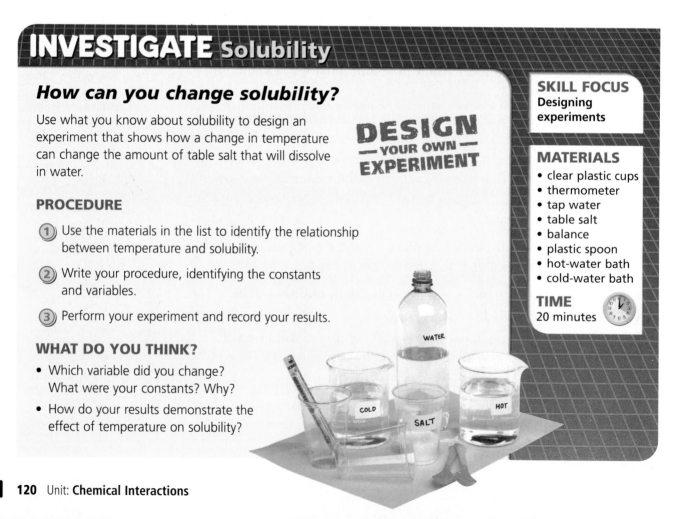

Think back to the earlier discussion of supersaturated solutions. One way in which a solution can become supersaturated is through a change in temperature. For example, suppose that a solution is saturated at 50°C (122°F), and is then

Temperature and Solubility		
Solute	Increased Temperature	Decreased Temperature
Solid	increase in solubility	decrease in solubility
Gas	decrease in solubility	increase in solubility

allowed to cool slowly. The solid is less soluble in the cooler solution, but the excess solute may not form a precipitate. As a result, the solution contains more of the dissolved solute than would be possible under normal conditions because of the change in temperature.

A change in temperature can produce changes in solutions in the environment. For example, a factory located on the shore of a lake may use the lake water as a coolant and then return heated water to the lake. This increase in temperature decreases the solubility of oxygen in the lake water. As a result, less oxygen will remain dissolved in the water. A decrease in the oxygen concentration can harm plant and animal life in the lake.

Changing Temperature Changes Solubility

More sugar dissolves in hot water than in cold water.

Solubility of Table Sugar (in 100 g H$_2$O)

Amount Dissolved (g) vs. Temperature (°C)

The solubility of most solids increases with a rise in temperature.

READING VISUALS About how much sugar will dissolve in 100 g of water at 70°C?

Pressure and Solubility

A change in pressure does not usually change the solubility of solid or liquid solutes. However, the solubility of any gas increases at higher pressures and decreases at lower pressures.

When manufacturers make carbonated beverages, such as soda, they add carbon dioxide gas at a pressure slightly greater than normal air pressure. When you open the can or bottle, the pressure decreases and the carbon dioxide bubbles out of solution with a fizz.

Another example is shown in the photograph on the left. When a diver's tank contains regular air, about 79 percent of the air is nitrogen. People breathe air like this all the time without any problem, but the pressure underwater is much greater than on Earth's surface. The higher pressure increases the solubility of nitrogen in the diver's blood.

When a diver heads up to the surface too fast, the pressure decreases, and so does the solubility of the nitrogen. The nitrogen comes out of solution, forming bubbles in the diver's blood vessels. These bubbles can cause a painful and sometimes fatal condition called the bends.

Divers can avoid the bends in two ways. They can rise to the surface very slowly, so that nitrogen bubbles stay small and pass through the bloodstream more easily. They can also breathe a different mixture of gases. Some professional divers breathe a mixture of oxygen and nitrogen that contains only about 66 percent nitrogen. For very deep dives, the mixture can also include helium because helium is less soluble in blood than nitrogen.

INFER If these divers are breathing regular air, why might they be looking at their depth gauges?

Pressure and Solubility		
Solute	Increased Pressure	Decreased Pressure
Solid	no effect on solubility	no effect on solubility
Gas	increase in solubility	decrease in solubility

 CHECK YOUR READING How does pressure affect the solubility of solids? of gases?

Solubility depends on molecular structure.

Everyone knows that oil and water do not mix. When a tanker spills oil near shore, the oil floats on the water and pollutes the beaches. Why do oil and water not mix? The answer involves their different molecular structures.

When a substance dissolves, its molecules or ions separate from one another and become evenly mixed with molecules of the solvent. Recall that water contains polar covalent bonds. As a result, water molecules have a negative region and a positive region. Water molecules are said to be polar. The molecules of an oil are nonpolar—the molecules do not have positive and negative regions. This difference makes oil insoluble in water.

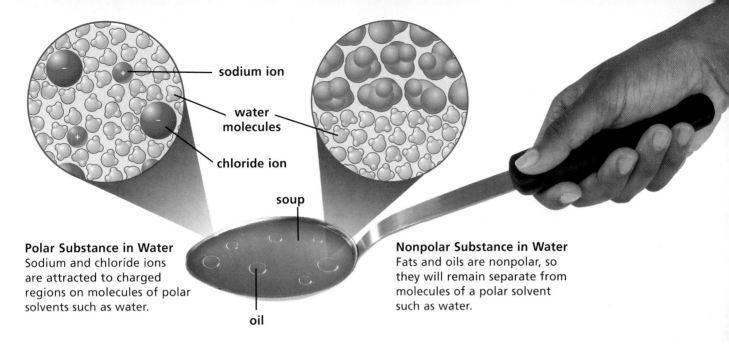

sodium ion

water molecules

chloride ion

soup

oil

Polar Substance in Water
Sodium and chloride ions are attracted to charged regions on molecules of polar solvents such as water.

Nonpolar Substance in Water
Fats and oils are nonpolar, so they will remain separate from molecules of a polar solvent such as water.

Because water is polar and oil is nonpolar, their molecules are not attracted to each other. The molecules of a polar solvent like water are attracted to other polar molecules, such as those of sugar. This explains why sugar has such a high solubility in water. Ionic compounds, such as sodium chloride, are also highly soluble in water. Because water molecules are polar, they interact with the sodium and chloride ions. In general, polar solvents dissolve polar solutes, and nonpolar solvents dissolve nonpolar solutes. This concept is often expressed as "Like dissolves like."

So many substances dissolve in water that it is sometimes called the universal solvent. Water is considered to be essential for life because it can carry so many different ions and molecules—just about anything the body needs or needs to get rid of—through the body.

Why will a nonpolar substance not dissolve in a polar substance?

4.2 Review

KEY CONCEPTS

1. How can a solution be made more concentrated? less concentrated?

2. What two factors can change the solubility of a gas?

3. Are nonpolar compounds highly soluble in water? Why or why not?

CRITICAL THINKING

4. **Predict** Suppose you stir sugar into ice water. Some sugar remains on the bottom of the glass. After the glass sits out for an hour, you stir it again. What will happen? Why?

5. **Infer** A powder dissolves easily in water but not in oil. Are the molecules in the powder probably polar or nonpolar? Explain.

○ CHALLENGE

6. **Synthesize** If mixing a substance with water forms a suspension, does the substance have a high or a low solubility in water? Explain.

Cool, Clear Water

The drinking water that comes out of a tap is a solution. Many minerals, chemicals, and even gases are dissolved in it. Some drinking water comes from rivers, lakes, or reservoirs, but about half of the drinking water in the United States is pumped from wells. Well water comes from underground aquifers. The water in aquifers flows through gaps in broken or porous rocks.

Filtering Impurities

The water in a puddle is not pure water. It contains suspended dirt and dissolved chemicals. This water can be cleaned underground. As the solution flows through soil and rocks, the soil and rocks filter and trap particles. Some chemicals in the water are removed from the solution by clay particles in the soil. Other chemicals, such as acids from acid rain, are neutralized by limestone and other rocks.

Adding Minerals

The rocks surrounding aquifers do not just remove chemicals from water. As water flows underground, minerals dissolve in the water. The solutes include compounds of calcium, magnesium, and iron. These compounds do not harm the quality of drinking water because they are necessary parts of your diet. Water with a high concentration of dissolved minerals is called hard water.

Copying Earth

Water that has been used by people must be cleaned before it is returned to the environment. Waste treatment plants copy some of the natural cleansing processes of Earth. Wastewater solutions may contain many dissolved impurities and harmful chemicals, but the water can be filtered through beds of sand and gravel. Water must be treated after it is used because so many substances dissolve in it.

Water that looks clear, clean, and pure may not be. The water you drink every day contains many dissolved substances.

Aquifer Layer

EXPLORE

1. **INFER** A white solid often forms around a tiny leak in a water pipe. Where does the white solid come from?

2. **CHALLENGE** Use the Internet or call your local water company to find out the source of your drinking water. Find out whether you have hard or soft water and what dissolved chemicals are in your drinking water.

RESOURCE CENTER
CLASSZONE.COM

Learn more about aquifers and water purification.

KEY CONCEPT

4.3 Solutions can be acidic, basic, or neutral.

  BEFORE, you learned

- Substances dissolved in solutions can break apart into ions
- Concentration is the amount of a substance dissolved in a solution
- Water is a common solvent

  NOW, you will learn

- What acids and bases are
- How to determine if a solution is acidic or basic
- How acids and bases react with each other

VOCABULARY

acid p. 126
base p. 126
pH p. 129
neutral p. 129

EXPLORE Acids and Bases

What happens when an antacid mixes with an acid?

PROCEDURE

1. Fill the cup halfway with vinegar.
2. Observe the vinegar in the cup. Record your observations.
3. Crush two antacid tablets and place them in the vinegar.
4. Observe the contents of the cup for 5 minutes. Record your observations.

MATERIALS
- clear plastic cup
- vinegar
- 2 antacid tablets

WHAT DO YOU THINK?
- What did you observe before adding the antacid tablets?
- What happened after you added the tablets?

Acids and bases have distinct properties.

Many solutions have certain properties that make us call them acids or bases. Acids are found in many foods, such as orange juice, tomatoes, and vinegar. They taste slightly sour when dissolved in water and produce a burning or itchy feeling on the skin. Strong acids should never be tasted or touched—these solutions are used in manufacturing and are dangerous chemicals.

Bases are the chemical opposite of acids. They tend to taste bitter rather than sour and often feel slippery to the touch. Bases are also found in common products around the home, including soap, ammonia, and antacids. Strong bases, like the lye used for unclogging drains, are also dangerous chemicals.

READING TiP

The prefix *ant-* means "against," so an antacid is a substance that works against an acid.

Acids, Bases, and Ions

RESOURCE CENTER
CLASSZONE.COM

Find out more about acids and bases.

Generally, a compound that is an acid or a base acts as an acid or a base only when it is dissolved in water. In a water-based solution, these compounds produce ions. Recall that an ion is a charged particle. For example, if a hydrogen atom, which consists of one proton and one electron, loses its electron, it becomes a hydrogen ion. The hydrogen ion is simply a proton and has a positive charge.

An **acid** can be defined as a substance that can donate a hydrogen ion—that is, a proton—to another substance. The diagram below shows what happens when the compound hydrogen chloride (HCl) is dissolved in water. The compound separates into hydrogen ions (H^+) and chloride ions (Cl^-). Hydrogen ions are free to react with other substances, so the solution is an acid. When hydrogen chloride is dissolved in water, the solution is called hydrochloric acid.

READING TiP

The H_2O above the arrow means the substance on the left is added to water and the substances on the right are dissolved in the water.

Acid

$$HCl \xrightarrow{\text{H}_2\text{O}} H^+ + Cl^-$$

In water, acids release a proton (H^+) into the solution.

A **base** can be defined as a substance that can accept a hydrogen ion from another substance. The diagram below shows what happens when the compound sodium hydroxide (NaOH) is dissolved in water. The compound separates into sodium ions (Na^+) and hydroxide ions (OH^-). The hydroxide ions are free to accept protons from other substances, so the solution is a base. The solution that results when NaOH is dissolved in water is called sodium hydroxide.

Base

$$NaOH \xrightarrow{\text{H}_2\text{O}} Na^+ + OH^-$$

In water, many bases release a hydroxide ion (OH^-), which can accept a proton.

On the atomic level, the difference between acids and bases is that acids donate protons and bases accept protons. When a proton—a hydrogen ion—from an acid is accepted by a hydroxide ion from a base, the two ions join together and form a molecule of water. This simple transfer of protons between substances is involved in a great many useful and important chemical reactions.

 CHECK YOUR READING · How are protons related to acids and bases?

Characteristics of Acids

As you read earlier, acids in foods taste sour and produce a burning or prickling feeling on the skin. However, since tasting or touching an unknown chemical is extremely dangerous, other methods are needed to tell whether a solution is an acid.

One safe way to test for an acid is to place a few drops of a solution on a compound that contains a carbonate (CO_3). For example, limestone is a rock that contains calcium carbonate ($CaCO_3$). When an acid touches a piece of limestone, a reaction occurs that produces carbon dioxide gas.

Acids also react with most metals. The reaction produces hydrogen gas, which you can see as bubbles in the photograph on the right. Such a reaction is characteristic of acids.

The feature of acids most often used to identify them is their ability to change the colors of certain compounds known as acid-base indicators. One common indicator is litmus, which is often prepared on slips of paper. When a drop of an acid is placed on litmus paper, the paper turns red.

Acids react with some metals, such as zinc, and release hydrogen gas.

$$2HCl + Zn \longrightarrow H_2 + ZnCl_2$$

 CHECK YOUR READING What are three safe methods to test for an acid?

Characteristics of Bases

Bases also have certain common characteristics. Mild bases in foods taste bitter and feel slippery, but as with acids, tasting and touching are not safe ways of testing whether a solution is a base. In fact, some strong bases can burn the skin as badly as strong acids.

Bases feel soapy or slippery because they react with acidic molecules in your skin called fatty acids. In fact, this is exactly how soap is made. Mixing a base—usually sodium hydroxide—with fatty acids produces soap. So, when a base touches your skin, the combination of the base with your own fatty acids actually makes a small amount of soap.

Like acids, bases change the colors of acid-base indicators, but the colors they produce are different. Bases turn litmus paper blue. A base will counteract the effect that an acid has on an acid-base indicator. You might put a few drops of acid on litmus paper to make it turn red. If you put a few drops of a base on the red litmus paper, the litmus paper will change colors again.

 CHECK YOUR READING How do the characteristics of bases differ from those of acids?

Bases are found in many cleaning agents, including soap.

The strengths of acids and bases can be measured.

MIND MAP
Remember to use a mind map to take notes about acid and base strength.

Battery fluid and many juices contain acids. Many people drink some type of juice every morning, but you would not want to drink, or even touch, the liquid in a car battery. Similarly, you probably wash your hands with soap several times a day, but you would not want to touch the liquid used to unclog drains. Both soap and drain cleaners are bases. Clearly, some acids and bases are stronger than others.

Acid and Base Strength

Strong acids break apart completely into ions. For example, when hydrogen chloride (HCl) dissolves in water to form hydrochloric acid, it breaks down into hydrogen ions and chloride ions. No hydrogen chloride remains in the solution. Because all of the hydrogen chloride forms separate ions, hydrochloric acid is a strong acid.

A weak acid does not form many ions in solution. When acetic acid ($HC_2H_3O_2$), which is the acid in vinegar, dissolves in water, only about 1 percent of the acetic acid breaks up into hydrogen ions and acetate ions. The other 99 percent of the acetic acid remains unchanged. Therefore, acetic acid is a weak acid.

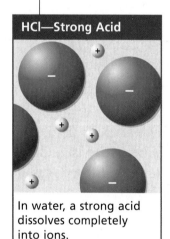

HCl—Strong Acid

In water, a strong acid dissolves completely into ions.

$HC_2H_3O_2$—Weak Acid

In water, a weak acid forms only a small number of ions.

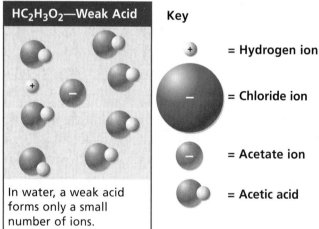

Key

$+$ = Hydrogen ion

$-$ = Chloride ion

$-$ = Acetate ion

= Acetic acid

Bases also can be strong or weak. When sodium hydroxide (NaOH) dissolves in water, it forms sodium ions (Na^+) and hydroxide ions (OH^-). None of the original NaOH remains in the solution, so sodium hydroxide is a strong base. However, when ammonia (NH_3) dissolves in water, only about 1 percent of the ammonia reacts with water to form OH^- ions.

$$NH_3 + H_2O \longrightarrow NH_4^+ + OH^-$$

The other 99 percent of the ammonia remains unchanged, so ammonia is a weak base. The ions formed when NaOH or NH_3 is dissolved in water are shown on the top of page 129.

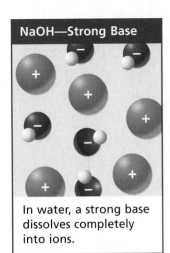

NaOH—Strong Base

In water, a strong base dissolves completely into ions.

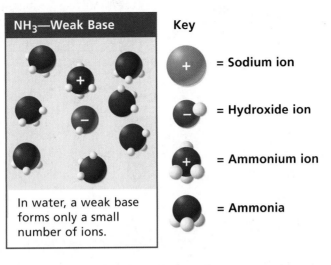

NH₃—Weak Base

In water, a weak base forms only a small number of ions.

Key

$+$ = Sodium ion

$-$ = Hydroxide ion

= Ammonium ion

= Ammonia

READING TiP

Look at the reaction on the bottom of page 128 for help with the illustration of NH_3 in water.

Note that the strength of an acid or base is not the same as its concentration. Dilute hydrochloric acid is still strong and can burn holes in your clothing, whereas acetic acid cannot. The strengths of acids and bases depend on the percentage of the substance that forms ions.

 CHECK YOUR READING What determines acid and base strength?

Measuring Acidity

The acidity of a solution depends on the concentration of H^+ ions in the solution. This concentration is often measured on the **pH** scale. In this scale, a high H^+ concentration is indicated by a low number, and a low H^+ concentration is indicated by a high number. The numbers of the pH scale usually range from 0 to 14, but numbers outside this range are possible. The middle number, 7, represents a neutral solution. A **neutral** substance is neither an acid nor a base. Pure water has a pH of 7.

Numbers below 7 indicate acidic solutions. A concentrated strong acid has a low pH value—the pH of concentrated hydrochloric acid, for example, is less than 0. Numbers above 7 indicate a basic solution. A concentrated strong base has a high pH value—the pH of concentrated sodium hydroxide, for example, is greater than 14. The illustration on page 130 shows the pH values of some common acids and bases.

Today, electronic pH meters are commonly used to measure pH. A probe is placed in a solution, and the pH value is indicated by the meter. An older method of measuring pH is to use an acid-base indicator. You read earlier that acids turn litmus paper red and bases turn litmus paper blue. Other acid-base indicators, such as a universal pH indicator, show a variety of colors at different pH values.

The strip of universal indicator paper in the bottom front of the photograph shows a nearly neutral pH.

 CHECK YOUR READING Is the pH of a base higher or lower than the pH of an acid?

Common Acids and Bases

Dilute acids and bases are found in many common products.

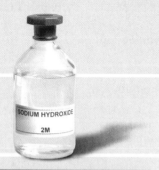

sodium hydroxide (NaOH)—pH > 14

Concentrated NaOH has a pH greater than 14 because it has a very low H⁺ concentration. Drain openers usually contain concentrated NaOH.

milk—pH 6.5

Milk contains molecules called fatty acids, which make milk slightly acidic.

lemon—pH 2

Lemons and other types of citrus fruit contain citric acid.

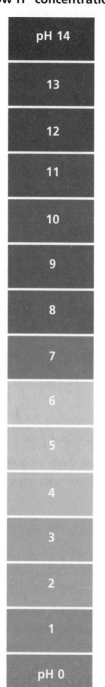

low H⁺ concentration

| pH 14 |
| 13 |
| 12 |
| 11 |
| 10 |
| 9 |
| 8 |
| 7 |
| 6 |
| 5 |
| 4 |
| 3 |
| 2 |
| 1 |
| pH 0 |

high H⁺ concentration

soap—pH 10

Soap is commonly made by mixing fats with NaOH. There is a relatively low concentration of NaOH in soap.

pure water (H₂O)—pH 7

In pure water, the H⁺ concentration is equal to the OH⁻ concentration. Pure water has a pH of 7 and is neutral.

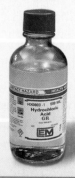

hydrochloric acid (HCl)—pH < 0

Concentrated HCl has a pH lower than 0 because it has a very high H⁺ concentration. HCl is used in many processes, including refining sugar from sugar cane.

READING VISUALS Where are the strong acids on the chart? Where are the strong bases? How does the concentration of hydrogen ions change?

Acids and bases neutralize each other.

Acids donate hydrogen ions, and bases accept hydrogen ions. Therefore, it is not surprising that acids and bases react when they come into contact with each other. Recall that when a hydrogen ion (H^+) from an acid collides with a hydroxide ion (OH^-) from a base, the two ions join to form a molecule of water (H_2O).

The negative ion of an acid (Cl^-) joins with the positive ion of a base (Na^+) to form a substance called a salt. Since both the salt and water are neutral, an acid-base reaction is called a neutralization (NOO-truh-lih-ZAY-shuhn) reaction. The reactants are an acid and a base, and the products are a salt and water.

READING TiP

The salt produced by a neutralization reaction is not necessarily table salt.

A common example of a neutralization reaction occurs when you swallow an antacid tablet to relieve an upset stomach. The acid in your stomach has a pH of about 1.5, due mostly to hydrochloric acid produced by the stomach lining. If your stomach produces more acid than is needed, you may feel a burning sensation. An antacid tablet contains a base, such as sodium bicarbonate, magnesium hydroxide, or calcium carbonate. The base reacts with the stomach acid and produces a salt and water. This reaction lowers the acidity—and raises the pH—to its normal value.

Acid rain forms when certain gases in the atmosphere dissolve in water vapor, forming acidic solutions. During rainstorms these acids fall to Earth. They can harm forests by making soil acidic and harm aquatic life by making lakes acidic. Acid rain can also dissolve marble and limestone in buildings and statues, because both marble and limestone contain calcium carbonate, which is a base.

 How is neutralization an example of a chemical reaction?

KEY CONCEPTS

1. Use the concept of ions to explain the difference between an acid and a base.

2. How do the properties of an acid differ from the properties of a base?

3. What happens when an acid and a base react with each other?

CRITICAL THINKING

4. **Infer** When an acid reacts with a metal, such as zinc, what is released? Where does that product come from?

5. **Infer** Suppose that you have 1 L of an acid solution with a pH of 2. You add 1 L of pure water. What happens to the pH of the solution? Explain.

CHALLENGE

6. **Synthesize** Suppose that equal amounts of solutions of HCl and NaOH with the same concentration are mixed together. What will the pH of the new solution be? What are the products of this reaction?

CHAPTER INVESTIGATION

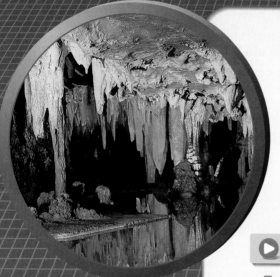

Acids and Bases

OVERVIEW AND PURPOSE Acids and bases are very common. For example, the limestone formations in the cave shown on the left are made of a substance that is a base when it is dissolved in water. In this activity you will use what you have learned about solutions, acids, and bases to

- test various household substances and place them in categories according to their pH values
- investigate the properties of common acids and bases

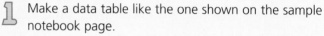

▶ Procedure

1. Make a data table like the one shown on the sample notebook page.

2. Set out 7 cups in your work area. Collect the substances that you will be testing: baking soda, fruit juice, shampoo, soda water, table salt, laundry detergent, and vinegar.

3. Label each cup. Be sure to wear goggles when pouring the substances that you will be testing. Pour 30 mL of each liquid substance into a separate cup. Dissolve 1 tsp of each solid substance in 30 mL of distilled water in a separate cup. To avoid contaminating the test solutions, wash and dry your measuring tools and hands between measurements.

MATERIALS
- plastic cups
- baking soda
- fruit juice
- shampoo
- soda water
- table salt
- detergent powder
- vinegar
- masking tape
- marking pen
- measuring spoons
- graduated cylinder
- distilled water
- paper towels
- pH indicator paper

4 Dip a piece of indicator paper into each solution. Compare the color of the test strip with the colors in the chart included in the package. Record the indicator color and the approximate pH number for each solution.

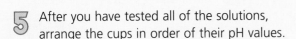
Step 4

5 After you have tested all of the solutions, arrange the cups in order of their pH values.

▶ Observe and Analyze
Write It Up

1. **RECORD DATA** Check to be sure that your data table is complete.

2. **ANALYZE DATA** What color range did the substances show when tested with the indicator paper? What do your results tell you about the pH of each substance you tested?

3. **CLASSIFY** Look for patterns in the pH values. Use your test results to place each household substance in one of three groups—acids, bases, or neutral.

4. **MODEL** Draw a diagram of the pH scale from 0 to 14. Use arrows and labels to show where the substances you tested fall on this scale.

▶ Conclude
Write It Up

1. **GENERALIZE** What general conclusions can you draw about the hydrogen ion concentration in many acids and bases found in the home? Are the hydrogen ion concentrations very high or very low? How do you know?

2. **EVALUATE** What limitations or difficulties did you experience in interpreting the results of your tests or other observations?

3. **APPLY** Antacid tablets react with stomach acid containing hydrochloric acid. What is this type of reaction called? What are the products of this type of reaction?

▶ INVESTIGATE Further

CHALLENGE Repeat the experiment, changing one variable. You might change the concentrations of the solutions you are testing or see what happens when you mix an acidic solution with a basic solution. Get your teacher's approval of your plan before proceeding. How does changing one particular variable affect the pH of the solutions?

Acids and Bases
Observe and Analyze
Table 1. Acid-Base Test Results

Substance	Indicator Color	pH	Group
baking soda			
juice			
shampoo			
soda water			
table salt			

Conclude

Metal alloys are solid mixtures.

◀ **BEFORE, you learned**

- A solution can be a solid
- Solutes change the properties of solvents
- The concentration of a solution can vary

▶ **NOW, you will learn**

- How metal alloys are made
- How a variety of alloys are used in modern society
- Why different alloys have different uses

VOCABULARY

alloy p. 134

THINK ABOUT

If gold jewelry is not pure gold, what is it?

People have prized gold since ancient times—archaeologists have found gold jewelry that was made thousands of years ago. Gold is a very soft metal, and jewelry made of pure gold bends very easily. Today, most gold jewelry is about 75 percent gold and 25 percent other metals. Why might these metals be mixed in?

Humans have made alloys for thousands of years.

VOCABULARY
Remember to use the strategy of your choice. You might use a description wheel diagram for *alloy*.

The gold used in jewelry is an example of an alloy. An **alloy** is a mixture of a metal and one or more other elements, usually metals as well. The gold alloys used in jewelry contain silver and copper in various amounts.

Many alloys are made by melting the metals and mixing them in the liquid state to form a solution. For example, bronze is made by melting and mixing copper and tin and then letting the solution cool. Bronze is not difficult to make, because both copper and tin melt at relatively low temperatures. Bronze was probably the first alloy made in ancient times—historians say it was discovered about 3800 B.C.

CHECK YOUR READING How is an alloy usually made?

Recall that the addition of a solute changes the properties of a solvent. The alloy bronze is harder than either copper or tin alone. This hardness made bronze a better material than stones or animal bones for making tools. The transition from the Stone Age to the Bronze Age, when humans first began to use metals, was an important period in human history.

Even though alloys have been made for thousands of years, new alloys with new properties are still being developed. One alloy with a very interesting property is nitinol, which is made of nickel and titanium. Nitinol is called a memory alloy because it can be given a particular shape and then reshaped. What makes nitinol unusual is that it will return to its original shape after being heated. Because of this property, nitinol is used in several common products, including eyeglass frames.

A short list of useful alloys is given in the table below. The percentages shown in the table are those for only one type of each alloy.

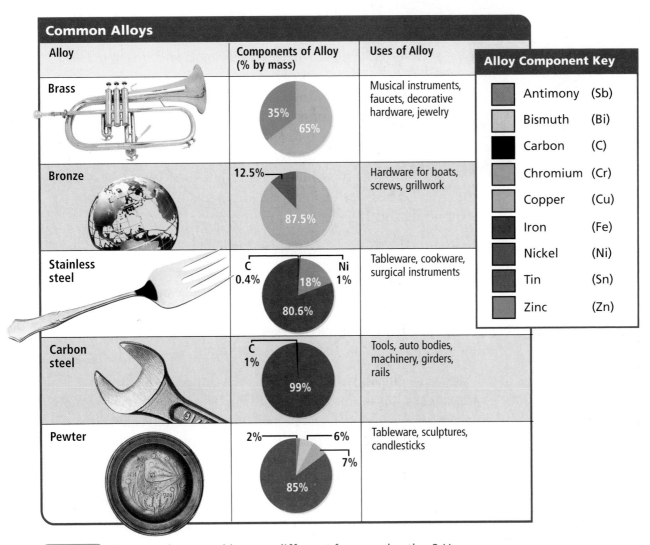

Common Alloys

Alloy	Components of Alloy (% by mass)	Uses of Alloy
Brass	35% / 65%	Musical instruments, faucets, decorative hardware, jewelry
Bronze	12.5% / 87.5%	Hardware for boats, screws, grillwork
Stainless steel	C 0.4% / 18% / Ni 1% / 80.6%	Tableware, cookware, surgical instruments
Carbon steel	C 1% / 99%	Tools, auto bodies, machinery, girders, rails
Pewter	2% / 6% / 7% / 85%	Tableware, sculptures, candlesticks

Alloy Component Key

Antimony	(Sb)
Bismuth	(Bi)
Carbon	(C)
Chromium	(Cr)
Copper	(Cu)
Iron	(Fe)
Nickel	(Ni)
Tin	(Sn)
Zinc	(Zn)

READING VISUALS How are brass and bronze different from each other? How are stainless steel and carbon steel different from each other?

Alloys have many uses in modern life.

The advances in materials science that began with bronze almost 6000 years ago continue today. Modern industry uses many different alloys. Some alloys, based on lightweight metals such as aluminum and titanium, are relatively recent developments. However, the most important alloy used today—steel—has been around for many years.

A major advance in technology occurred in the 1850s with the development of the Bessemer process. This process made it possible to manufacture large amounts of steel in a short time. Until then, steel could be made only in batches of less than 100 pounds. The Bessemer process made it possible to produce up to 30 tons of steel in about 20 minutes. Since it began to be mass-produced, steel has been used in everything from bridges to cars to spoons.

Steel is the main material used in the structure of this sphere at Epcot Center in Florida.

Most steel used in construction is an alloy of iron and carbon. Iron is too soft to be a good building material by itself, but adding only a small amount of carbon—about 1 percent by mass—makes a very hard and strong material. Some types of steel contain small amounts of other metals as well, which give the alloys different properties. As you can see on the chart on page 135, one type of stainless steel contains only 1 percent nickel. However, different types of stainless steel can be made, and they have different uses. For instance, stainless steel used in appliances has 8 to 10 percent nickel and 18 percent chromium in it.

Alloys in Transportation

Different forms of transportation rely on steel. Wooden sailing ships were replaced by steel ships in the late 1800s. Today, steel cargo ships carry steel containers. Railroads depended on steel from their very beginning. Today's high-speed trains still run on steel wheels and tracks.

Modern vehicles use more recently developed alloys as well. For example, aluminum and titanium are lightweight metals that are relatively soft, like iron. However, their alloys are strong, like steel, and light. Airplane engines are made from aluminum alloys, and both aluminum and titanium alloys are used in aircraft bodies. Aluminum alloys are also commonly used in high-speed passenger ferries and in the bodies of cars. Because the alloys are light, they help to improve the fuel efficiency of these vehicles.

 CHECK YOUR READING How are alloys used in transportation?

Alloys in Medicine

You may have noticed that most medical equipment is shiny and silver-colored. This equipment is made of stainless steel, which contains nickel and chromium in addition to iron and carbon. Surgical instruments are often made of stainless steel because it can be honed to a very sharp edge and is also rust resistant.

Cobalt and titanium alloys are also widely used in medicine because they do not easily react with substances in the body, such as blood and digestive juices. These alloys can be surgically placed inside the body with a minimum of harm to either the body or the metal. The photographs on the right show one use of alloys—making artificial joints.

Memory alloys similar to the nitinol alloy described earlier also have a wide range of medical uses. These alloys are used in braces for teeth, and as implants that hold open blocked arteries or correct a curve in the spine. Medical devices made of memory alloys can be made in a particular shape and then reshaped for implantation. After the device is in place, the person's body heat causes it to return to its original shape.

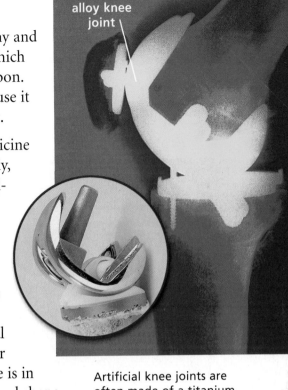
alloy knee joint

Artificial knee joints are often made of a titanium alloy. The x-ray image shows the device in place.

 CHECK YOUR READING What properties make alloys useful in medicine?

INVESTIGATE Alloys

How is a pure metal different from its alloy?

PROCEDURE

1. Examine the iron nails and the alloy (steel or stainless steel) nails. Record your observations.

2. Find and record the mass of the three iron nails. Repeat with the three alloy nails.

3. Find the volume of the nails by displacement, as follows: Into the empty graduated cylinder, pour water to a height that is higher than the nails are long. Note the water level. Add the iron nails and record the change in water level. Repeat this step with the alloy nails.

4. Calculate the density of each type of nail. **Density = $\dfrac{mass}{Volume}$**

WHAT DO YOU THINK?

- Compare your observations of the metals contained in the nails.
- Which metal has the greater density? How might a metal's density be important in how it is used?

CHALLENGE How can you identify different alloys of a metal?

SKILL FOCUS
Observing

MATERIALS
- 3 iron nails
- 3 steel nails or 3 stainless steel nails
- balance
- graduated cylinder
- water

TIME
30 minutes

Alloys in Space Flight

The aerospace industry develops and uses some of the newest and most advanced alloys. The same qualities that make titanium and aluminum alloys useful in airplanes—lightness, strength, and heat resistance—also make them useful in spacecraft. Titanium alloys were used in the Gemini space program of the 1960s. Large portions of the wings of today's space shuttle are made of aluminum alloys.

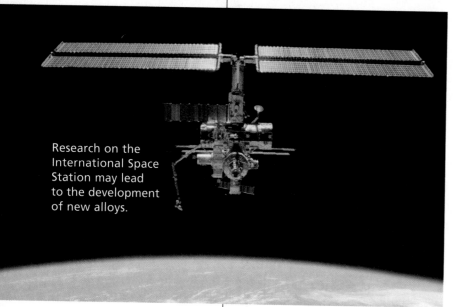

Research on the International Space Station may lead to the development of new alloys.

For more than 20 years, the heat shield on the shuttle's belly has been made from ceramic tiles. However, engineers have experimented with a titanium heat shield as well.

Construction of the International Space Station, which is shown in the photograph on the left, began in 1998. Alloys are a major part of the space station's structure. More important, research on the space station may lead to the development of new alloys.

One of the goals of research on the space station is to make alloys in a microgravity environment, which cannot be done on Earth. For example, astronauts have experimented with thick liquids, made with iron, that harden or change shape when a magnet is placed nearby, and then return to their previous shapes when the magnet is removed. These liquid alloys may be useful in robots or in artificial organs for humans.

 CHECK YOUR READING Why is research into new alloys on the International Space Station important?

KEY CONCEPTS

1. How can one metal be made to dissolve in another metal?

2. Name three metal alloys and a use for each one.

3. Why are alloys of cobalt or titanium, instead of pure iron, used for medical devices that are implanted inside people?

CRITICAL THINKING

4. **Infer** In industry, all titanium alloys are simply called titanium. What might this tell you about the use of pure titanium?

5. **Compare and Contrast** How are modern alloys similar to alloys made hundreds or thousands of years ago? How are they different?

CHALLENGE

6. **Synthesize** The melting point of copper is 1083°C. Tin is dissolved in copper to make bronze. Will bronze have a melting point of 1083°C? Why or why not?

MATH TUTORIAL
CLASSZONE.COM
Click on Math
Tutorial for more help
understanding percents.

The Mixtures in Alloys

An alloy is a mixture of a metal with other substances. Because even a small change in the percentages of materials in an alloy can change its properties, alloys are made according to strict specifications. For example, steel is an alloy of iron and carbon. Steel that contains 0.6 percent carbon by mass is used in steel beams, whereas steel that contains 1.0 percent carbon by mass, which makes the steel harder, is used to make tools and springs. How can the percentages of materials in an alloy be calculated?

Example

Calculate the percentage of nickel in an alloy if a small portion of the alloy has 10 atoms, 3 of which are nickel.

(1) Convert the number of atoms into a fraction.

3 of 10 atoms in the alloy are nickel $= \dfrac{3}{10}$

(2) To calculate a percentage, first find an equivalent fraction that has a denominator of 100. Use x as the numerator.

$$\dfrac{3}{10} = \dfrac{x}{100}$$

(3) Convert the fraction into a percentage by using cross products

$$3 \cdot 100 = 10 \cdot x$$
$$300 = 10x$$
$$30 = x$$

ANSWER The percentage of nickel atoms in the alloy is 30%.

Answer the following questions.

1. A sample of an alloy contains 4 iron atoms, 3 zinc atoms, 2 aluminum atoms, and 1 copper atom.

   a. What percentage of the alloy is aluminum by number of atoms?

   b. What percentage is zinc by number of atoms?

2. A sample of an alloy contains 12 titanium atoms, 4 niobium atoms, and 4 aluminum atoms.

   a. What percentage of the alloy is titanium by number of atoms?

   b. What percentage is niobium by number of atoms?

CHALLENGE Suppose there is an alloy in which 2 of every 3 atoms are silver atoms, 1 of every 4 atoms is a copper atom, and 1 of every 12 atoms is a tin atom. What are the percentages of each metal in the alloy by number of atoms?

The steel in girders like these contains iron and 0.6 percent carbon by mass.

Chapter Review

the BIG idea

When substances dissolve to form a solution, the properties of the mixture change.

CONTENT REVIEW
CLASSZONE.COM

KEY CONCEPTS SUMMARY

4.1 **A solution is a type of mixture.**

- A solution is a mixture in which one or more solutes are dissolved in a solvent.
- A solution is a homogeneous mixture.

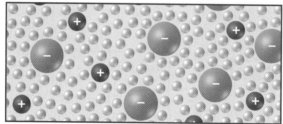
Ionic compound dissolved in solvent

VOCABULARY
solution p. 111
solute p. 112
solvent p. 112
suspension p. 113

4.2 **The amount of solute that dissolves can vary.**

- The amount of dissolved solute determines a solution's concentration.
- The more soluble a substance is, the more of it will dissolve in a solution.

Dilute   **Concentrated**

VOCABULARY
concentration p. 117
dilute p. 118
saturated p. 118
solubility p. 119

4.3 **Solutions can be acidic, basic, or neutral.**

- Acids donate protons (H+) in solutions, and bases accept protons in solutions.
- Acidity is measured by the H+ concentration on the pH scale.

$$\textbf{Acid} \quad HCl \xrightarrow{H_2O} H^+ + Cl^-$$

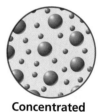

$$\textbf{Base} \quad NaOH \xrightarrow{H_2O} Na^+ + OH^-$$

VOCABULARY
acid p. 126
base p. 126
pH p. 129
neutral p. 129

4.4 **Metal alloys are solid mixtures.**

- Many of the metals used in modern transportation and medicine are alloys.
- The properties of a metal can be changed by adding one or more substances to produce a more useful material.

VOCABULARY
alloy p. 134

Reviewing Vocabulary

Draw a diagram similar to the example shown below to connect and organize the concepts of related vocabulary terms. After you have completed your diagram, explain in two or three sentences why you organized the terms in that way. Underline each of the terms in your explanation.

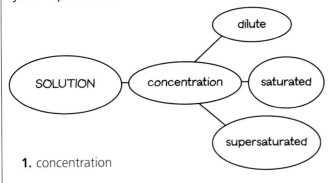

1. concentration

2. acid

3. base

4. neutral

5. pH

Latin Roots *Several of the vocabulary terms in this chapter come from the Latin word* solvere, *which means "to loosen." Describe how each of the following terms is related to the Latin word.*

6. solution

7. solute

8. solvent

9. solubility

Reviewing Key Concepts

Multiple Choice *Choose the letter of the best answer.*

10. What makes a solution different from other types of mixtures?
    a. Its parts can be separated.
    b. It is the same throughout.
    c. Its parts can be seen.
    d. It is a liquid.

11. When a solute is dissolved in a solvent, the solvent's
    a. boiling point decreases
    b. boiling point decreases and its freezing point increases
    c. freezing point increases
    d. freezing point decreases and its boiling point increases

12. When a compound held together by ionic bonds dissolves, the compound
    a. releases molecules into the solution
    b. forms a suspension
    c. releases ions into the solution
    d. becomes nonpolar

13. Water is called the universal solvent because it
    a. dissolves many substances
    b. dissolves very dense substances
    c. has no charged regions
    d. is nonpolar

14. How does an increase in temperature affect the solubility of solids and gases?
    a. It increases solubility of most solids and decreases the solubility of gases.
    b. It decreases solubility of most solids and gases.
    c. It increases solubility of gases and decreases the solubility of most solids.
    d. It increases solubility of both solids and gases.

15. A solution with a very high H^+ concentration has a
    a. very high pH   c. pH close to 5
    b. very low pH   d. pH close to 7

16. Why are oils insoluble in water?
    a. They are acids.   c. They are bases.
    b. They are polar.   d. They are nonpolar.

Short Answer *Write a short answer to each question.*

17. Describe the reaction that occurs when a strong acid reacts with a strong base.

18. How might an alloy be changed for different uses? Explain.

Thinking Critically

The illustration below shows the results of pH tests of four different solutions. Assume the solutions are made with strong acids or strong bases. Use the diagram to answer the next four questions.

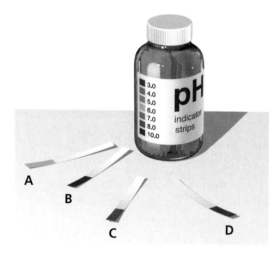

19. OBSERVE Which of the indicator strips show an acidic solution? Which show a basic solution?

20. INFER Which strip of indicator paper detected the highest concentration of H^+ ions? How do you know?

21. PREDICT What would happen if you mixed together equal amounts of the solutions that produced the results of strip B and strip D?

22. INFER Suppose you mix together equal amounts of the solutions that produced the results of strip C and strip D, then test the pH of this new solution. What color will the indicator paper be? Explain.

23. CAUSE AND EFFECT Suppose that you place a beaker containing a solution in a refrigerator. An hour later there is a white solid on the bottom of the beaker. What happened? Why?

24. INFER Do you think iron by itself would be a good material to use in the frame of a bridge? Why or why not?

25. SYNTHESIZE How might the concentration of a solute in an alloy be related to the properties of the alloy? Explain.

Using Math Skills in Science

Use the graph below to answer the next three questions.

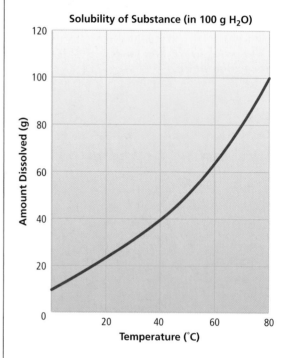

26. What happens to the solubility of the substance as the temperature increases? decreases?

27. Approximately how many grams of the substance dissolve at 20°C? 60°C?

28. Is the substance a solid or a gas? Explain.

the BIG idea

29. APPLY Look back at pages 108–109. Think about the answer you gave to the question about the photograph. How has your understanding of solutions and their properties changed?

30. COMPARE Describe the similarities and differences between solutions of table salt (NaCl) in water and sugar in water. Do both solutes have similar effects on the properties of the solvent? Explain.

UNIT PROJECTS

Check your schedule for your unit project. How are you doing? Be sure that you have placed data or notes from your research in your project folder.

Interpreting Graphs

Use the information in the paragraph and the graph to answer the questions.

Acid rain is an environmental concern in the United States and in other countries. Acid rain is produced when the burning of fuels releases certain chemicals into the air. These chemicals can react with water vapor in Earth's atmosphere to form acids. The acids then fall back to the ground in either rain or snow. The acids can damage plants, animals, and buildings. Normally, rain has a pH of about 5.6, which is slightly acidic. But rain in some areas of the United States has a pH that is lower than 4.0. The graph shows the pH of water in several lakes.

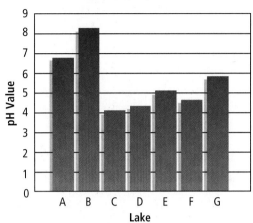

Lake Water pH Values

1. Which lake is the most acidic?
   a. Lake A   **c.** Lake C
   b. Lake B   **d.** Lake D

2. Which lake is the least acidic?
   a. Lake A   **c.** Lake C
   b. Lake B   **d.** Lake D

3. Which lake has water the closest to neutral?
   a. Lake A   **c.** Lake E
   b. Lake B   **d.** Lake G

4. Lakes that form on a bed of limestone are less likely to suffer from high acidity. The limestone reacts with acids to neutralize them. Which of the following lakes is most likely to have a limestone bed?
   a. Lake C   **c.** Lake F
   b. Lake D   **d.** Lake G

5. Lake trout are fish that live in many freshwater lakes. When the pH of the water in a lake drops below 5.5, this species of fish can no longer reproduce, because its eggs cannot hatch. Which of the following statements is most likely true?
   a. Lake trout have probably stopped reproducing in all the lakes.
   b. In terms of reproducing, lake trout are not in danger in any of the lakes.
   c. Lake trout will probably be able to reproduce in lakes A, B, and G but not in the others.
   d. Lake trout have probably stopped reproducing only in lakes C, D, and F.

Extended Response

Answer the following two questions in detail. Include some of the terms from the list in the box. Underline each term you use in your answers.

concentration	solute	solubility
polar	solution	solvent

6. Suppose you are trying to make two solutions. One contains water and salt. The other contains water and oil. What do you think will happen in both cases? How might charges on particles affect your results?

7. Explain why some substances dissolve more easily than others. How can this characteristic of a solute be changed by changing the temperature or pressure of a solution?

Carbon in Life and Materials

the **BIG** idea

Carbon is essential to living things and to modern materials.

Where in this photograph might you find carbon-based molecules?

Key Concepts

SECTION

5.1 **Carbon-based molecules have many structures.**
Learn why carbon forms many different compounds.

SECTION

5.2 **Carbon-based molecules are life's building blocks.**
Learn about the four main types of carbon-based molecules in living things.

SECTION

5.3 **Carbon-based molecules are in many materials.**
Learn how common materials are made from carbon-based molecules.

Internet Preview

CLASSZONE.COM

Chapter 5 online resources: Content Review, Simulation, Visualization, four Resource Centers, Math Tutorial, Test Practice

EXPLORE (the BIG idea)

Structure and Function

Drop a hollow rubber ball on the ground and observe what happens. Then cut the ball in half and glue the two pieces together back-to-back. Predict what will happen when you drop the glued ball. Will it bounce? If so, how high? Test your prediction.

Observe and Think What happened when you dropped the glued ball? How does the ball's behavior depend on its structure?

Sweet Crackers

Eat an unsalted cracker, but chew it for a long time. Keep the cracker in your mouth for a few minutes before you swallow it.

Observe and Think What happened to the taste of the cracker during the time it was in your mouth? What does the change in taste tell you about the molecules in the cracker?

Internet Activity: Polymers

Visit **ClassZone.com** to explore the Polymer Resource Center. Discover some of the common polymers that you use every day. Investigate how a change in a polymer's structure can make a very different material.

Observe and Think What things around you might be polymers? How might the variety of polymers be related to the way in which carbon atoms bond to each other?

NSTA scilinks.org SCILINKS

Organic Compounds **Code: MDL026**

Getting Ready to Learn

◀ **CONCEPT REVIEW**

- Atoms share electrons when they form covalent bonds.
- Some atoms can form multiple bonds with another atom.
- Chemical reactions alter the arrangement of atoms.

◀ **VOCABULARY REVIEW**

electron p. 11

covalent bond p. 50

chemical reaction p. 69

catalyst p. 76

CONTENT REVIEW
CLASSZONE.COM
Review concepts and vocabulary.

▶ **TAKING NOTES**

SUPPORTING MAIN IDEAS

Make a chart to show main ideas and the information that supports them. Copy each blue heading. Below each heading, add supporting information, such as reasons, explanations, and examples.

VOCABULARY STRATEGY

Think about a vocabulary term as a **magnet word** diagram. Write the other terms or ideas related to that term around it.

See the Note-Taking Handbook on pages R45–R51.

SCIENCE NOTEBOOK

Living and nonliving things contain carbon.

→ All life on Earth is based on carbon.

→ All organic compounds contain carbon.

→ Compounds that do not contain carbon are inorganic.

compounds that contain the same atoms in different places

ISOMER

carbon-based molecules

butane and isobutane

Carbon-based molecules have many structures.

 BEFORE, you learned

- Atoms of one element differ from atoms of other elements
- The structure and properties of compounds depend on bonds
- Atoms of different elements can form different numbers of bonds

▶ **NOW, you will learn**

- About the importance of carbon in living things
- Why carbon can form many different compounds
- About different structures of carbon-based molecules

VOCABULARY

organic compound p. 147
inorganic compound
  p. 148
isomer p. 152

THINK ABOUT

Where can you find carbon?

The wood of a pencil consists of carbon-based molecules. These molecules are considered to be organic. The graphite in the center of the pencil is also made of carbon. In fact, graphite is pure carbon, but it is not considered to be organic. What makes the carbon in wood different from the carbon in graphite?

Living and nonliving things contain carbon.

Just about every substance that makes up living things contains carbon atoms. In fact, carbon is the most important element for life. Molecules containing carbon atoms were originally called organic because a large number of carbon-based molecules were found in living organisms. Sugars are organic. They are formed by plants, which are living organisms, and they contain carbon. Notice that the term *organic* is closely related to the term *organism*.

Organic compounds are based on carbon. Besides carbon, organic compounds often contain atoms of the elements hydrogen and oxygen, but they can also contain atoms of nitrogen, sulfur, and phosphorus. Scientists once thought that organic compounds could be made only in living organisms by an organism's life processes. Then an organic compound was made in a laboratory. This discovery showed that organic substances were not unique to living things. Instead, organic compounds could be made in a laboratory just like all other chemical compounds.

VOCABULARY
Remember to make a magnet word diagram for *organic compound* and for other vocabulary terms.

CHECK YOUR READING Why were carbon compounds called organic compounds?

Organic Compound

Sugar, shown here as cubes, is organic and contains carbon atoms. It is made by plants from inorganic substances.

Inorganic Compound

Carbon dioxide, shown here as dry ice, is inorganic even though it contains carbon atoms. It is used by plants to make sugars.

There are several exceptions to the rule that carbon-based molecules are organic. These include diamond and graphite, which are made entirely of carbon but are not considered to be organic. The same is true of other compounds, such as cyanides (which contain a CN^- group), carbonates (which contain a CO_3^{2-} group), and carbon dioxide (CO_2). These carbon-containing compounds, among others, and all compounds without carbon are called **inorganic compounds.**

READING TiP

The prefix *in-* means "not," so *inorganic* means "not organic."

Carbon forms many different compounds.

Millions of different carbon-based molecules exist. Consider the number of molecules that make up living things and all of the processes that occur in living things. Carbon-based molecules are vital for all of them.

The large variety of carbon-based molecules results from the number of bonds that each carbon atom forms in a molecule and from a carbon atom's ability to form bonds with atoms of many different elements. In compounds, carbon atoms always share four pairs of electrons in four covalent bonds. This means that one carbon atom can form single bonds with up to four other atoms. Carbon atoms can also form multiple bonds—the atoms can share more than one pair of electrons—with other atoms including, most importantly, other carbon atoms. Different ways of showing the same carbon-based molecules are illustrated below and on page 149.

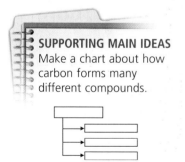

SUPPORTING MAIN IDEAS
Make a chart about how carbon forms many different compounds.

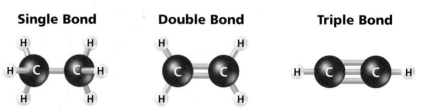

Single Bond   **Double Bond**   **Triple Bond**

CHECK YOUR READING How many bonds can one carbon atom form with another?

As you can see in the compounds shown, two carbon atoms can form single, double, or even triple bonds with one another. The compounds have different numbers of hydrogen atoms and different numbers of bonds between their carbon atoms. Count the bonds for each carbon atom. Each carbon atom makes a total of four bonds and always makes just one bond with each hydrogen atom.

Organic molecules are often shown in a simplified way. Instead of models that include all of a molecule's atoms and bonds, structural formulas—such as those shown below—can be used.

▼ REMINDER

One pair of electrons is shared in a single covalent bond.

Full Structural Formulas

$$
\begin{array}{ccc}
\overset{\displaystyle H}{\underset{\displaystyle H}{\overset{|}{\underset{|}{H-C}}}} \quad \overset{\displaystyle H}{\underset{\displaystyle H}{\overset{|}{\underset{|}{C-H}}}}
&
\overset{\displaystyle H}{\underset{\displaystyle H}{\overset{|}{\underset{|}{C}}}} = \overset{\displaystyle H}{\underset{\displaystyle H}{\overset{|}{\underset{|}{C}}}}
&
H-C\equiv C-H
\end{array}
$$

Simplified Structural Formulas

$$CH_3 - CH_3 \qquad CH_2 = CH_2 \qquad CH \equiv CH$$

Carbon-based molecules can have many different structures. Some of the most important structures are molecules shaped like chains and molecules shaped like rings.

INVESTIGATE Carbon Bonding

How do carbon-based molecules depend on the number of bonds between carbon atoms?

SKILL FOCUS
Modeling

PROCEDURE

(1) Label the large foam balls "C" for carbon, and label the small foam balls "H" for hydrogen.

(2) Using a toothpick to represent a bond, construct a model of a molecule with two carbons, six hydrogens, and seven toothpicks. Carbon has four bonds and hydrogen has one.

(3) Make a new model, using two carbons, two hydrogens, and five toothpicks.

MATERIALS
• marking pen
• 2 large foam balls
• 6 small foam balls
• toothpicks

TIME
10 minutes

WHAT DO YOU THINK?

• How many bonds are there between carbon atoms in the first model? in the second model?

• Which molecule might be more tightly held together? Why?

CHALLENGE In the model on the right, would it be possible for an additional hydrogen atom to bond to each carbon atom? Why or why not?

Carbon Chains

Unlike atoms of other elements, carbon atoms have the unusual property of being able to bond to each other to form very long chains. One carbon chain might have hundreds of carbon atoms bonded together. A carbon chain can be straight or branched.

Straight Chain

$$CH_3 - CH_2 - CH_2 - CH_2 - CH_2 - CH_3$$

Branched Chain

In a branched carbon chain, additional carbon atoms, or even other carbon chains, can bond to carbon atoms in the main carbon chain. Straight chains and branched chains are both results of carbon's ability to form four bonds.

CHECK YOUR READING How is it possible for carbon atoms to form both straight and branched chains?

Carbon Rings

Carbon-based molecules also can be shaped like rings. Carbon rings containing either 5 or 6 carbon atoms are the most common ones, and carbon rings containing more than 20 carbon atoms do not occur naturally.

Just as there are different types of carbon chains, there are different types of carbon ring molecules. One of the most important carbon-based ring molecules is a molecule called benzene (BEHN–ZEEN). Benzene contains six carbon atoms and six hydrogen atoms. Benzene differs from other carbon-based rings because it contains alternating single and double bonds between carbon atoms, as shown below. The benzene molecule is often shown as a circle inside a hexagon.

Benzene Ring

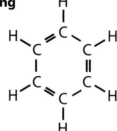

Simplified Benzene Ring

Many compounds are based on benzene's ring structure. These carbon-based molecules often have very strong smells, or aromas, and so are called aromatic compounds. One aromatic compound that contains a benzene ring is a molecule called vanillin. Vanillin is the molecule that gives vanilla its distinctive smell.

Carbon Chains and Carbon Rings

Carbon-based molecules shaped like chains or rings are found in the world around you.

Carbon Chains

One of the carbon chains in the diesel fuel for this locomotive has the formula $C_{15}H_{32}$. It contains 13 CH_2 groups between the CH_3 groups that are on both ends of the molecule. This molecule can be written as $CH_3(CH_2)_{13}CH_3$.

$$CH_3 - CH_2 - CH_2 - CH_2 - CH_2 - CH_2 - CH_2 - CH_2 - CH_2 - CH_2 - CH_2 - CH_2 - CH_2 - CH_2 - CH_3$$

Carbon Rings

Vanilla ice cream gets its flavor from vanilla, which is also used to enhance other flavors. The molecule that gives vanilla its strong smell is based on the benzene carbon ring.

Carbon Chains and Rings

The molecules in polystyrene, which make up this foam container, contain carbon rings attached to a long carbon chain. The dashed lines at both ends of the structural formula tell you that the molecule continues in both directions.

$$---CH_2 - CH - CH_2 - CH - CH_2 - CH---$$

Isomers

READING TiP

The prefix *iso-* means "equal," and the root *mer-* means "part."

Another reason there is such a large number of carbon-based molecules is that carbon can form different molecules with the same atoms. The atoms in these molecules are in different places, and the molecules have different structures. Because the atoms are arranged differently, they are actually two different substances. Compounds that contain the same atoms, but in different places, are called **isomers.**

The formulas below show a pair of compounds—butane and isobutane—that are isomers. Both molecules contain four carbon atoms and ten hydrogen atoms. However, butane molecules are straight chains of carbon atoms. Isobutane molecules are branched chains of carbon atoms. Even though both butane and isobutane contain the same atoms, the structures of the molecules are different, so they are isomers.

Butane

$$CH_3 — CH_2 — CH_2 — CH_3$$

Butane contains four carbon atoms and ten hydrogen atoms. It has a straight chain structure.

Isobutane

$$CH_3 — CH — CH_3$$
with CH_3 branching from the middle CH.

Isobutane also contains four carbon atoms and ten hydrogen atoms. It has a branched chain structure.

Some carbon-based molecules can shift from one isomer to another, and then back to the original structure. For example, isomers of a molecule called retinal are necessary for your eyesight. When light strikes retinal, its structure changes from one isomer to another. The new isomer of retinal starts a process that sends a signal from the eye to the brain. After the retinal isomer starts the signaling process, the molecule shifts back to its original structure.

CHECK YOUR READING If two substances are isomers of each other, how are they the same? different?

5.1 Review

KEY CONCEPTS

1. Why were carbon-based compounds first called organic? How has the understanding of organic compounds changed?

2. How is the way in which carbon atoms bond to each other important for the number of carbon-based compounds?

3. Describe three structures of carbon-based molecules.

CRITICAL THINKING

4. **Infer** Could the last carbon atom in a carbon chain make bonds with four hydrogen atoms? Why or why not?

5. **Synthesize** Do you think molecules based on carbon rings can have isomers? Why or why not?

CHALLENGE

6. **Communicate** A molecule called naphthalene consists of ten carbon atoms and eight hydrogen atoms in two linked benzene rings. Draw a diagram of a molecule that could be naphthalene. Be sure to include the atoms and the bonds between the atoms.

Stronger Than Steel

Can you imagine something that is much smaller than a human hair yet much stronger than steel? Welcome to the world of carbon nanotubes. Carbon nanotubes are made of pure carbon. They are 10 to 100 times as strong as the same weight of steel, but they can be 10,000 times smaller than a hair from your head. Carbon nanotubes were discovered in 1991 as a byproduct of a chemical reaction, but they may have many uses in the near future.

The Tiniest Test Tube

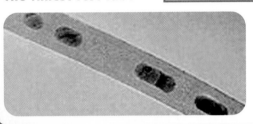

Because a carbon nanotube is hollow, atoms and small molecules can fit inside the tube. Chemists have even used them as tiny test tubes. This photograph shows beads of silver inside a carbon nanotube.

Really Tiny Axles

Carbon nanotubes are not all the same size. Smaller tubes can be placed inside larger tubes. The atoms of the two tubes do not interact much, so the inner nanotube can turn inside the outer one. Nested carbon nanotubes might one day be used as axles for extremely tiny machines.

Conductor or Insulator

Depending on their structure, some carbon nanotubes can conduct an electric current just as well as metal, whereas others will not. Computer scientists have built simple nanotube electrical circuits that could someday become the brains of new supercomputers.

Flash and It's Gone

Some carbon nanotubes are sensitive to bright flashes of light. In fact, when scientists tried to take flash photographs of fluffy masses of tubes, the material caught fire. This property might make them useful as a precise way to control explosives.

EXPLORE

1. **CLASSIFY** Is a carbon nanotube an element, a compound, or a mixture? Explain.
2. **CHALLENGE** Use the Internet to find information about carbon nanotube research. What are some of the uses, in addition to those listed above, that scientists have proposed for carbon nanotubes? Which of these possibilities is most interesting to you? Why?

RESOURCE CENTER CLASSZONE.COM — Learn more about carbon nanotubes.

This carbon nanotube, shown in blue, has been made into a very small wire. How small? The yellow shapes behind the nanotube are parts of circuits on a microchip.

KEY CONCEPT

5.2 Carbon-based molecules are life's building blocks.

BEFORE, you learned

- Carbon is the basis of life on Earth
- Carbon atoms can form multiple bonds
- Carbon can form molecules shaped like chains or rings

NOW, you will learn

- About the functions of carbohydrates and lipids in living things
- About structures and functions of proteins
- How nucleic acids carry instructions for building proteins

VOCABULARY

carbohydrate p. 155
lipid p. 156
protein p. 158
enzyme p. 159
nucleic acid p. 161

EXPLORE Carbon in Food

How can you see the carbon in food?

PROCEDURE

① Place the candle in the pie plate and light the candle.

② Use the tongs to hold each food sample in the candle flame for 20 seconds. Record your observations.

WHAT DO YOU THINK?

- What changes did you observe in the samples?
- What type of chemical reaction might have caused these changes?

MATERIALS

- aluminum pie plate
- candle
- wooden matches
- tongs
- small marshmallow
- piece of carrot

Carbon-based molecules have many functions in living things.

You depend on carbon-based molecules for all of the activities in your life. For example, when you play softball, you need energy to swing the bat and run the bases. Carbon-based molecules are the source of the chemical energy needed by your muscle cells. Carbon-based molecules make up your muscle cells and provide those cells with the ability to contract and relax. Carbon-based molecules carry oxygen to your muscle cells so that your muscles can function properly. Carbon-based molecules even provide the information for building new molecules.

The many carbon-based molecules in all living things have certain similarities. They all contain carbon and elements such as hydrogen, oxygen, nitrogen, sulfur, and phosphorus. Many of the molecules are also very large molecules called macromolecules. However, these molecules have different structures and different functions.

READING TIP

The prefix *macro-* means "large," so a macromolecule is a large molecule.

Living things contain four major types of carbon-based molecules.

The organic molecules found in living things are classified into four major groups—carbohydrates, lipids, proteins, and nucleic acids. You may already be familiar with these types of molecules and their functions in living things.

Carbohydrates include sugars and starches found in foods such as bread and pasta. Many lipids are fats or oils. Proteins are necessary for many functions in the body, including the formation of muscle tissue. Nucleic acids are the molecules that carry the genetic code for all living things. As you read about each of these types of molecules, look for ways in which the molecule's function depends on its structure.

Carbohydrates

Carbohydrates (KAHR-boh-HY-DRAYTZ) include sugars, starches, and cellulose, and contain atoms of three elements—carbon, hydrogen, and oxygen. They serve two main functions. Carbohydrates are a source of chemical energy for cells in many living things. They are also part of the structural materials of plants.

One important carbohydrate is the sugar glucose, which has the chemical formula $C_6H_{12}O_6$. Cells in both plants and animals break down glucose for energy. In plants glucose molecules also can be joined together to form more complex carbohydrates, such as starch and cellulose. Starch is a macromolecule that consists of many glucose molecules, or units, bonded together. Many foods, such as pasta, contain starch. When starch is broken back down into individual glucose molecules, those glucose molecules can be used as an energy source by cells.

Modeling Glucose

The glucose molecule can be represented by a hexagon. The red O shows that an oxygen atom is in the ring.

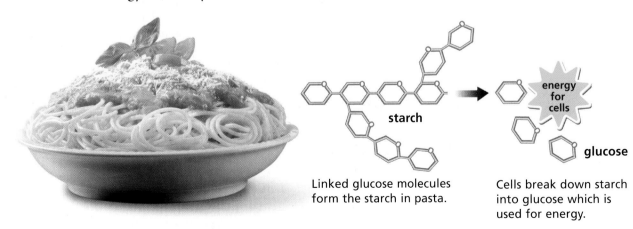

Linked glucose molecules form the starch in pasta.

starch

energy for cells

glucose

Cells break down starch into glucose which is used for energy.

Moss Leaf Cells

Plants make their own glucose through a process called photosynthesis, which you read about in Chapter 3. Some of the glucose made during photosynthesis is used to make the complex carbohydrate molecules that form a plant's structure.

Cellulose

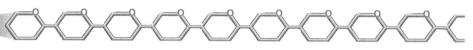

Cellulose is a long chain-like molecule that forms part of a plant's structure.

Unlike animal cells, plant cells have a tough, protective layer outside the cell membrane called the cell wall. Cellulose (SEHL-yuh-LOHS) is a macromolecule found in plant cell walls, and it is a large part of vegetables such as lettuce and celery. The illustration shows moss leaf cells with their cell walls, and a diagram of part of a cellulose molecule.

Cellulose and starch are both carbohydrates composed of glucose molecules, but the glucose molecules that make up these larger macro-molecules are linked in different ways. Because of their different structures, starch and cellulose have different functions. In fact, this structural difference also prevents your body from breaking down and using cellulose as it would starch.

 CHECK YOUR READING What are some functions of carbohydrates in animals? in plants?

Lipids

Lipids include fats and oils and are used mainly for energy and as structural materials in living things. Like carbohydrates, most lipids are made of carbon, hydrogen, and oxygen. Even though lipids and carbohydrates have many similarities, they have different structures and properties.

Animals store chemical energy in fat. Plants store chemical energy in oils, such as olive oil and peanut oil. Fats and oils store energy very efficiently—one gram of fat contains about twice as much energy as one gram of carbohydrate or protein. Fats and oils contain three carbon chains called fatty acids. The illustration below shows the general structure of a fatty acid.

Modeling Fatty Acids

$$CH_3 - CH_2 - CH_2 \} \{ CH_2 - CH_2 - CH_2 - COOH \ = \ \text{(zig-zag structure)} \ \overset{O}{\underset{\|}{C}} - OH$$

The carbon chains in lipids are called fatty acids. A carbon atom is at each bend of the zig-zag model above. The break in the middle of the chain shows that some carbon atoms have been left out.

You may have heard the terms *saturated* and *unsaturated* in relation to fats. If all of the bonds between carbon atoms in the fatty acids are single bonds, the lipid is a saturated fat. If one or more of these bonds is a double bond, the lipid is an unsaturated fat. Most animal fats are saturated, and most oils from plants are unsaturated. Diets high in saturated fats have been linked to heart disease. Lipids in the butter in the photograph on the right are saturated fats.

Fat Structure

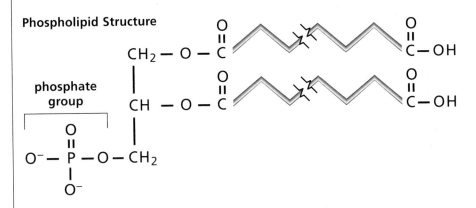

Fats in butter contain three fatty acids and are used for energy. Butter contains saturated fats.

○ **CHECK YOUR READING** What is the difference between a saturated fat and an unsaturated fat?

Some lipids are important parts of cell structure. Structural lipids often contain the element phosphorus and are called phospholipids. Phospholipids are a significant part of cell membranes such as the one shown in the photograph of the nerve cell on the right.

Phospholipid Structure

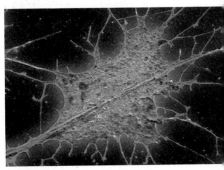

Some lipids in this nerve cell's membrane have two fatty acids and one phosphate group. These lipids are called phospholipids.

Another lipid involved in cell structure is cholesterol, which is a part of cell membranes. Cholesterol has other functions as well. It is necessary to make substances called hormones. Hormones, such as adrenaline, are chemical messengers in your body.

Your body makes some of the cholesterol that it needs, but it also uses cholesterol from foods you eat. Cholesterol is found in many foods that come from animals, such as meat and eggs. Even some plant products, such as coconut oil, can increase the amount of cholesterol in your body. Although you need cholesterol, eating too much of it—just like eating too much saturated fat—can lead to heart disease.

INVESTIGATE Organic Molecules

Where can you find organic molecules?

PROCEDURE

① Place a dropper of cornstarch solution into one jar lid and a dropper of liquid gelatin into a second jar lid.

② Add a drop of iodine solution to the cornstarch sample and to the gelatin sample.

③ Examine the jar lids after 1 minute. Record your observations.

④ Using the remaining two jar lids, repeat steps 2 and 3 with the bread and the tofu instead of the cornstarch and gelatin.

WHAT DO YOU THINK?

- What changes occurred after the addition of iodine to the cornstarch and to the gelatin?

- Iodine can be used to detect the presence of starches. What carbon-based molecules might be in the bread and tofu? How do you know?

CHALLENGE Suppose you tested a piece of pepperoni pizza with iodine. Which ingredients (crust, sauce, cheese, pepperoni) would likely contain starch?

MATERIALS
- 4 small jar lids
- 3 eyedroppers
- cornstarch solution
- liquid gelatin
- iodine solution
- bread
- tofu
- stopwatch

TIME
20 minutes

Proteins

Proteins are macromolecules that are made of smaller molecules called amino acids. Proteins, like carbohydrates and lipids, contain carbon, hydrogen, and oxygen. However, proteins differ from carbohydrates and lipids in that they also contain nitrogen, sulfur, and other elements. Unlike carbohydrates and lipids, which are used primarily for energy and structure, proteins have many different functions.

Think of a protein as being like a word, with amino acids as the letters in that word. The meaning of a word depends on the order of letters in the word. For example, rearranging the letters in the word "eat" makes different words with different meanings. Similarly, proteins depend on the order of their amino acids.

Linked Amino Acids

| tyrosine | lysine | cysteine | serine | leucine |

Just as 26 letters of the alphabet make up all words in the English language, 20 amino acids make up all of the proteins in your body. The structure of a protein is determined by the order of its amino acids. If two amino acids change places, the entire protein changes.

The function of a protein depends on its structure. There are at least 100,000 proteins in your body, each with a different structure that gives it a specific function. Some proteins are structural materials, some control chemical reactions, and others transport substances within cells and through the body. Still others are a part of the immune system, which protects you from infections.

 CHECK YOUR READING How does the function of a protein depend on its structure?

Proteins that are part of the structure of living things are often shaped like coils. One coil-shaped protein, keratin, is part of human hair as shown on the left below. Proteins called actin and myosin are coil-shaped proteins that help your muscles contract.

Other types of proteins have coiled regions but curl up into shapes like balls. One example is hemoglobin, shown on the right below. Hemoglobin is a transport protein that carries oxygen in the blood.

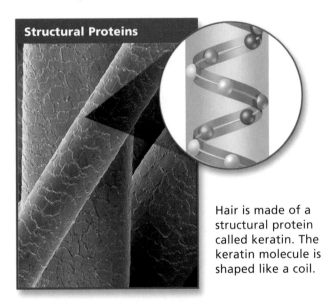

Structural Proteins

Hair is made of a structural protein called keratin. The keratin molecule is shaped like a coil.

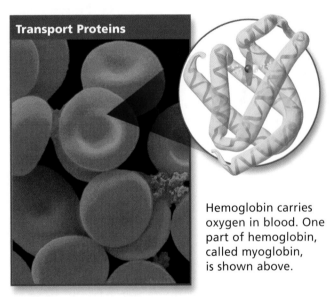

Transport Proteins

Hemoglobin carries oxygen in blood. One part of hemoglobin, called myoglobin, is shown above.

Some proteins that curl up into a shape like a ball are enzymes. An **enzyme** (EHN-zym) is a catalyst for a chemical reaction in living things. Catalysts increase the rate of chemical reactions. Enzymes are necessary for many chemical reactions in your body. Without enzymes, these reactions would occur too slowly to keep you alive.

It is important to have proteins in your diet so that your body can make its own proteins. Proteins in foods such as meats, soybeans, and nuts are broken down into amino acids by your body. These amino acids are then used by your cells to make new proteins.

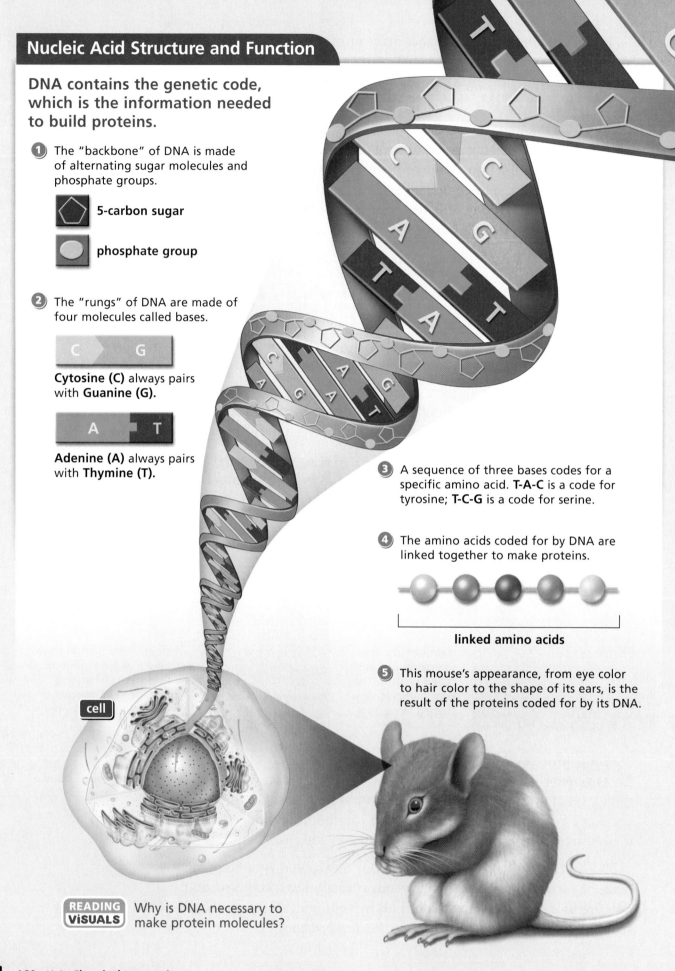

Nucleic Acid Structure and Function

DNA contains the genetic code, which is the information needed to build proteins.

① The "backbone" of DNA is made of alternating sugar molecules and phosphate groups.

⬠ **5-carbon sugar**

⬭ **phosphate group**

② The "rungs" of DNA are made of four molecules called bases.

C　**G**

Cytosine (C) always pairs with **Guanine (G)**.

A　**T**

Adenine (A) always pairs with **Thymine (T)**.

③ A sequence of three bases codes for a specific amino acid. **T-A-C** is a code for tyrosine; **T-C-G** is a code for serine.

④ The amino acids coded for by DNA are linked together to make proteins.

linked amino acids

⑤ This mouse's appearance, from eye color to hair color to the shape of its ears, is the result of the proteins coded for by its DNA.

cell

READING VISUALS Why is DNA necessary to make protein molecules?

Nucleic Acids

Nucleic acids (noo-KLEE-ihk AS-ihdz) are huge, complex carbon-based molecules that contain the information that cells use to make proteins. These macromolecules are made of carbon, hydrogen, and oxygen, as well as nitrogen and phosphorus. Each of the cells in your body contains a complete set of nucleic acids. This means that each cell has all of the instructions necessary for making any protein in your body.

The illustration on page 160 shows part of a nucleic acid molecule called DNA, which looks like a twisted ladder. The sides of the ladder are made of sugar molecules and phosphate groups. Each rung of the ladder is composed of two nitrogen-containing molecules called bases. DNA has four types of bases, represented by the letters A, C, T, and G. The order of the bases in a DNA molecule is the way in which DNA stores the instructions for making proteins. How do just four molecules—A, C, T, and G—carry all of this important information?

Recall that a protein is composed of amino acids that have to be linked in a certain order. Each of the 20 amino acids is represented by a particular series of three DNA bases. For example, the sequence T–A–C corresponds to—or is a code for—the amino acid tyrosine. There are 64 different three-base sequences in DNA, all of which have a specific meaning. This genetic code works in the same way in every living thing on Earth. It provides a complete set of instructions for linking amino acids in the right order to make each specific protein molecule. The DNA code is only one part of making proteins, though. Other types of nucleic acids, called RNA, are responsible for reading the code and assembling a protein with the correct amino acids.

READING TiP

The *NA* in DNA stands for nucleic acid. The *D* stands for deoxyribose, which is the type of sugar in the molecule.

RESOURCE CENTER
CLASSZONE.COM

Find out more about carbohydrates, lipids, proteins, and nucleic acids.

> **CHECK YOUR READING** How many different types of bases make up the genetic code in DNA?

5.2 Review

KEY CONCEPTS

1. How does the function of a lipid depend on its structure?

2. What determines the structure of a protein?

3. What role does DNA perform in the making of proteins?

CRITICAL THINKING

4. **Synthesize** Give two examples of carbon-based molecules in living things that are based on a chain structure. Explain.

5. **Compare and Contrast** How are carbohydrates and lipids similar? How are they different?

CHALLENGE

6. **Infer** Suppose the order of bases in a DNA molecule is changed. What do you think will happen to the structure of the protein that is coded for by that region of DNA? Why?

MATH TUTORIAL
CLASSZONE.COM

Click on Math Tutorial for more help with bar graphs.

Graphing Good Food

People need to eat carbohydrates, proteins, and lipids to have a healthy diet. Different amounts of each type of organic molecule are recommended for different groups of people. In general, grains, vegetables, and fruits contain carbohydrates. Dairy products, meats, and beans contain proteins and lipids. The table on the right shows dietary recommendations. The information could also be shown in a bar graph.

Recommended Servings

Food group	Young children	Teen girls	Teen boys
Grains	6	9	11
Vegetables	3	4	5
Fruits	2	3	4
Dairy	3	3	3
Meats, beans	2	2	3

SOURCE: *U.S. Department of Agriculture, Home and Garden Bulletin Number 252, 1996*

Example

Create a bar graph that shows the dietary recommendation of grains for each group.

(1) Use the height of the bar to indicate the numerical value of a piece of data.

(2) Show the number of servings on the vertical axis. Label each group of bars on the horizontal axis.

(3) Use a different color for each group.

ANSWER

■ Young Children
■ Teen Girls
■ Teen Boys

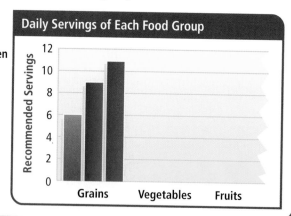

Daily Servings of Each Food Group

Use the Recommended Servings table above to answer the following questions.

1. Copy and complete the bar graph to show the dietary recommendations for the other four food groups.

2. Which group has the tallest bars on the graph? the shortest?

CHALLENGE Choose one group of people and make a pie graph showing recommendations for them. (**Hint:** First convert the numbers of servings into fractions of the whole diet.)

5.3 Carbon-based molecules are in many materials.

◀ **BEFORE**, you learned

- Organic compounds are based on carbon
- Carbon can form molecules shaped like chains or rings
- Four types of carbon-based compounds are common in living things

▶ **NOW**, you will learn

- How carbon-based molecules are obtained from petroleum
- How carbon-based molecules are designed for specific uses
- How a material's properties depend on its molecular structure

VOCABULARY

hydrocarbon p. 163
polymer p. 166
monomer p. 166
plastic p. 167

THINK ABOUT

What do windbreakers and motor oil have in common?

Motor oil and windbreakers are both made of carbon-based molecules. The motor oil is composed mostly of carbon and hydrogen. The nylon windbreaker is also composed mostly of carbon and hydrogen. How can two materials that are so different be made of similar molecules?

RESOURCE CENTER
CLASSZONE.COM

Find out more about petroleum and hydrocarbons.

Carbon-based compounds from ancient organisms are used to make new materials.

Many of the things you see around you every day contain carbon-based molecules. Some, such as people, plants, and animals, are easy to spot. Others are not so easy to identify. These objects include clothing, furniture, packing materials, sports equipment, and more. You have read that a large number of substances that make up living things are based on carbon. Where do we get carbon-based molecules that we use to make modern materials?

The carbon-based compounds that are the basis of many materials are called hydrocarbons. A **hydrocarbon** is simply a compound made of only carbon and hydrogen. Many different hydrocarbons are found in large deposits underground and under the sea. The story of how they got there began a long time ago and is related to the way carbon moves through the environment in a cycle.

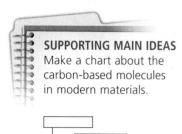

SUPPORTING MAIN IDEAS
Make a chart about the carbon-based molecules in modern materials.

READING TiP

As you read the numbered steps, follow the process shown on page 165.

VISUALIZATION
CLASSZONE.COM

Observe the process involved in the separation of the hydrocarbons in petroleum.

In the carbon cycle, plants use carbon dioxide from the air to make carbohydrates. Animals eat plants and absorb carbon, and then release carbon dioxide into the air when they exhale. When animals and plants die, they decompose and carbon returns to the environment. Most carbon returns to the atmosphere as part of the carbon cycle, but some does not. This carbon is the source of the carbon-based compounds that are so important for modern life.

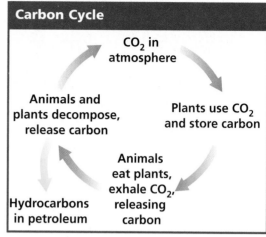

Carbon Cycle

CO_2 in atmosphere

Plants use CO_2 and store carbon

Animals eat plants, exhale CO_2, releasing carbon

Hydrocarbons in petroleum

Animals and plants decompose, release carbon

1 **Obtaining Petroleum** Some living things that died hundreds of millions of years ago fell into mud or sediment. Instead of returning to the atmosphere, the carbon-based molecules from these organisms became trapped in the ground. Over time, and through a process of chemical changes, some of this organic material became petroleum, which is a mixture of hundreds of different hydrocarbons. People pump petroleum from underground and undersea deposits. Liquid petroleum is called crude oil.

2 **Refining Petroleum** In its raw form, petroleum is not a useful substance. However, when it is processed at a refinery, it is separated into many useful parts.

3 **Using Products Made from Petroleum** Many products, including gasoline, plastics, and fibers such as nylon are made from the separated parts of petroleum.

The refining of petroleum is an example of the separation of a mixture based on physical properties. Each type of hydrocarbon in petroleum has a different boiling point. In general, each boiling point depends on the number and arrangement of carbon atoms in the molecule. For example, lubricating oil contains long carbon chains and boils at temperatures above 350°C. The hydrocarbons that make up gasoline are smaller molecules, and they boil between 35°C and 220°C.

At a refinery, petroleum is heated until all but the largest of the hydrocarbons are in gaseous form. This gaseous petroleum is released into a distillation tower. As the gases rise in the tower, they gradually cool. When each specific hydrocarbon cools to its boiling point, it condenses back into a liquid. Thus, lubricating oil cools to its boiling point quickly and is collected from a low level in the tower. Hydrocarbons in gasoline take longer to become liquids and are collected higher in the tower.

CHECK YOUR READING   How are hydrocarbons in petroleum separated from each other?

Using Petroleum

Carbon-based compounds in petroleum are used to make a wide range of products.

① Obtaining Petroleum

Petroleum is trapped underground between rock layers that it cannot move through. People have pumped petroleum out of the ground since the 1850s.

rock layer containing petroleum

② Refining Petroleum

Petroleum is separated into different parts, or fractions, at an oil refinery. Different fractions are used for different purposes.

Petroleum Products

Petroleum Fraction	Number of Carbon Atoms per Molecule	Uses
Gases	1 to 4	Cooking, heating, manufacturing
Gasoline	5 to 12	Automobile fuel
Kerosene	12 to 16	Airplane fuel
Fuel oil	15 to 18	Diesel fuel, heating oil
Greases	16 to 20	Lubrication

SOURCE: *Mortimer, Chemistry, 6th edition*

③ Using Products Made from Petroleum

The gas fraction of petroleum is often used to make such products as fibers and plastics. The gasoline fraction is often used as a fuel for cars.

fibers

fuels

plastics

Polymers contain repeating carbon-based units.

READING **TiP**

The prefix *mono-* means "one," and the prefix *poly-* means "many."

Many everyday materials made of carbon-based molecules contain macromolecules called polymers. **Polymers** are very large carbon-based molecules made of smaller, repeating units. These small, repeating units, called **monomers,** are linked together one after another. By themselves, monomers are also carbon-based molecules.

Some of the carbon-based molecules that you read about in the previous section are polymers. For example, both cellulose and starch are polymers. They are chains of linked glucose units. The glucose units are the monomers. Many common materials that are manufactured for specific purposes are polymers. Plastics and fibers are two examples of these kinds of polymers.

 CHECK YOUR READING What do starch and plastic have in common?

Formation of Polymers

The properties of a polymer depend on the size and structure of the polymer molecule. The size and structure of a polymer depend both on its particular monomers and how many monomers are added together to make the final product.

The process of making a polymer involves chemical reactions that bond monomers together. Think back to the different types of reactions described in Chapter 3. The process of making a polymer is a synthesis reaction that yields a more complex product from simpler reactants.

The diagram on the top of page 167 shows one way in which a polymer can be made. The monomer that is the building block of the polymer in the illustration is called propylene (PROH-puh-LEEN). The propylene molecule consists of three carbon atoms and six hydrogen atoms. By itself, propylene is a gas. Notice that propylene has a double bond between two of its carbon atoms.

During the reaction that links the monomers, one of the bonds that makes up the double bond is broken. When that bond is broken, a new bond can form between two of the monomer units. A large number of the propylene monomers bonded together form a polymer called polypropylene. Polypropylene is a strong, solid plastic used to make such items as plastic crates, toys, bicycle helmets, and even indoor-outdoor carpeting.

 CHECK YOUR READING How do the properties of polypropylene differ from those of propylene?

Building Polymers

Polymers such as polypropylene are made by linking many monomers together.

This bicycle helmet is made of polypropylene.

1 Propylene (C_3H_6) can be used as a monomer.

Monomer

$CH_2 = CH - CH_3$

2 Propylene monomers are linked together.

Monomers Are Linked Together

$CH_2 = CH - CH_3$ $CH_2 = CH - CH_3$ $CH_2 = CH - CH_3$

3 Linked propylene monomers make polypropylene.

Polymer

$$CH_2 - CH - CH_2 - CH - CH_2 - CH ---$$
$$\qquad\quad | \qquad\qquad\quad | \qquad\qquad\quad |$$
$$\qquad\quad CH_3 \qquad\quad CH_3 \qquad\quad CH_3$$

— = double bond changed to single bond
— = new bond formed between monomers

Polymers may be composed of more than one type of monomer. Polyester fabric is an example of a polymer that contains two different monomers. Protein is another example. In fact, as you read earlier, proteins in living things contain several different monomers. The monomers in proteins are amino acids.

Plastics

Polypropylene is one of many polymers that are called plastics. As an adjective, *plastic* means "capable of being molded or shaped." A **plastic** is a polymer that can be molded or shaped. If you look around, you can see how common plastics are in everyday life.

The first plastic made by chemists was celluloid, which was patented in 1870. It was based on cellulose molecules from cotton plants and was used to make such things as billiard balls and movie film. Celluloid is different from many of the plastics that are made today. It was made by chemically changing an existing, naturally occurring polymer—cellulose.

Many of today's plastics are made artificially, by building polymers from monomers. The first completely artificial polymer made by scientists was a plastic called Bakelite, which was invented in 1907. Chemists made Bakelite by linking individual monomers together. Because Bakelite is moldable and nonflammable, it was used for many household items such as pot handles, jewelry, lamps, buttons, and radio cases.

 CHECK YOUR READING How does the term plastic describe a polymer's properties?

Recycling Plastics				
Code	Chemical Name	Monomers	Properties	Uses
1	Polyethylene terephthalate (PET or PETE)	$C_2H_6O_2$ and $C_8H_6O_4$	Transparent, high strength, does not stretch	Clothing, soft-drink bottles, audiotapes, videotapes
2	High Density Polyethylene (HDPE)	C_2H_4	Similar to LDPE (code 4) but denser, tougher, more rigid	Milk and water jugs, gasoline tanks, cups
3	Polyvinyl chloride (PVC)	C_2H_3Cl	Rigid, transparent, high strength	Shampoo bottles, garden hoses, plumbing pipes
4	Low Density Polyethylene (LDPE)	C_2H_4	White, soft, subject to cracking	Plastic bags, toys, electrical insulation
5	Polypropylene (PP)	C_3H_6	High strength and rigidity, impermeable to liquids and gases	Battery cases, indoor-outdoor carpeting, bottle caps, auto trim
6	Polystyrene (PS)	C_8H_8	Glassy, rigid, brittle	Insulation, drinking cups, packing materials

SOURCE: *American Chemical Society*

The chart above lists some common plastics and their uses. You may have noticed the symbols shown in the first column of the chart on plastic bottles and containers that you have around your home. The numbers stand for different types of plastic, with different uses. After a plastic has been used in a certain way, such as in soft drink bottles, it can recycled and used again. When a plastic is recycled it can be made into a new product that has a different use. For example, recycled soft drink bottles can be made into fibers for carpeting.

Designing Materials

Chemists have been designing and making polymers for many years. However, new polymers are always being developed. One way in which scientists make new polymers is by chemically changing an original monomer. When scientists change a monomer and then link the monomers together, a new material is produced.

Teflon is very strong and light in weight. It was used to make the roof of this stadium in Minneapolis.

Teflon is a common polymer that is made by chemically changing a hydrocarbon monomer. Chemists replace the hydrogen atoms in the monomer with fluorine atoms and link the monomers together. You have probably seen Teflon as a nonstick coating on pots and pans. Teflon is also very strong, and it was used as a part of the structure of the stadium's dome in the photograph on the left.

$$--- CF_2 - CF_2 - CF_2 - CF_2 ---$$

Nomex

Kevlar

Nomex is used to make fireproof clothing worn by firefighters.

Kevlar is used in bulletproof vests worn by police officers and police dogs.

Chemists have developed several other materials by changing the monomers in nylon, a polymer that is often used in clothing. By adding a carbon-based ring to the nylon monomer, chemists made Nomex, which is used in fireproof clothing. Then scientists changed the placement of this ring on the monomer. This change resulted in the polymer called Kevlar, which is used in bulletproof vests.

Nomex and Kevlar are isomers. The monomers that are the basis of each contain the same atoms but have different structures. As a result, the polymers have different properties and uses. The structure of the polymer in Nomex gives the fibers flexibility along with fire resistance. As a result, Nomex can be made into relatively comfortable fireproof clothing for firefighters and race car drivers. Kevlar, however, is very rigid because of its structure and is the strongest known fiber. In fact, Kevlar is five times stronger than an equal amount of steel, which helps explain why Kevlar is used in bulletproof vests.

 CHECK YOUR READING Why are Nomex and Kevlar isomers?

5.3 Review

KEY CONCEPTS

1. What physical property allows the hydrocarbons in petroleum to be separated? Explain.

2. What are monomers? How are monomers related to polymers?

3. How are polymers such as Kevlar and Nomex similar to each other? How are they different?

CRITICAL THINKING

4. **Synthesize** What general type of chemical reaction makes polymers from monomers? Explain.

5. **Compare and Contrast** How are plastics such as polypropylene similar to celluloid, the first plastic? How are they different?

CHALLENGE

6. **Synthesize** A petroleum deposit is full of carbon compounds. How did that carbon get out of the atmosphere and into the petroleum?

CHAPTER INVESTIGATION

Polymers

OVERVIEW AND PURPOSE Polymers are used in many common items. For example, the substance that is being pulled out of the beaker in the photograph on the left is raw nylon, which is a polymer. The properties of polymers are influenced by the way in which the chains are linked together. In this activity, you will use what you have learned about carbon-based molecules to

- make a polymer
- study the properties of a polymer

▶ Procedure

1. Create a data table like the one shown on the sample notebook page.

2. Follow the instructions to mix the polymer called Glurch. After you have made the polymer, store it in a zip-top bag.

MATERIALS
- measuring spoons
- 2 plastic containers
- tap water
- white glue
- food coloring
- borax
- jar with lid
- plastic spoon
- zip-top plastic bags
- scissors
- 2 L plastic bottle
- ring stand with ring
- stopwatch
- straws

GLURCH
40 mL (8 tsp) water
40 mL (8 tsp) white glue
6 drops of food coloring

2 tsp powdered borax
30 mL (6 tsp) water

- Make a glue mixture by mixing 40 mL of water with 40 mL of white glue in a plastic container.
- Add food coloring and mix the color evenly.
- Make a borax solution by adding 2 tsp of borax to 30 mL of water. Shake the mixture in a covered jar for 30 seconds.
- Combine the borax solution with the glue mixture. Stir.
- Knead until the mixture is smooth, with a rubberlike consistency.

3. Remove some of the polymer from the bag. Try each test below in order. Observe each test and record your results.

4. **SQUEEZE TEST** Put some of the polymer in your hand. Squeeze the polymer to test its shape and its feel. Is it a solid, a liquid, or a little like both? Record your observations.

5. **PULL TEST** Hold the polymer between your hands and pull it apart slowly. Try again, and pull it apart very quickly. What happens to the polymer? Record the results of this test.

BOUNCE TEST Roll some of the polymer into a ball between your palms. Test whether the polymer ball will bounce. Record your observations about the polymer's behavior.

CREEP TEST
Setup Cut the top off a 2 L bottle. Keep the bottle cap on. Set up a ring stand. To use the bottle top as a funnel, place it upside down in the ring. Put a plastic container under the funnel.

step 7

Trials Place approximately 100 mL of the polymer in the funnel. Remove the bottle cap and time how long it takes for the polymer to flow completely through the funnel. Record the time. If time allows, conduct one or two more trials.

BUBBLE TEST Take a small amount of the polymer and roll it into a ball around the end of a straw. Pinch the polymer closed around the straw. Hold the ball in one hand as you gently blow into the other end of the straw. Try to make a bubble by filling the polymer with air. Record your observations.

Observe and Analyze

Write It Up

1. **RECORD OBSERVATIONS** Be sure that your data table is complete. Describe how the polymer feels, as well as its state, shape, and behavior.

2. **COMMUNICATE** Include drawings of any observations for which a picture is helpful in understanding your results.

3. **INTERPRET DATA** Make a list of the polymer's physical properties. Which test was most helpful in identifying these properties? Which test was the least helpful?

Conclude

Write It Up

1. **INFER** The more complex a polymer is, the more rigid it is. Do you think that the polymer you made contains molecules with extremely long or complex carbon chains? Why or why not? What properties of your polymer provide evidence for your answer?

2. **EVALUATE** What limitations or difficulties did you experience in interpreting the results of your tests or other observations?

3. **APPLY** Based upon your results, what uses could you suggest for the polymer? What further tests would you need to do to make sure it would stand up to the demands of that use?

INVESTIGATE Further

CHALLENGE Investigate the properties of your polymer by varying the proportions of the ingredients. Change only one ingredient. Be sure to record the change you made in the polymer. Make a new data table. Record the results of the experimental tests. How do changes in the polymer recipe change the physical properties of the polymer?

Polymers
Observe and Analyze

Table 1. Polymer Properties

Test	Observations
Squeeze test	
Pull test	
Bounce test	
Creep test	Trial 1 (time) Trial 2 (time) Trial 3 (time)
Bubble test	

Conclude

Chapter Review

the **BIG** idea

Carbon is essential to living things and to modern materials.

CONTENT REVIEW
CLASSZONE.COM

◀ **KEY CONCEPTS SUMMARY**

5.1 Carbon-based molecules have many structures.

Carbon forms a large number of different compounds because of the number of bonds it can make with other atoms.

Single Bond

Double Bond

Triple Bond

Carbon can form chains and rings.

Hexane

$$CH_3 - CH_2 - CH_2 - CH_2 - CH_2 - CH_3$$

Vanillin

VOCABULARY
organic compound p. 147
inorganic compound p. 148
isomer p. 152

5.2 Carbon-based molecules are life's building blocks.

There are four main types of carbon-based molecules in living things.

Carbon-Based Molecules			
Carbohydrates	**Lipids**	**Proteins**	**Nucleic Acids**
• include sugars and starches	• include fats and oils	• function depends on order of amino acids	• DNA
• energy for cells	• energy for cells	• structure, transport, immune system, enzymes	• carries genetic code
• plant cell walls	• cell membranes		• sequence of three DNA bases is the code for an amino acid

VOCABULARY
carbohydrate p. 155
lipid p. 156
protein p. 158
enzyme p. 159
nucleic acid p. 161

5.3 Carbon-based molecules are in many materials.

Carbon from ancient organisms is used to make many common items, such as clothing and plastics. These items are based on polymers.

Monomer $CH_2 = CH - CH_3$

Polymer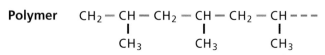

VOCABULARY
hydrocarbon p. 163
polymer p. 166
monomer p. 166
plastic p. 167

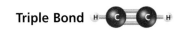

Reviewing Vocabulary

Copy and complete the chart below. Fill in the blanks with the missing term, example, or function. See the example in the chart.

Term	Example	Function
inorganic compound	*carbon dioxide*	*used by plants to make glucose*
1. organic compound	glucose	
2. carbohydrate	sugar	
3.	fat	stores chemical energy
4.	keratin	found in hair and feathers
5. nucleic acid		instructions for proteins
6. plastic	polypropylene	

Greek Roots *Describe how each of the following terms is related to one or more of the following Greek roots.*

iso- means "equal"   *mono-* means "one"
-mer means "part"   *poly-* means "many"

7. isomer

8. polymer

9. monomer

10. polyunsaturated

Reviewing Key Concepts

Multiple Choice *Choose the letter of the best answer.*

11. All life on Earth is based on atoms of which element?
   a. oxygen
   b. nitrogen
   c. carbon
   d. hydrogen

12. One reason that carbon atoms can form large numbers of compounds is that a carbon atom forms
   a. two bonds with a hydrogen atom
   b. four bonds in its compounds
   c. ionic bonds in its compounds
   d. bonds with up to five hydrogen atoms

13. Which of the following is not found in living things?
   a. proteins   **c.** lipids
   b. petroleum   **d.** carbohydrates

14. What functions do carbohydrates and lipids perform in living things?
   a. They provide energy and instructions.
   b. They provide water and oxygen.
   c. They provide water and immunity.
   d. They provide energy and structure.

15. The molecules that carry instructions to make other molecules are called
   a. nucleic acids   **c.** carbohydrates
   b. proteins   **d.** lipids

16. Which kinds of molecules are best for storing chemical energy in living things?
   a. enzymes   **c.** lipids
   b. proteins   **d.** nucleic acids

17. The properties of artificial polymers are determined by
   a. the structure of the molecule
   b. the reaction used to make the polymer
   c. the time it took to make the polymer
   d. a series of DNA bases

Short Answer *Write a short answer to each question.*

18. Explain how carbon's ability to form isomers is related to the large number of carbon-based molecules that exist.

19. Describe the movement of carbon through the environment in a cycle. How does a break in the cycle provide carbon for modern materials?

Thinking Critically

The illustration below models linked amino acids. Use the illustration to answer the next four questions.

20. SYNTHESIZE Why can the model shown by the illustration be considered to be a polymer?

21. CONCLUDE What would cause the amino acids in the illustration to be placed in that particular order? Explain.

22. APPLY If the order of amino acids shown in the illustration changes, would the protein formed likely still have the same function? Why or why not?

23. PREDICT Suppose the protein formed by the amino acids has a coiled shape. What might be the general function of that protein? What if the protein is coiled but also curls up into a ball?

24. COMPARE AND CONTRAST Copy and complete the chart below. Provide two similarities and two differences for each pair of items.

Items	Similarities	Differences
starch/ cellulose	both carbohydrates; both polymers	starch used for energy, cellulose for structure; starch molecule branched, cellulose molecule straight
carbon chains/ carbon rings		
proteins/lipids		
glucose/ amino acids		

Using Math Skills in Science

The nutrition label below shows the Calories and the amount of fat, carbohydrates, and protein in a type of cracker. Use the information on the label to answer the following three questions.

Nutrition Facts

Servings Per Container   about 15

Amount Per Serving

Calories	150
Total Fat	6g
Total Carbohydrates	20g
Protein	2g

25. Fats contain about twice as many Calories per gram as carbohydrates and proteins. Assume that all of the Calories on the label come from the carbohydrates, fats, and proteins. About how many Calories come from each substance?

26. Make a pie chart that compares the number of Calories from carbohydrates, fats, and proteins contained in this food.

27. Adult athletes are recommended to eat a diet that provides 15% of its Calories from protein, 30% from fats, and 55% from carbohydrates. Does this food have the recommended balance of nutrients? Why or why not?

the BIG idea

28. DRAW CONCLUSIONS Look at the photographs on pages 144–145. Describe three ways in which carbon is important in the activities taking place.

29. SYNTHESIZE Write one or more paragraphs describing how plants, animals, and plastics are related to each other.

UNIT PROJECTS

Evaluate all the data, results, and information from your project folder. Prepare to present your project.

Interpreting Tables

The following table contains information about some of the different products that can be separated from petroleum. Use the information in the table to answer questions 1–5.

Characteristics of Petroleum Products		
Product	Number of Carbon Atoms per Molecule	Boiling Point (°C)
Natural gas	1 to 4	lower than 20
Gasoline	5 to 12	35 to 220
Kerosene	12 to 16	200 to 315
Jet fuel	12 to 16	200 to 315
Diesel fuel	15 to 18	250 to 375
Heating oil	15 to 18	250 to 375
Lubricating oil	16 to 20	350 and higher
Asphalt	More than 25	600 and higher

SOURCE: *Mortimer, Chemistry, 6th edition*

1. Which petroleum product has the lowest boiling point?

a. diesel fuel

b. gasoline

c. kerosene

d. natural gas

2. Which petroleum product has the highest boiling point?

a. asphalt

b. heating oil

c. jet fuel

d. kerosene

3. Petroleum is heated and turned into gas. The gas rises in a distillation tower. The lightest gases—those with the smallest molecules—rise highest. The heaviest gases—those with the largest molecules—stay lowest. Which of the following products would be found lowest in the tower?

a. diesel fuel

b. kerosene

c. lubricating oil

d. natural gas

4. Petroleum is split into fractions. Each fraction includes all the products that have the same boiling point. Which of the following pairs of products are in the same fraction?

a. gasoline and natural gas

b. jet fuel and kerosene

c. lubricating oil and diesel fuel

d. natural gas and asphalt

5. What might be the boiling point of a petroleum product that contains 22 carbon atoms?

a. 100°C

b. 300°C

c. 500°C

d. 700°C

Extended Response

Answer the following two questions in detail. Include some of the terms from the list in the box at right. Underline each term that you use in your answers.

atoms	carbon chains	carbon rings
molecules	properties	structure
function	monomer	

6. How are polymers made? Give examples of a natural polymer and an artificial polymer.

7. Carbohydrates, lipids, and proteins are all carbon-based molecules. How are they similar? How are they different?

Student Resource Handbooks

Scientific Thinking Handbook

Making Observations

An **observation** is an act of noting and recording an event, characteristic, behavior, or anything else detected with an instrument or with
the senses.

Observations allow you to make informed hypotheses and to gather data for
experiments. Careful observations often lead to ideas for new experiments.
There are two categories of observations:

- **Quantitative observations** can be expressed in numbers and include
  records of time, temperature, mass, distance, and volume.

- **Qualitative observations** include descriptions of sights, sounds, smells,
  and textures.

EXAMPLE

A student dissolved 30 grams of Epsom salts in water, poured the solution into
a dish, and let the dish sit out uncovered overnight. The next day, she made
the following observations of the Epsom salt crystals that grew in the dish.

Table 1. Observations of Epsom Salt Crystals

To determine the mass, the
student found the mass of
the dish before and after
growing the crystals and
then used subtraction to
find the difference.

The student measured several crystals and calculated the
mean length. (To learn how
to calculate the mean of a
data set, see page R36.)

Quantitative Observations	Qualitative Observations
• mass = 30 g • mean crystal length = 0.5 cm • longest crystal length = 2 cm	• Crystals are clear. • Crystals are long, thin, and rectangular. • White crust has formed around edge of dish.

Photographs or sketches
are useful for recording
qualitative observations.

Epsom salt crystals

MORE ABOUT OBSERVING

- Make quantitative observations whenever possible. That way, others will
  know exactly what you observed and be able to compare their results
  with yours.

- It is always a good idea to make qualitative observations too. You never
  know when you might observe something unexpected.

Predicting and Hypothesizing

A **prediction** is an expectation of what will be observed or what will happen. A **hypothesis** is a tentative explanation for an observation or scientific problem that can be tested by further investigation.

EXAMPLE

Suppose you have made two paper airplanes and you wonder why one of them tends to glide farther than the other one.

1. Start by asking a question.

2. Make an educated guess. After examination, you notice that the wings of the airplane that flies farther are slightly larger than the wings of the other airplane.

3. Write a prediction based upon your educated guess, in the form of an "If . . . , then . . ." statement. Write the independent variable after the word *if,* and the dependent variable after the word *then.*

4. To make a hypothesis, explain why you think what you predicted will occur. Write the explanation after the word *because.*

> 1. Why does one of the paper airplanes glide farther than the other?
>
> 2. The size of an airplane's wings may affect how far the airplane will glide.
>
> 3. Prediction: If I make a paper airplane with larger wings, then the airplane will glide farther.

To read about independent and dependent variables, see page R30.

> 4. Hypothesis: If I make a paper airplane with larger wings, then the airplane will glide farther, because the additional surface area of the wing will produce more lift.

Notice that the part of the hypothesis after *because* adds an explanation of why the airplane will glide farther.

MORE ABOUT HYPOTHESES

- The results of an experiment cannot prove that a hypothesis is correct. Rather, the results either support or do not support the hypothesis.

- Valuable information is gained even when your hypothesis is not supported by your results. For example, it would be an important discovery to find that wing size is not related to how far an airplane glides.

- In science, a hypothesis is supported only after many scientists have conducted many experiments and produced consistent results.

Inferring

An **inference** is a logical conclusion drawn from the available evidence and prior knowledge. Inferences are often made from observations.

EXAMPLE

A student observing a set of acorns noticed something unexpected about one of them. He noticed a white, soft-bodied insect eating its way out of the acorn.

> The student recorded these observations.

Observations

- There is a hole in the acorn, about 0.5 cm in diameter, where the insect crawled out.
- There is a second hole, which is about the size of a pinhole, on the other side of the acorn.
- The inside of the acorn is hollow.

> Here are some inferences that can be made on the basis of the observations.

Inferences

- The insect formed from the material inside the acorn, grew to its present size, and ate its way out of the acorn.
- The insect crawled through the smaller hole, ate the inside of the acorn, grew to its present size, and ate its way out of the acorn.
- An egg was laid in the acorn through the smaller hole. The egg hatched into a larva that ate the inside of the acorn, grew to its present size, and ate its way out of the acorn.

> When you make inferences, be sure to look at all of the evidence available and combine it with what you already know.

MORE ABOUT INFERENCES

Inferences depend both on observations and on the knowledge of the people making the inferences. Ancient people who did not know that organisms are produced only by similar organisms might have made an inference like the first one. A student today might look at the same observations and make the second inference. A third student might have knowledge about this particular insect and know that it is never small enough to fit through the smaller hole, leading her to the third inference.

Identifying Cause and Effect

In a **cause-and-effect relationship,** one event or characteristic is the result of another. Usually an effect follows its cause in time.

There are many examples of cause-and-effect relationships in everyday life.

Cause	Effect
Turn off a light.	Room gets dark.
Drop a glass.	Glass breaks.
Blow a whistle.	Sound is heard.

Scientists must be careful not to infer a cause-and-effect relationship just because one event happens after another event. When one event occurs after another, you cannot infer a cause-and-effect relationship on the basis of that information alone. You also cannot conclude that one event caused another if there are alternative ways to explain the second event. A scientist must demonstrate through experimentation or continued observation that an event was truly caused by another event.

EXAMPLE

Make an Observation

Suppose you have a few plants growing outside. When the weather starts getting colder, you bring one of the plants indoors. You notice that the plant you brought indoors is growing faster than the others are growing. You cannot conclude from your observation that the change in temperature was the cause of the increased plant growth, because there are alternative explanations for the observation. Some possible explanations are given below.

- The humidity indoors caused the plant to grow faster.

- The level of sunlight indoors caused the plant to grow faster.

- The indoor plant's being noticed more often and watered more often than the outdoor plants caused it to grow faster.

- The plant that was brought indoors was healthier than the other plants to begin with.

To determine which of these factors, if any, caused the indoor plant to grow faster than the outdoor plants, you would need to design and conduct an experiment.

See pages R28–R35 for information about designing experiments.

Recognizing Bias

Television, newspapers, and the Internet are full of experts claiming to have scientific evidence to back up their claims. How do you know whether the claims are really backed up by good science?

Bias is a slanted point of view, or personal prejudice. The goal of scientists is to be as objective as possible and to base their findings on facts instead of opinions. However, bias often affects the conclusions of researchers, and it is important to learn to recognize bias.

When scientific results are reported, you should consider the source of the information as well as the information itself. It is important to critically analyze the information that you see and read.

SOURCES OF BIAS

There are several ways in which a report of scientific information may be biased. Here are some questions that you can ask yourself:

1. **Who is sponsoring the research?**

   Sometimes, the results of an investigation are biased because an organization paying for the research is looking for a specific answer. This type of bias can affect how data are gathered and interpreted.

2. **Is the research sample large enough?**

   Sometimes research does not include enough data. The larger the sample size, the more likely that the results are accurate, assuming a truly random sample.

3. **In a survey, who is answering the questions?**

   The results of a survey or poll can be biased. The people taking part in the survey may have been specifically chosen because of how they would answer. They may have the same ideas or lifestyles. A survey or poll should make use of a random sample of people.

4. **Are the people who take part in a survey biased?**

   People who take part in surveys sometimes try to answer the questions the way they think the researcher wants them to answer. Also, in surveys or polls that ask for personal information, people may be unwilling to answer questions truthfully.

SCIENTIFIC BIAS

It is also important to realize that scientists have their own biases because of the types of research they do and because of their scientific viewpoints. Two scientists may look at the same set of data and come to completely different conclusions because of these biases. However, such disagreements are not necessarily bad. In fact, a critical analysis of disagreements is often responsible for moving science forward.

Identifying Faulty Reasoning

Faulty reasoning is wrong or incorrect thinking. It leads to mistakes and to wrong conclusions. Scientists are careful not to draw unreasonable conclusions from experimental data. Without such caution, the results of scientific investigations may be misleading.

EXAMPLE

Scientists try to make generalizations based on their data to explain as much about nature as possible. If only a small sample of data is looked at, however, a conclusion may be faulty. Suppose a scientist has studied the effects of the El Niño and La Niña weather patterns on flood damage in California from 1989 to 1995. The scientist organized the data in the bar graph below.

The scientist drew the following conclusions:

1. The La Niña weather pattern has no effect on flooding in California.

2. When neither weather pattern occurs, there is almost no flood damage.

3. A weak or moderate El Niño produces a small or moderate amount of flooding.

4. A strong El Niño produces a lot of flooding.

For the six-year period of the scientist's investigation, these conclusions may seem to be reasonable. However, a six-year study of weather patterns may be too small of a sample for the conclusions to be supported. Consider the following graph, which shows information that was gathered from 1949 to 1997.

Flood and Storm Damage in California

Estimated damage (millions of dollars)

Weak–moderate El Niño
Strong El Niño

Starting year of season
(July 1–June 30)

SOURCE: *Governor's Office of Emergency Services, California*

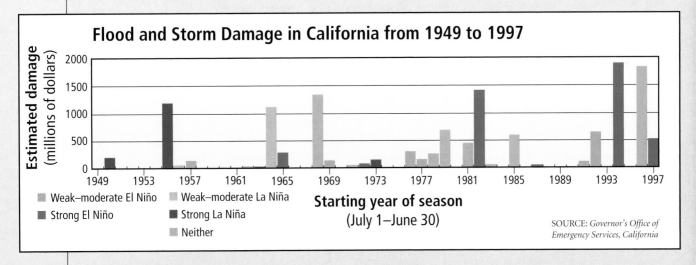

Flood and Storm Damage in California from 1949 to 1997

Estimated damage (millions of dollars)

Weak–moderate El Niño   Weak–moderate La Niña
Strong El Niño   Strong La Niña
Neither

Starting year of season
(July 1–June 30)

SOURCE: *Governor's Office of Emergency Services, California*

The only one of the conclusions that all of this information supports is number 3: a weak or moderate El Niño produces a small or moderate amount of flooding. By collecting more data, scientists can be more certain of their conclusions and can avoid faulty reasoning.

Analyzing Statements

To **analyze** a statement is to examine its parts carefully. Scientific findings are often reported through media such as television or the Internet. A report that is made public often focuses on only a small part of research. As a result, it is important to question the sources of information.

Evaluate Media Claims

To **evaluate** a statement is to judge it on the basis of criteria you've established. Sometimes evaluating means deciding whether a statement is true.

Reports of scientific research and findings in the media may be misleading or incomplete. When you are exposed to this information, you should ask yourself some questions so that you can make informed judgments about the information.

1. **Does the information come from a credible source?**

   Suppose you learn about a new product and it is stated that scientific evidence proves that the product works. A report from a respected news source may be more believable than an advertisement paid for by the product's manufacturer.

2. **How much evidence supports the claim?**

   Often, it may seem that there is new evidence every day of something in the world that either causes or cures an illness. However, information that is the result of several years of work by several different scientists is more credible than an advertisement that does not even cite the subjects of the experiment.

3. **How much information is being presented?**

   Science cannot solve all questions, and scientific experiments often have flaws. A report that discusses problems in a scientific study may be more believable than a report that addresses only positive experimental findings.

4. **Is scientific evidence being presented by a specific source?**

   Sometimes scientific findings are reported by people who are called experts or leaders in a scientific field. But if their names are not given or their scientific credentials are not reported, their statements may be less credible than those of recognized experts.

Differentiate Between Fact and Opinion

Sometimes information is presented as a fact when it may be an opinion. When scientific conclusions are reported, it is important to recognize whether they are based on solid evidence. Again, you may find it helpful to ask yourself some questions.

1. **What is the difference between a fact and an opinion?**

   A **fact** is a piece of information that can be strictly defined and proved true. An **opinion** is a statement that expresses a belief, value, or feeling. An opinion cannot be proved true or false. For example, a person's age is a fact, but if someone is asked how old they feel, it is impossible to prove the person's answer to be true or false.

2. **Can opinions be measured?**

   Yes, opinions can be measured. In fact, surveys often ask for people's opinions on a topic. But there is no way to know whether or not an opinion is the truth.

HOW TO DIFFERENTIATE FACT FROM OPINION

Human Activities and the Environment

Unfortunately, human use of fossil fuels is one of the most significant developments of the past few centuries. Humans rely on fossil fuels, a non-renewable energy resource, for more than 90 percent of their energy needs.

This careless misuse of our planet's resources has resulted in pollution, global warming, and the destruction of fragile ecosystems. For example, oil pipelines carry more than one million barrels of oil each day across tundra regions. Transporting oil across such areas can only result in oil spills that poison the land for decades.

Opinions
Notice words or phrases that express beliefs or feelings. The words *unfortunately* and *careless* show that opinions are being expressed.

Opinion
Look for statements that speculate about events. These statements are opinions, because they cannot be proved.

Facts
Statements that contain statistics tend to be facts. Writers often use facts to support their opinions.

Lab Handbook

Safety Rules

Before you work in the laboratory, read these safety rules twice. Ask your teacher to explain any rules that you do not completely understand. Refer to these rules later on if you have questions about safety in the science classroom.

Directions

- Read all directions and make sure that you understand them before starting an investigation or lab activity. If you do not understand how to do a procedure or how to use a piece of equipment, ask your teacher.
- Do not begin any investigation or touch any equipment until your teacher has told you to start.
- Never experiment on your own. If you want to try a procedure that the directions do not call for, ask your teacher for permission first.
- If you are hurt or injured in any way, tell your teacher immediately.

Dress Code

goggles

apron

gloves

- Wear goggles when
  — using glassware, sharp objects, or chemicals
  — heating an object
  — working with anything that can easily fly up into the air and hurt someone's eye
- Tie back long hair or hair that hangs in front of your eyes.
- Remove any article of clothing—such as a loose sweater or a scarf—that hangs down and may touch a flame, chemical, or piece of equipment.
- Observe all safety icons calling for the wearing of eye protection, gloves, and aprons.

Heating and Fire Safety

fire safety

heating safety

- Keep your work area neat, clean, and free of extra materials.
- Never reach over a flame or heat source.
- Point objects being heated away from you and others.
- Never heat a substance or an object in a closed container.
- Never touch an object that has been heated. If you are unsure whether something is hot, treat it as though it is. Use oven mitts, clamps, tongs, or a test-tube holder.
- Know where the fire extinguisher and fire blanket are kept in your classroom.
- Do not throw hot substances into the trash. Wait for them to cool or use the container your teacher puts out for disposal.

Electrical Safety

electrical safety

- Never use lamps or other electrical equipment with frayed cords.
- Make sure no cord is lying on the floor where someone can trip over it.
- Do not let a cord hang over the side of a counter or table so that the equipment can easily be pulled or knocked to the floor.
- Never let cords hang into sinks or other places where water can be found.
- Never try to fix electrical problems. Inform your teacher of any problems immediately.
- Unplug an electrical cord by pulling on the plug, not the cord.

Chemical Safety

chemical safety

poison

fumes

- If you spill a chemical or get one on your skin or in your eyes, tell your teacher right away.
- Never touch, taste, or sniff any chemicals in the lab. If you need to determine odor, waft. Wafting consists of holding the chemical in its container 15 centimeters (6 in.) away from your nose, and using your fingers to bring fumes from the container to your nose.
- Keep lids on all chemicals you are not using.
- Never put unused chemicals back into the original containers. Throw away extra chemicals where your teacher tells you to.
- Pour chemicals over a sink or your work area, not over the floor.
- If you get a chemical in your eye, use the eyewash right away.
- Always wash your hands after handling chemicals, plants, or soil.

Wafting

Glassware and Sharp-Object Safety

sharp objects

- If you break glassware, tell your teacher right away.
- Do not use broken or chipped glassware. Give these to your teacher.
- Use knives and other cutting instruments carefully. Always wear eye protection and cut away from you.

Animal Safety

- Never hurt an animal.
- Touch animals only when necessary. Follow your teacher's instructions for handling animals.
- Always wash your hands after working with animals.

Cleanup

disposal

- Follow your teacher's instructions for throwing away or putting away supplies.
- Clean your work area and pick up anything that has dropped to the floor.
- Wash your hands.

Using Lab Equipment

Different experiments require different types of equipment. But even though experiments differ, the ways in which the equipment is used are the same.

Beakers

- Use beakers for holding and pouring liquids.
- Do not use a beaker to measure the volume of a liquid. Use a graduated cylinder instead. (See page R16.)
- Use a beaker that holds about twice as much liquid as you need. For example, if you need 100 milliliters of water, you should use a 200- or 250-milliliter beaker.

Test Tubes

- Use test tubes to hold small amounts of substances.
- Do not use a test tube to measure the volume of a liquid.
- Use a test tube when heating a substance over a flame. Aim the mouth of the tube away from yourself and other people.
- Liquids easily spill or splash from test tubes, so it is important to use only small amounts of liquids.

Test-Tube Holder

- Use a test-tube holder when heating a substance in a test tube.
- Use a test-tube holder if the substance in a test tube is dangerous to touch.
- Make sure the test-tube holder tightly grips the test tube so that the test tube will not slide out of the holder.
- Make sure that the test-tube holder is above the surface of the substance in the test tube so that you can observe the substance.

Test-Tube Rack

- Use a test-tube rack to organize test tubes before, during, and after an experiment.

- Use a test-tube rack to keep test tubes upright so that they do not fall over and spill their contents.

- Use a test-tube rack that is the correct size for the test tubes that you are using. If the rack is too small, a test tube may become stuck. If the rack is too large, a test tube may lean over, and some of its contents may spill or splash.

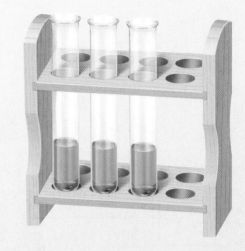

Forceps

- Use forceps when you need to pick up or hold a very small object that should not be touched with your hands.

- Do not use forceps to hold anything over a flame, because forceps are not long enough to keep your hand safely away from the flame. Plastic forceps will melt, and metal forceps will conduct heat and burn your hand.

Hot Plate

- Use a hot plate when a substance needs to be kept warmer than room temperature for a long period of time.

- Use a hot plate instead of a Bunsen burner or a candle when you need to carefully control temperature.

- Do not use a hot plate when a substance needs to be burned in an experiment.

- Always use "hot hands" safety mitts or oven mitts when handling anything that has been heated on a hot plate.

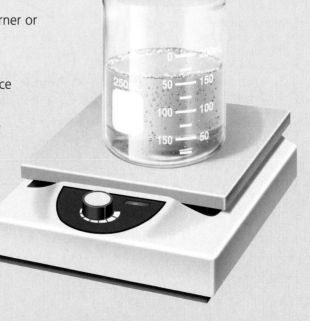

Microscope

Scientists use microscopes to see very small objects that cannot easily be seen with the eye alone. A microscope magnifies the image of an object so that small details may be observed. A microscope that you may use can magnify an object 400 times—the object will appear 400 times larger than its actual size.

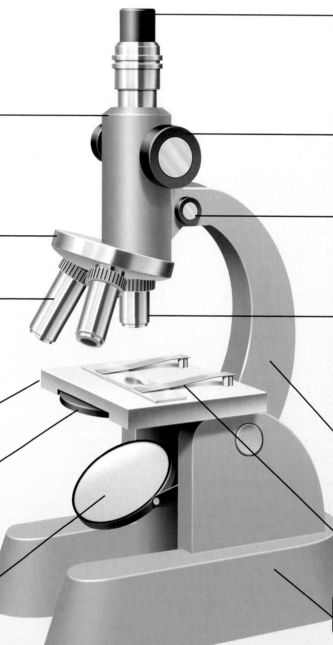

Body The body separates the lens in the eyepiece from the objective lenses below.

Nosepiece The nosepiece holds the objective lenses above the stage and rotates so that all lenses may be used.

High-Power Objective Lens This is the largest lens on the nosepiece. It magnifies an image approximately 40 times.

Stage The stage supports the object being viewed.

Diaphragm The diaphragm is used to adjust the amount of light passing through the slide and into an objective lens.

Mirror or Light Source Some microscopes use light that is reflected through the stage by a mirror. Other microscopes have their own light sources.

Eyepiece Objects are viewed through the eyepiece. The eyepiece contains a lens that commonly magnifies an image 10 times.

Coarse Adjustment This knob is used to focus the image of an object when it is viewed through the low-power lens.

Fine Adjustment This knob is used to focus the image of an object when it is viewed through the high-power lens.

Low-Power Objective Lens This is the smallest lens on the nosepiece. It magnifies an image approximately 10 times.

Arm The arm supports the body above the stage. Always carry a microscope by the arm and base.

Stage Clip The stage clip holds a slide in place on the stage.

Base The base supports the microscope.

VIEWING AN OBJECT

1. Use the coarse adjustment knob to raise the body tube.

2. Adjust the diaphragm so that you can see a bright circle of light through the eyepiece.

3. Place the object or slide on the stage. Be sure that it is centered over the hole in the stage.

4. Turn the nosepiece to click the low-power lens into place.

5. Using the coarse adjustment knob, slowly lower the lens and focus on the specimen being viewed. Be sure not to touch the slide or object with the lens.

6. When switching from the low-power lens to the high-power lens, first raise the body tube with the coarse adjustment knob so that the high-power lens will not hit the slide.

7. Turn the nosepiece to click the high-power lens into place.

8. Use the fine adjustment knob to focus on the specimen being viewed. Again, be sure not to touch the slide or object with the lens.

MAKING A SLIDE, OR WET MOUNT

1 Place the specimen in the center of a clean slide.

2 Place a drop of water on the specimen.

3 Place a cover slip on the slide. Put one edge of the cover slip into the drop of water and slowly lower it over the specimen.

4 Remove any air bubbles from under the cover slip by gently tapping the cover slip.

5 Dry any excess water before placing the slide on the microscope stage for viewing.

Spring Scale (Force Meter)

- Use a spring scale to measure a force pulling on the scale.
- Use a spring scale to measure the force of gravity exerted on an object by Earth.
- To measure a force accurately, a spring scale must be zeroed before it is used. The scale is zeroed when no weight is attached and the indicator is positioned at zero.
- Do not attach a weight that is either too heavy or too light to a spring scale. A weight that is too heavy could break the scale or exert too great a force for the scale to measure. A weight that is too light may not exert enough force to be measured accurately.

Graduated Cylinder

- Use a graduated cylinder to measure the volume of a liquid.
- Be sure that the graduated cylinder is on a flat surface so that your measurement will be accurate.
- When reading the scale on a graduated cylinder, be sure to have your eyes at the level of the surface of the liquid.
- The surface of the liquid will be curved in the graduated cylinder. Read the volume of the liquid at the bottom of the curve, or meniscus (muh-NIHS-kuhs).
- You can use a graduated cylinder to find the volume of a solid object by measuring the increase in a liquid's level after you add the object to the cylinder.

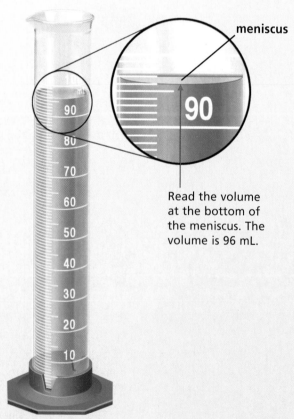

meniscus

Read the volume at the bottom of the meniscus. The volume is 96 mL.

Metric Rulers

- Use metric rulers or meter sticks to measure objects' lengths.

- Do not measure an object from the end of a metric ruler or meter stick, because the end is often imperfect. Instead, measure from the 1-centimeter mark, but remember to subtract a centimeter from the apparent measurement.

- Estimate any lengths that extend between marked units. For example, if a meter stick shows centimeters but not millimeters, you can estimate the length that an object extends between centimeter marks to measure it to the nearest millimeter.

- **Controlling Variables** If you are taking repeated measurements, always measure from the same point each time. For example, if you're measuring how high two different balls bounce when dropped from the same height, measure both bounces at the same point on the balls—either the top or the bottom. Do not measure at the top of one ball and the bottom of the other.

EXAMPLE

How to Measure a Leaf

1. Lay a ruler flat on top of the leaf so that the 1-centimeter mark lines up with one end. Make sure the ruler and the leaf do not move between the time you line them up and the time you take the measurement.

2. Look straight down on the ruler so that you can see exactly how the marks line up with the other end of the leaf.

3. Estimate the length by which the leaf extends beyond a marking. For example, the leaf below extends about halfway between the 4.2-centimeter and 4.3-centimeter marks, so the apparent measurement is about 4.25 centimeters.

4. Remember to subtract 1 centimeter from your apparent measurement, since you started at the 1-centimeter mark on the ruler and not at the end. The leaf is about 3.25 centimeters long (4.25 cm − 1 cm = 3.25 cm).

Triple-Beam Balance

This balance has a pan and three beams with sliding masses, called riders. At one end of the beams is a pointer that indicates whether the mass on the pan is equal to the masses shown on the beams.

1. Make sure the balance is zeroed before measuring the mass of an object. The balance is zeroed if the pointer is at zero when nothing is on the pan and the riders are at their zero points. Use the adjustment knob at the base of the balance to zero it.

2. Place the object to be measured on the pan.

3. Move the riders one notch at a time away from the pan. Begin with the largest rider. If moving the largest rider one notch brings the pointer below zero, begin measuring the mass of the object with the next smaller rider.

4. Change the positions of the riders until they balance the mass on the pan and the pointer is at zero. Then add the readings from the three beams to determine the mass of the object.

300 g	position of largest rider
90 g	position of middle rider
+ 3 g	position of smallest rider
393 g	mass of beaker

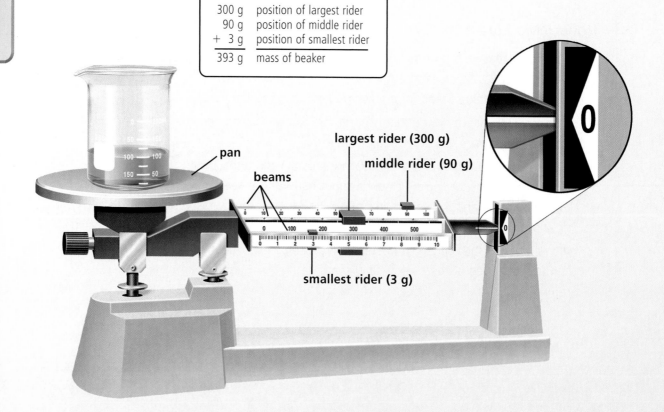

pan

beams

largest rider (300 g)

middle rider (90 g)

smallest rider (3 g)

Double-Pan Balance

This type of balance has two pans. Between the pans is a pointer that indicates whether the masses on the pans are equal.

1. Make sure the balance is zeroed before measuring the mass of an object. The balance is zeroed if the pointer is at zero when there is nothing on either of the pans. Many double-pan balances have sliding knobs that can be used to zero them.

2. Place the object to be measured on one of the pans.

3. Begin adding standard masses to the other pan. Begin with the largest standard mass. If this adds too much mass to the balance, begin measuring the mass of the object with the next smaller standard mass.

4. Add standard masses until the masses on both pans are balanced and the pointer is at zero. Then add the standard masses together to determine the mass of the object being measured.

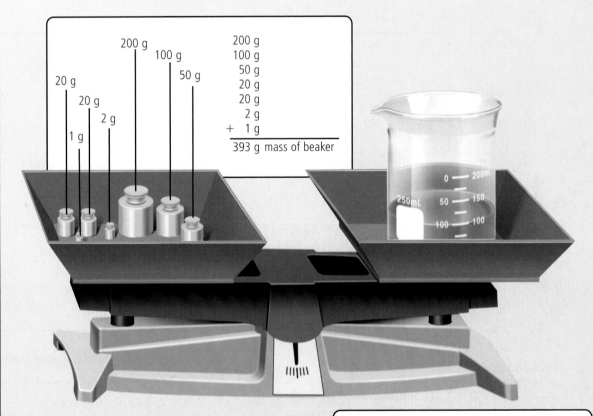

200 g
100 g
50 g
20 g
20 g
2 g
+ 1 g
393 g mass of beaker

Never place chemicals or liquids directly on a pan. Instead, use the following procedure:

1. Determine the mass of an empty container, such as a beaker.

2. Pour the substance into the container, and measure the total mass of the substance and the container.

3. Subtract the mass of the empty container from the total mass to find the mass of the substance.

The Metric System and SI Units

Scientists use International System (SI) units for measurements of distance, volume, mass, and temperature. The International System is based on multiples of ten and the metric system of measurement.

Basic SI Units		
Property	**Name**	**Symbol**
length	meter	m
volume	liter	L
mass	kilogram	kg
temperature	kelvin	K

SI Prefixes		
Prefix	**Symbol**	**Multiple of 10**
kilo-	k	1000
hecto-	h	100
deca-	da	10
deci-	d	$0.1 \left(\frac{1}{10}\right)$
centi-	c	$0.01 \left(\frac{1}{100}\right)$
milli-	m	$0.001 \left(\frac{1}{1000}\right)$

Changing Metric Units

You can change from one unit to another in the metric system by multiplying or dividing by a power of 10.

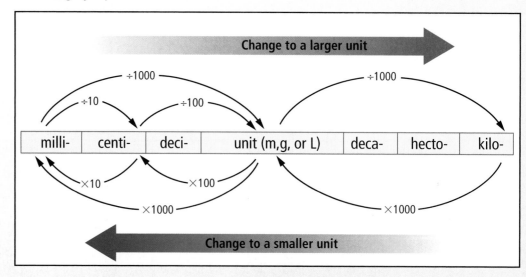

Example

Change 0.64 liters to milliliters.

(1) Decide whether to multiply or divide.

(2) Select the power of 10.

ANSWER 0.64 L = 640 mL

Change to a smaller unit by multiplying.

mL ◄——— × 1000 ——— L

0.64 × 1000 = 640.

Example

Change 23.6 grams to kilograms.

(1) Decide whether to multiply or divide.

(2) Select the power of 10.

ANSWER 23.6 g = 0.0236 kg

Change to a larger unit by dividing.

g ——— ÷ 1000 ——► kg

23.6 ÷ 1000 = 0.0236

LAB HANDBOOK

Temperature Conversions

Even though the kelvin is the SI base unit of temperature, the degree Celsius will be the unit you use most often in your science studies. The formulas below show the relationships between temperatures in degrees Fahrenheit (°F), degrees Celsius (°C), and kelvins (K).

$$°C = \frac{5}{9}(°F - 32)$$

$$°F = \frac{9}{5}°C + 32$$

$$K = °C + 273$$

See page R42 for help with using formulas.

Examples of Temperature Conversions

Condition	Degrees Celsius	Degrees Fahrenheit
Freezing point of water	0	32
Cool day	10	50
Mild day	20	68
Warm day	30	86
Normal body temperature	37	98.6
Very hot day	40	104
Boiling point of water	100	212

Converting Between SI and U.S. Customary Units

Use the chart below when you need to convert between SI units and U.S. customary units.

SI Unit	From SI to U.S. Customary			From U.S. Customary to SI		
Length	When you know	multiply by	to find	When you know	multiply by	to find
kilometer (km) = 1000 m	kilometers	0.62	miles	miles	1.61	kilometers
meter (m) = 100 cm	meters	3.28	feet	feet	0.3048	meters
centimeter (cm) = 10 mm	centimeters	0.39	inches	inches	2.54	centimeters
millimeter (mm) = 0.1 cm	millimeters	0.04	inches	inches	25.4	millimeters
Area	When you know	multiply by	to find	When you know	multiply by	to find
square kilometer (km²)	square kilometers	0.39	square miles	square miles	2.59	square kilometers
square meter (m²)	square meters	1.2	square yards	square yards	0.84	square meters
square centimeter (cm²)	square centimeters	0.155	square inches	square inches	6.45	square centimeters
Volume	When you know	multiply by	to find	When you know	multiply by	to find
liter (L) = 1000 mL	liters	1.06	quarts	quarts	0.95	liters
	liters	0.26	gallons	gallons	3.79	liters
	liters	4.23	cups	cups	0.24	liters
	liters	2.12	pints	pints	0.47	liters
milliliter (mL) = 0.001 L	milliliters	0.20	teaspoons	teaspoons	4.93	milliliters
	milliliters	0.07	tablespoons	tablespoons	14.79	milliliters
	milliliters	0.03	fluid ounces	fluid ounces	29.57	milliliters
Mass	When you know	multiply by	to find	When you know	multiply by	to find
kilogram (kg) = 1000 g	kilograms	2.2	pounds	pounds	0.45	kilograms
gram (g) = 1000 mg	grams	0.035	ounces	ounces	28.35	grams

Precision and Accuracy

When you do an experiment, it is important that your methods, observations, and data be both precise and accurate.

low precision

precision, but not accuracy

precision and accuracy

Precision

In science, **precision** is the exactness and consistency of measurements. For example, measurements made with a ruler that has both centimeter and millimeter markings would be more precise than measurements made with a ruler that has only centimeter markings. Another indicator of precision is the care taken to make sure that methods and observations are as exact and consistent as possible. Every time a particular experiment is done, the same procedure should be used. Precision is necessary because experiments are repeated several times and if the procedure changes, the results will change.

EXAMPLE

Suppose you are measuring temperatures over a two-week period. Your precision will be greater if you measure each temperature at the same place, at the same time of day, and with the same thermometer than if you change any of these factors from one day to the next.

Accuracy

In science, it is possible to be precise but not accurate. **Accuracy** depends on the difference between a measurement and an actual value. The smaller the difference, the more accurate the measurement.

EXAMPLE

Suppose you look at a stream and estimate that it is about 1 meter wide at a particular place. You decide to check your estimate by measuring the stream with a meter stick, and you determine that the stream is 1.32 meters wide. However, because it is hard to measure the width of a stream with a meter stick, it turns out that you didn't do a very good job. The stream is actually 1.14 meters wide. Therefore, even though your estimate was less precise than your measurement, your estimate was actually more accurate.

Making Data Tables and Graphs

Data tables and graphs are useful tools for both recording and communicating scientific data.

Making Data Tables

You can use a **data table** to organize and record the measurements that you make. Some examples of information that might be recorded in data tables are frequencies, times, and amounts.

EXAMPLE

Suppose you are investigating photosynthesis in two elodea plants. One sits in direct sunlight, and the other sits in a dimly lit room. You measure the rate of photosynthesis by counting the number of bubbles in the jar every ten minutes.

1. Title and number your data table.

2. Decide how you will organize the table into columns and rows.

3. Any units, such as seconds or degrees, should be included in column headings, not in the individual cells.

Table 1. Number of Bubbles from Elodea

Time (min)	Sunlight	Dim Light
0	0	0
10	15	5
20	25	8
30	32	7
40	41	10
50	47	9
60	42	9

> Always number and title data tables.

The data in the table above could also be organized in a different way.

Table 1. Number of Bubbles from Elodea

Light Condition	Time (min)						
	0	10	20	30	40	50	60
Sunlight	0	15	25	32	41	47	42
Dim light	0	5	8	7	10	9	9

> Put units in column heading.

Making Line Graphs

You can use a **line graph** to show a relationship between variables. Line graphs are particularly useful for showing changes in variables over time.

EXAMPLE

Suppose you are interested in graphing temperature data that you collected over the course of a day.

Table 1. Outside Temperature During the Day on March 7

	Time of Day						
	7:00 A.M.	9:00 A.M.	11:00 A.M.	1:00 P.M.	3:00 P.M.	5:00 P.M.	7:00 P.M.
Temp (°C)	8	9	11	14	12	10	6

1. Use the vertical axis of your line graph for the variable that you are measuring—temperature.

2. Choose scales for both the horizontal axis and the vertical axis of the graph. You should have two points more than you need on the vertical axis, and the horizontal axis should be long enough for all of the data points to fit.

3. Draw and label each axis.

4. Graph each value. First find the appropriate point on the scale of the horizontal axis. Imagine a line that rises vertically from that place on the scale. Then find the corresponding value on the vertical axis, and imagine a line that moves horizontally from that value. The point where these two imaginary lines intersect is where the value should be plotted.

5. Connect the points with straight lines.

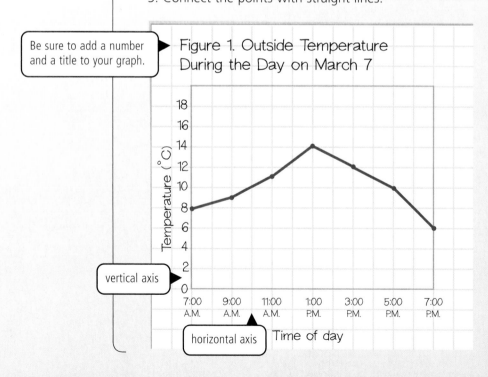

Be sure to add a number and a title to your graph.

Figure 1. Outside Temperature During the Day on March 7

vertical axis

horizontal axis   Time of day

Making Circle Graphs

You can use a **circle graph,** sometimes called a pie chart, to represent data as parts of a circle. Circle graphs are used only when the data can be expressed as percentages of a whole. The entire circle shown in a circle graph is equal to 100 percent of the data.

EXAMPLE

Suppose you identified the species of each mature tree growing in a small wooded area. You organized your data in a table, but you also want to show the data in a circle graph.

1. To begin, find the total number of mature trees.

    $56 + 34 + 22 + 10 + 28 = 150$

2. To find the degree measure for each sector of the circle, write a fraction comparing the number of each tree species with the total number of trees. Then multiply the fraction by 360°.

    Oak: $\frac{56}{150} \times 360° = 134.4°$

3. Draw a circle. Use a protractor to draw the angle for each sector of the graph.

4. Color and label each sector of the graph.

5. Give the graph a number and title.

Table 1. Tree Species in Wooded Area

Species	Number of Specimens
Oak	56
Maple	34
Birch	22
Willow	10
Pine	28

Figure 1. Tree Species in Wooded Area

Willow 10
Birch 22
Oak 56
Pine 28
Maple 34

Instead of labeling each sector, you could make a color key.

Oak 56
Maple 34
Pine 28
Birch 22
Willow 10

Bar Graph

A **bar graph** is a type of graph in which the lengths of the bars are used to represent and compare data. A numerical scale is used to determine the lengths of the bars.

EXAMPLE

To determine the effect of water on seed sprouting, three cups were filled with sand, and ten seeds were planted in each. Different amounts of water were added to each cup over a three-day period.

Table 1. Effect of Water on Seed Sprouting

Daily Amount of Water (mL)	Number of Seeds That Sprouted After 3 Days in Sand
0	1
10	4
20	8

1. Choose a numerical scale. The greatest value is 8, so the end of the scale should have a value greater than 8, such as 10. Use equal increments along the scale, such as increments of 2.

2. Draw and label the axes. Mark intervals on the vertical axis according to the scale you chose.

3. Draw a bar for each data value. Use the scale to decide how long to make each bar.

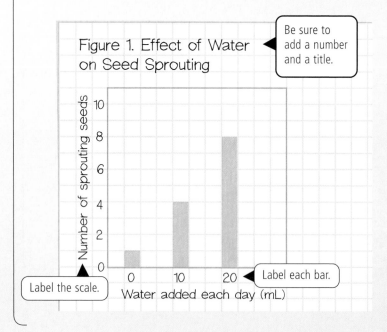

Be sure to add a number and a title.

Figure 1. Effect of Water on Seed Sprouting

Number of sprouting seeds

Water added each day (mL)

Label the scale.

Label each bar.

Double Bar Graph

A **double bar graph** is a bar graph that shows two sets of data. The two bars for each measurement are drawn next to each other.

EXAMPLE

The seed-sprouting experiment was done using both sand and potting soil. The data for sand and potting soil can be plotted on one graph.

1. Draw one set of bars, using the data for sand, as shown below.
2. Draw bars for the potting-soil data next to the bars for the sand data. Shade them a different color. Add a key.

Table 2. Effect of Water and Soil on Seed Sprouting

Daily Amount of Water (mL)	Number of Seeds That Sprouted After 3 Days in Sand	Number of Seeds That Sprouted After 3 Days in Potting Soil
0	1	2
10	4	5
20	8	9

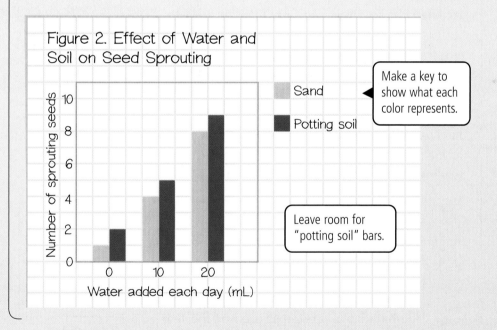

Figure 2. Effect of Water and Soil on Seed Sprouting

Make a key to show what each color represents.

Leave room for "potting soil" bars.

Designing an Experiment

Use this section when designing or conducting an experiment.

Determining a Purpose

You can find a purpose for an experiment by doing research, by examining the results of a previous experiment, or by observing the world around you. An **experiment** is an organized procedure to study something under controlled conditions.

> Don't forget to learn as much as possible about your topic before you begin.

1. Write the purpose of your experiment as a question or problem that you want to investigate.

2. Write down research questions and begin searching for information that will help you design an experiment. Consult the library, the Internet, and other people as you conduct your research.

EXAMPLE

Middle school students observed an odor near the lake by their school. They also noticed that the water on the side of the lake near the school was greener than the water on the other side of the lake. The students did some research to learn more about their observations. They discovered that the odor and green color in the lake

came from algae. They also discovered that a new fertilizer was being used on a field nearby. The students inferred that the use of the fertilizer might be related to the presence of the algae and designed a controlled experiment to find out whether they were right.

Problem

How does fertilizer affect the presence of algae in a lake?

Research Questions

- Have other experiments been done on this problem? If so, what did those experiments show?

- What kind of fertilizer is used on the field? How much?

- How do algae grow?

- How do people measure algae?

- Can fertilizer and algae be used safely in a lab? How?

> **Research**
> As you research, you may find a topic that is more interesting to you than your original topic, or learn that a procedure you wanted to use is not practical or safe. It is OK to change your purpose as you research.

Writing a Hypothesis

A **hypothesis** is a tentative explanation for an observation or scientific problem that can be tested by further investigation. You can write your hypothesis in the form of an "If . . . , then . . . , because . . ." statement.

Hypothesis

If the amount of fertilizer in lake water is increased, then the amount of algae will also increase, because fertilizers provide nutrients that algae need to grow.

◄ **Hypotheses**
For help with hypotheses, refer to page R3.

Determining Materials

Make a list of all the materials you will need to do your experiment. Be specific, especially if someone else is helping you obtain the materials. Try to think of everything you will need.

Materials

- 1 large jar or container
- 4 identical smaller containers
- rubber gloves that also cover the arms
- sample of fertilizer-and-water solution
- eyedropper
- clear plastic wrap
- scissors
- masking tape
- marker
- ruler

Determining Variables and Constants

EXPERIMENTAL GROUP AND CONTROL GROUP

An experiment to determine how two factors are related always has two groups—a control group and an experimental group.

1. Design an experimental group. Include as many trials as possible in the experimental group in order to obtain reliable results.

2. Design a control group that is the same as the experimental group in every way possible, except for the factor you wish to test.

> **Experimental Group:** two containers of lake water with one drop of fertilizer solution added to each
>
> **Control Group:** two containers of lake water with no fertilizer solution added

> Go back to your materials list and make sure you have enough items listed to cover both your experimental group and your control group.

VARIABLES AND CONSTANTS

Identify the variables and constants in your experiment. In a controlled experiment, a **variable** is any factor that can change. **Constants** are all of the factors that are the same in both the experimental group and the control group.

1. Read your hypothesis. The **independent variable** is the factor that you wish to test and that is manipulated or changed so that it can be tested. The independent variable is expressed in your hypothesis after the word *if*. Identify the independent variable in your laboratory report.

2. The **dependent variable** is the factor that you measure to gather results. It is expressed in your hypothesis after the word *then*. Identify the dependent variable in your laboratory report.

> **Hypothesis**
> If the amount of fertilizer in lake water is increased, then the amount of algae will also increase, because fertilizers provide nutrients that algae need to grow.

Table 1. Variables and Constants in Algae Experiment

Independent Variable	Dependent Variable	Constants
Amount of fertilizer in lake water	Amount of algae that grow	• Where the lake water is obtained • Type of container used • Light and temperature conditions where water will be stored

> Set up your experiment so that you will test only one variable.

MEASURING THE DEPENDENT VARIABLE

Before starting your experiment, you need to define how you will measure the dependent variable. An **operational definition** is a description of the one particular way in which you will measure the dependent variable.

Your operational definition is important for several reasons. First, in any experiment there are several ways in which a dependent variable can be measured. Second, the procedure of the experiment depends on how you decide to measure the dependent variable. Third, your operational definition makes it possible for other people to evaluate and build on your experiment.

EXAMPLE 1

An operational definition of a dependent variable can be qualitative. That is, your measurement of the dependent variable can simply be an observation of whether a change occurs as a result of a change in the independent variable. This type of operational definition can be thought of as a "yes or no" measurement.

Table 2. Qualitative Operational Definition of Algae Growth

Independent Variable	Dependent Variable	Operational Definition
Amount of fertilizer in lake water	Amount of algae that grow	Algae grow in lake water

A qualitative measurement of a dependent variable is often easy to make and record. However, this type of information does not provide a great deal of detail in your experimental results.

EXAMPLE 2

An operational definition of a dependent variable can be quantitative. That is, your measurement of the dependent variable can be a number that shows how much change occurs as a result of a change in the independent variable.

Table 3. Quantitative Operational Definition of Algae Growth

Independent Variable	Dependent Variable	Operational Definition
Amount of fertilizer in lake water	Amount of algae that grow	Diameter of largest algal growth (in mm)

A quantitative measurement of a dependent variable can be more difficult to make and analyze than a qualitative measurement. However, this type of data provides much more information about your experiment and is often more useful.

Writing a Procedure

Write each step of your procedure. Start each step with a verb, or action word, and keep the steps short. Your procedure should be clear enough for someone else to use as instructions for repeating your experiment.

> If necessary, go back to your materials list and add any materials that you left out.

Procedure

1. Put on your gloves. Use the large container to obtain a sample of lake water.

2. Divide the sample of lake water equally among the four smaller containers.

> **Controlling Variables**
> The same amount of fertilizer solution must be added to two of the four containers.

3. Use the eyedropper to add one drop of fertilizer solution to two of the containers.

4. Use the masking tape and the marker to label the containers with your initials, the date, and the identifiers "Jar 1 with Fertilizer," "Jar 2 with Fertilizer," "Jar 1 without Fertilizer," and "Jar 2 without Fertilizer."

5. Cover the containers with clear plastic wrap. Use the scissors to punch ten holes in each of the covers.

> **Controlling Variables**
> All four containers must receive the same amount of light.

6. Place all four containers on a window ledge. Make sure that they all receive the same amount of light.

7. Observe the containers every day for one week.

8. Use the ruler to measure the diameter of the largest clump of algae in each container, and record your measurements daily.

Recording Observations

Once you have obtained all of your materials and your procedure has been approved, you can begin making experimental observations. Gather both quantitative and qualitative data. If something goes wrong during your procedure, make sure you record that too.

> **Observations**
> For help with making qualitative and quantitative observations, refer to page R2.

> For more examples of data tables, see page R23.

Table 4. Fertilizer and Algae Growth

Date and Time	Experimental Group		Control Group		Observations
	Jar 1 with Fertilizer (diameter of algae in mm)	Jar 2 with Fertilizer (diameter of algae in mm)	Jar 1 without Fertilizer (diameter of algae in mm)	Jar 2 without Fertilizer (diameter of algae in mm)	
5/3 4:00 P.M.	0	0	0	0	condensation in all containers
5/4 4:00 P.M.	0	3	0	0	tiny green blobs in jar 2 with fertilizer
5/5 4:15 P.M.	4	5	0	3	green blobs in jars 1 and 2 with fertilizer and jar 2 without fertilizer
5/6 4:00 P.M.	5	6	0	4	water light green in jar 2 with fertilizer
5/7 4:00 P.M.	8	10	0	6	water light green in jars 1 and 2 with fertilizer and in jar 2 without fertilizer
5/8 3:30 P.M.	10	18	0	6	cover off jar 2 with fertilizer
5/9 3:30 P.M.	14	23	0	8	drew sketches of each container

> Notice that on the sixth day, the observer found that the cover was off one of the containers. It is important to record observations of unintended factors because they might affect the results of the experiment.

> Use technology, such as a microscope, to help you make observations when possible.

Drawings of Samples Viewed Under Microscope on 5/9 at 100x

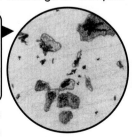
Jar 1 with Fertilizer

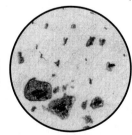
Jar 2 with Fertilizer

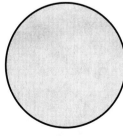
Jar 1 without Fertilizer

Jar 2 without Fertilizer

Summarizing Results

To summarize your data, look at all of your observations together. Look for meaningful ways to present your observations. For example, you might average your data or make a graph to look for patterns. When possible, use spreadsheet software to help you analyze and present your data. The two graphs below show the same data.

EXAMPLE 1

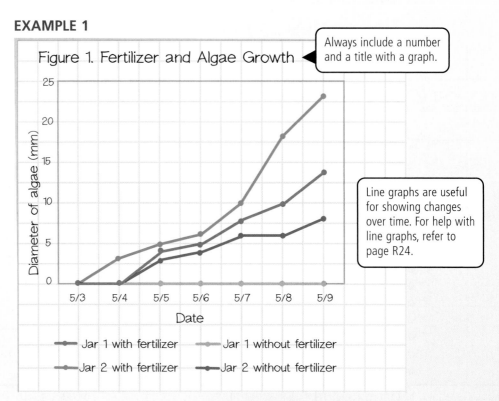

Figure 1. Fertilizer and Algae Growth

> Always include a number and a title with a graph.

> Line graphs are useful for showing changes over time. For help with line graphs, refer to page R24.

EXAMPLE 2

> Bar graphs are useful for comparing different data sets. This bar graph has four bars for each day. Another way to present the data would be to calculate averages for the tests and the controls, and to show one test bar and one control bar for each day.

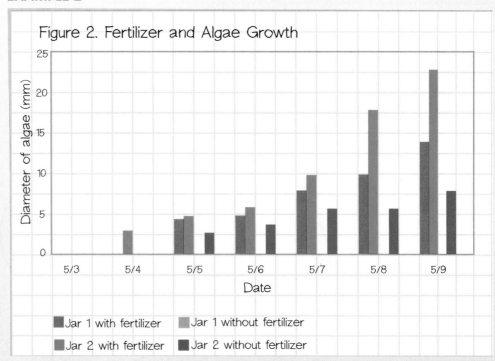

Figure 2. Fertilizer and Algae Growth

Drawing Conclusions

RESULTS AND INFERENCES

To draw conclusions from your experiment, first write your results. Then compare your results with your hypothesis. Do your results support your hypothesis? Be careful not to make inferences about factors that you did not test.

> For help with making inferences, see page R4.

Results and Inferences

The results of my experiment show that more algae grew in lake water to which fertilizer had been added than in lake water to which no fertilizer had been added. My hypothesis was supported. I infer that it is possible that the growth of algae in the lake was caused by the fertilizer used on the field.

> Notice that you cannot conclude from this experiment that the presence of algae in the lake was due only to the fertilizer.

QUESTIONS FOR FURTHER RESEARCH

Write a list of questions for further research and investigation. Your ideas may lead you to new experiments and discoveries.

Questions for Further Research

- What is the connection between the amount of fertilizer and algae growth?
- How do different brands of fertilizer affect algae growth?
- How would algae growth in the lake be affected if no fertilizer were used on the field?
- How do algae affect the lake and the other life in and around it?
- How does fertilizer affect the lake and the life in and around it?
- If fertilizer is getting into the lake, how is it getting there?

Math Handbook

Describing a Set of Data

Means, medians, modes, and ranges are important math tools for describing data sets such as the following widths of fossilized clamshells.

13 mm   25 mm   14 mm   21 mm   16 mm   23 mm   14 mm

Mean

The **mean** of a data set is the sum of the values divided by the number of values.

Example

To find the mean of the clamshell data, add the values and then divide the sum by the number of values.

$$\frac{13 \text{ mm} + 25 \text{ mm} + 14 \text{ mm} + 21 \text{ mm} + 16 \text{ mm} + 23 \text{ mm} + 14 \text{ mm}}{7} = \frac{126 \text{ mm}}{7} = 18 \text{ mm}$$

ANSWER The mean is 18 mm.

Median

The **median** of a data set is the middle value when the values are written in numerical order. If a data set has an even number of values, the median is the mean of the two middle values.

Example

To find the median of the clamshell data, arrange the values in order from least to greatest. The median is the middle value.

13 mm   14 mm   14 mm   16 mm   21 mm   23 mm   25 mm

ANSWER The median is 16 mm.

Mode

The **mode** of a data set is the value that occurs most often.

> ### Example
>
> To find the mode of the clamshell data, arrange the values in order from least to greatest and determine the value that occurs most often.
>
> 13 mm   14 mm   14 mm   16 mm   21 mm   23 mm   25 mm
>
> **ANSWER** The mode is 14 mm.

A data set can have more than one mode or no mode. For example, the following data set has modes of 2 mm and 4 mm:

2 mm   2 mm   3 mm   4 mm   4 mm

The data set below has no mode, because no value occurs more often than any other.

2 mm   3 mm   4 mm   5 mm

Range

The **range** of a data set is the difference between the greatest value and the least value.

> ### Example
>
> To find the range of the clamshell data, arrange the values in order from least to greatest.
>
> 13 mm   14 mm   14 mm   16 mm   21 mm   23 mm   25 mm
>
> Subtract the least value from the greatest value.
>
> 13 mm is the least value.
> 25 mm is the greatest value.
>
> 25 mm − 13 mm = 12 mm
>
> **ANSWER** The range is 12 mm.

Using Ratios, Rates, and Proportions

You can use ratios and rates to compare values in data sets. You can use proportions to find unknown values.

Ratios

A **ratio** uses division to compare two values. The ratio of a value a to a nonzero value b can be written as $\frac{a}{b}$.

> ### Example
>
> The height of one plant is 8 centimeters. The height of another plant is 6 centimeters. To find the ratio of the height of the first plant to the height of the second plant, write a fraction and simplify it.
>
> $$\frac{8 \text{ cm}}{6 \text{ cm}} = \frac{4 \times \overset{1}{\cancel{2}}}{3 \times \underset{1}{\cancel{2}}} = \frac{4}{3}$$
>
> **ANSWER** The ratio of the plant heights is $\frac{4}{3}$.

You can also write the ratio $\frac{a}{b}$ as "a to b" or as $a:b$. For example, you can write the ratio of the plant heights as "4 to 3" or as $4:3$.

Rates

A **rate** is a ratio of two values expressed in different units. A unit rate is a rate with a denominator of 1 unit.

> ### Example
>
> A plant grew 6 centimeters in 2 days. The plant's rate of growth was $\frac{6 \text{ cm}}{2 \text{ days}}$. To describe the plant's growth in centimeters per day, write a unit rate.
>
> *Divide numerator and denominator by 2:* $\quad \frac{6 \text{ cm}}{2 \text{ days}} = \frac{6 \text{ cm} \div 2}{2 \text{ days} \div 2}$ ◄ You divide 2 days by 2 to get 1 day, so divide 6 cm by 2 also.
>
> *Simplify:* $\quad = \frac{3 \text{ cm}}{1 \text{ day}}$
>
> **ANSWER** The plant's rate of growth is 3 centimeters per day.

Proportions

A **proportion** is an equation stating that two ratios are equivalent. To solve for an unknown value in a proportion, you can use cross products.

Example

If a plant grew 6 centimeters in 2 days, how many centimeters would it grow in 3 days (if its rate of growth is constant)?

Write a proportion: $\dfrac{6 \text{ cm}}{2 \text{ days}} = \dfrac{x}{3 \text{ days}}$

Set cross products: $6 \text{ cm} \cdot 3 = 2x$

Multiply 6 and 3: $18 \text{ cm} = 2x$

Divide each side by 2: $\dfrac{18 \text{ cm}}{2} = \dfrac{2x}{2}$

Simplify: $9 \text{ cm} = x$

ANSWER The plant would grow 9 centimeters in 3 days.

Using Decimals, Fractions, and Percents

Decimals, fractions, and percentages are all ways of recording and representing data.

Decimals

A **decimal** is a number that is written in the base-ten place value system, in which a decimal point separates the ones and tenths digits. The values of each place is ten times that of the place to its right.

Example

A caterpillar traveled from point *A* to point *C* along the path shown.

A —— 36.9 cm —— B —— 52.4 cm —— C

ADDING DECIMALS To find the total distance traveled by the caterpillar, add the distance from *A* to *B* and the distance from *B* to *C*. Begin by lining up the decimal points. Then add the figures as you would whole numbers and bring down the decimal point.

```
  36.9 cm
+ 52.4 cm
─────────
  89.3 cm
```

ANSWER The caterpillar traveled a total distance of 89.3 centimeters.

SUBTRACTING DECIMALS To find how much farther the caterpillar traveled on the second leg of the journey, subtract the distance from *A* to *B* from the distance from *B* to *C*.

$$
\begin{array}{r}
52.4 \text{ cm} \\
- \ 36.9 \text{ cm} \\
\hline
15.5 \text{ cm}
\end{array}
$$

ANSWER The caterpillar traveled 15.5 centimeters farther on the second leg of the journey.

Example

A caterpillar is traveling from point *D* to point *F* along the path shown. The caterpillar travels at a speed of 9.6 centimeters per minute.

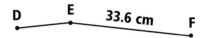

D   E   33.6 cm   F

MULTIPLYING DECIMALS You can multiply decimals as you would whole numbers. The number of decimal places in the product is equal to the sum of the number of decimal places in the factors.

For instance, suppose it takes the caterpillar 1.5 minutes to go from *D* to *E*. To find the distance from *D* to *E*, multiply the caterpillar's speed by the time it took.

$$
\begin{array}{rl}
9.6 & \quad 1 \quad \text{decimal place} \\
\times \ 1.5 & \quad + 1 \quad \text{decimal place} \\
\hline
480 \\
96 \\
\hline
14.40 & \quad 2 \quad \text{decimal places}
\end{array}
$$

Align as shown.

ANSWER The distance from *D* to *E* is 14.4 centimeters.

DIVIDING DECIMALS When you divide by a decimal, move the decimal points the same number of places in the divisor and the dividend to make the divisor a whole number.

For instance, to find the time it will take the caterpillar to travel from *E* to *F*, divide the distance from *E* to *F* by the caterpillar's speed.

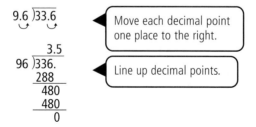

Move each decimal point one place to the right.

Line up decimal points.

ANSWER The caterpillar will travel from *E* to *F* in 3.5 minutes.

MATH HANDBOOK

Fractions

A **fraction** is a number in the form $\frac{a}{b}$, where b is not equal to 0. A fraction is in **simplest form** if its numerator and denominator have a greatest common factor (GCF) of 1. To simplify a fraction, divide its numerator and denominator by their GCF.

Example

A caterpillar is 40 millimeters long. The head of the caterpillar is 6 millimeters long. To compare the length of the caterpillar's head with the caterpillar's total length, you can write and simplify a fraction that expresses the ratio of the two lengths.

$$\text{Write the ratio of the two lengths:} \quad \frac{\text{Length of head}}{\text{Total length}} = \frac{6 \text{ mm}}{40 \text{ mm}}$$

$$\textit{Write numerator and denominator as products of numbers and the GCF:} \quad = \frac{3 \times 2}{20 \times 2}$$

$$\textit{Divide numerator and denominator by the GCF:} \quad = \frac{3 \times \overset{1}{\cancel{2}}}{20 \times \underset{1}{\cancel{2}}}$$

$$\textit{Simplify:} \quad = \frac{3}{20}$$

ANSWER In simplest form, the ratio of the lengths is $\frac{3}{20}$.

Percents

A **percent** is a ratio that compares a number to 100. The word *percent* means "per hundred" or "out of 100." The symbol for *percent* is %.

For instance, suppose 43 out of 100 caterpillars are female. You can represent this ratio as a percent, a decimal, or a fraction.

Percent	Decimal	Fraction
43%	0.43	$\frac{43}{100}$

Example

In the preceding example, the ratio of the length of the caterpillar's head to the caterpillar's total length is $\frac{3}{20}$. To write this ratio as a percent, write an equivalent fraction that has a denominator of 100.

$$\textit{Multiply numerator and denominator by 5:} \quad \frac{3}{20} = \frac{3 \times 5}{20 \times 5}$$

$$= \frac{15}{100}$$

$$\textit{Write as a percent:} \quad = 15\%$$

ANSWER The caterpillar's head represents 15 percent of its total length.

Using Formulas

A **formula** is an equation that shows the general relationship between two or more quantities.

The term *variable* is also used in science to refer to a factor that can change during an experiment.

In science, a formula often has a word form and a symbolic form. The formula below expresses Ohm's law.

Word Form

$$\text{Current} = \frac{\text{voltage}}{\text{resistance}}$$

Symbolic Form

$$I = \frac{V}{R}$$

In this formula, I, V, and R are variables. A mathematical **variable** is a symbol or letter that is used to represent one or more numbers.

Example

Suppose that you measure a voltage of 1.5 volts and a resistance of 15 ohms. You can use the formula for Ohm's law to find the current in amperes.

Write the formula for Ohm's law: $\quad I = \dfrac{V}{R}$

Substitute 1.5 volts for V and 15 ohms for R: $\quad I = \dfrac{1.5 \text{ volts}}{15 \text{ ohms}}$

Simplify: $\quad I = 0.1 \text{ amp}$

ANSWER The current is 0.1 ampere.

If you know the values of all variables but one in a formula, you can solve for the value of the unknown variable. For instance, Ohm's law can be used to find a voltage if you know the current and the resistance.

Example

Suppose that you know that a current is 0.2 amperes and the resistance is 18 ohms. Use the formula for Ohm's law to find the voltage in volts.

Write the formula for Ohm's law: $\qquad I = \dfrac{V}{R}$

Substitute 0.2 amp for I and 18 ohms for R: $\qquad 0.2 \text{ amp} = \dfrac{V}{18 \text{ ohms}}$

Multiply both sides by 18 ohms: $\quad 0.2 \text{ amp} \cdot 18 \text{ ohms} = V$

Simplify: $\qquad 3.6 \text{ volts} = V$

ANSWER The voltage is 3.6 volts.

Finding Areas

The area of a figure is the amount of surface the figure covers.

Area is measured in square units, such as square meters (m^2) or square centimeters (cm^2). Formulas for the areas of three common geometric figures are shown below.

Area = (side length)^2
$A = s^2$

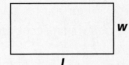

Area = length × width
$A = lw$

Area = $\frac{1}{2}$ × base × height
$A = \frac{1}{2} bh$

Example

Each face of a halite crystal is a square like the one shown. You can find the area of the square by using the steps below.

Write the formula for the area of a square: $A = s^2$

Substitute 3 mm for s: $= (3 \text{ mm})^2$

Simplify: $= 9 \text{ mm}^2$

3 mm

3 mm

ANSWER The area of the square is 9 square millimeters.

Finding Volumes

The volume of a solid is the amount of space contained by the solid.

Volume is measured in cubic units, such as cubic meters (m^3) or cubic centimeters (cm^3). The volume of a rectangular prism is given by the formula shown below.

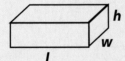

Volume = length × width × height
$V = lwh$

Example

A topaz crystal is a rectangular prism like the one shown. You can find the volume of the prism by using the steps below.

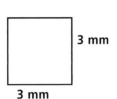

10 mm

12 mm

20 mm

Write the formula for the volume of a rectangular prism: $V = lwh$

Substitute dimensions: $= 20 \text{ mm} \times 12 \text{ mm} \times 10 \text{ mm}$

Simplify: $= 2400 \text{ mm}^3$

ANSWER The volume of the rectangular prism is 2400 cubic millimeters.

Using Significant Figures

The **significant figures** in a decimal are the digits that are warranted by the accuracy of a measuring device.

When you perform a calculation with measurements, the number of significant figures to include in the result depends in part on the number of significant figures in the measurements. When you multiply or divide measurements, your answer should have only as many significant figures as the measurement with the fewest significant figures.

Example

Using a balance and a graduated cylinder filled with water, you determined that a marble has a mass of 8.0 grams and a volume of 3.5 cubic centimeters. To calculate the density of the marble, divide the mass by the volume.

Write the formula for density: $\text{Density} = \dfrac{\text{mass}}{\text{Volume}}$

Substitute measurements: $= \dfrac{8.0 \text{ g}}{3.5 \text{ cm}^3}$

Use a calculator to divide: $\approx 2.285714286 \text{ g/cm}^3$

ANSWER Because the mass and the volume have two significant figures each, give the density to two significant figures. The marble has a density of 2.3 grams per cubic centimeter.

Using Scientific Notation

Scientific notation is a shorthand way to write very large or very small numbers. For example, 73,500,000,000,000,000,000,000 kg is the mass of the Moon. In scientific notation, it is 7.35×10^{22} kg.

Example

You can convert from standard form to scientific notation.

Standard Form	Scientific Notation
720,000	7.2×10^5
5 decimal places left	Exponent is 5.
0.000291	2.91×10^{-4}
4 decimal places right	Exponent is −4.

You can convert from scientific notation to standard form.

Scientific Notation	Standard Form
4.63×10^7	46,300,000
Exponent is 7.	7 decimal places right
1.08×10^{-6}	0.00000108
Exponent is −6.	6 decimal places left

Note-Taking Handbook

Note-Taking Strategies

Taking notes as you read helps you understand the information. The notes you take can also be used as a study guide for later review. This handbook presents several ways to organize your notes.

Content Frame

1. Make a chart in which each column represents a category.

2. Give each column a heading.

3. Write details under the headings.

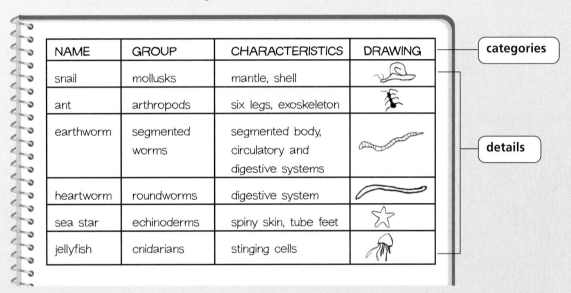

categories

details

NAME	GROUP	CHARACTERISTICS	DRAWING
snail	mollusks	mantle, shell	
ant	arthropods	six legs, exoskeleton	
earthworm	segmented worms	segmented body, circulatory and digestive systems	
heartworm	roundworms	digestive system	
sea star	echinoderms	spiny skin, tube feet	
jellyfish	cnidarians	stinging cells	

Combination Notes

1. For each new idea or concept, write an informal outline of the information.

2. Make a sketch to illustrate the concept, and label it.

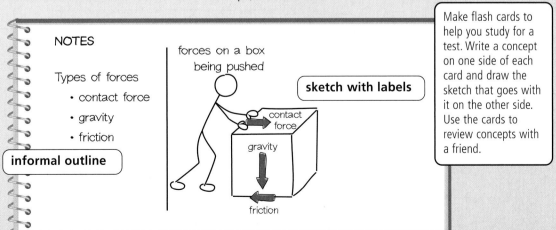

NOTES

Types of forces
- contact force
- gravity
- friction

informal outline

forces on a box being pushed

contact force

gravity

friction

sketch with labels

Make flash cards to help you study for a test. Write a concept on one side of each card and draw the sketch that goes with it on the other side. Use the cards to review concepts with a friend.

Main Idea and Detail Notes

1. In the left-hand column of a two-column chart, list main ideas. The blue headings express main ideas throughout this textbook.

2. In the right-hand column, write details that expand on each main idea.

You can shorten the headings in your chart. Be sure to use the most important words.

When studying for tests, cover up the detail notes column with a sheet of paper. Then use each main idea to form a question—such as "How does latitude affect climate?" Answer the question, and then uncover the detail notes column to check your answer.

MAIN IDEAS	DETAIL NOTES
1. Latitude affects climate. **main idea 1**	1. Places close to the equator are usually warmer than places close to the poles. 1. Latitude has the same effect in both hemispheres.
2. Altitude affects climate. **main idea 2**	2. Temperature decreases with altitude. 2. Altitude can overcome the effect of latitude on temperature.

details about main idea 1

details about main idea 2

Main Idea Web

1. Write a main idea in a box.

2. Add boxes around it with related vocabulary terms and important details.

You can find definitions near highlighted terms.

definition of work
Work is the use of force to move an object.

formula
Work = force · distance

main idea Force is necessary to do work.

The joule is the unit used to measure work.
definition of joule

Work depends on the size of a force.
important detail

Mind Map

1. Write a main idea in the center.

2. Add details that relate to one another and to the main idea.

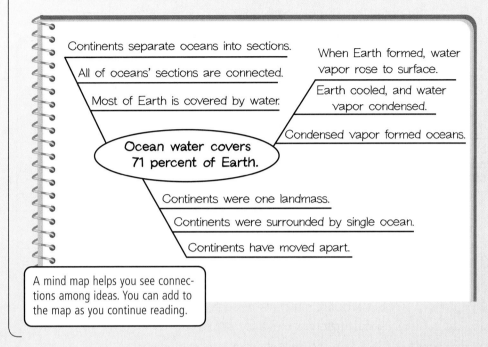

Continents separate oceans into sections.

All of oceans' sections are connected.

Most of Earth is covered by water.

When Earth formed, water vapor rose to surface.

Earth cooled, and water vapor condensed.

Condensed vapor formed oceans.

Ocean water covers 71 percent of Earth.

Continents were one landmass.

Continents were surrounded by single ocean.

Continents have moved apart.

A mind map helps you see connections among ideas. You can add to the map as you continue reading.

Supporting Main Ideas

1. Write a main idea in a box.

2. Add boxes underneath with information—such as reasons, explanations, and examples—that supports the main idea.

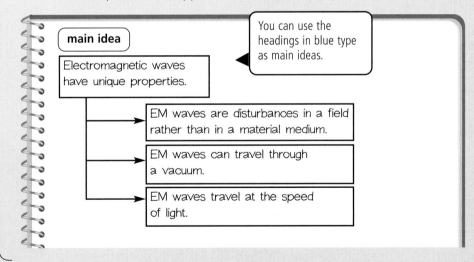

main idea

Electromagnetic waves have unique properties.

You can use the headings in blue type as main ideas.

EM waves are disturbances in a field rather than in a material medium.

EM waves can travel through a vacuum.

EM waves travel at the speed of light.

Outline

1. Copy the chapter title and headings from the book in the form of an outline.

2. Add notes that summarize in your own words what you read.

Cell Processes

1st key idea

I. Cells capture and release energy.

1st subpoint of I

A. All cells need energy.

2nd subpoint of I

B. Some cells capture light energy.

1st detail about B

  1. Process of photosynthesis

2nd detail about B

  2. Chloroplasts (site of photosynthesis)

  3. Carbon dioxide and water as raw materials

  4. Glucose and oxygen as products

C. All cells release energy.

  1. Process of cellular respiration

  2. Fermentation of sugar to carbon dioxide

  3. Bacteria that carry out fermentation

II. Cells transport materials through membranes.

A. Some materials move by diffusion.

  1. Particle movement from higher to lower concentrations

  2. Movement of water through membrane (osmosis)

B. Some transport requires energy.

  1. Active transport

  2. Examples of active transport

Correct Outline Form

Include a title.

Arrange key ideas, subpoints, and details as shown.

Indent the divisions of the outline as shown.

Use the same grammatical form for items of the same rank. For example, if A is a sentence, B must also be a sentence.

You must have at least two main ideas or subpoints. That is, every A must be followed by a B, and every 1 must be followed by a 2.

Concept Map

1. Write an important concept in a large oval.

2. Add details related to the concept in smaller ovals.

3. Write linking words on arrows that connect the ovals.

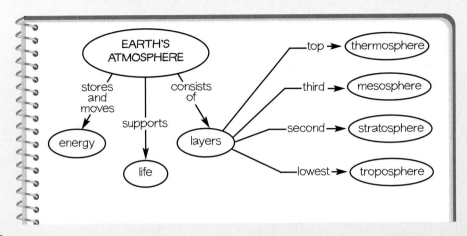

The main ideas or concepts can often be found in the blue headings. An example is "The atmosphere stores and moves energy." Use nouns from these concepts in the ovals, and use the verb or verbs on the lines.

Venn Diagram

1. Draw two overlapping circles, one for each item that you are comparing.

2. In the overlapping section, list the characteristics that are shared by both items.

3. In the outer sections, list the characteristics that are peculiar to each item.

4. Write a summary that describes the information in the Venn diagram.

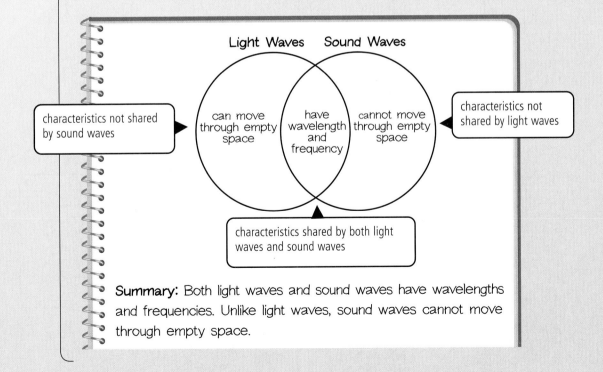

Summary: Both light waves and sound waves have wavelengths and frequencies. Unlike light waves, sound waves cannot move through empty space.

Vocabulary Strategies

Important terms are highlighted in this book. A definition of each term can be found in the sentence or paragraph where the term appears. You can also find definitions in the Glossary. Taking notes about vocabulary terms helps you understand and remember what you read.

Description Wheel

1. Write a term inside a circle.
2. Write words that describe the term on "spokes" attached to the circle.

When studying for a test with a friend, read the phrases on the spokes one at a time until your friend identifies the correct term.

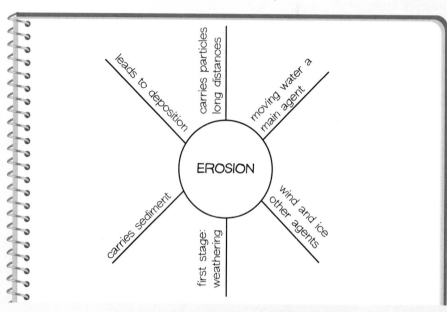

Four Square

1. Write a term in the center.
2. Write details in the four areas around the term.

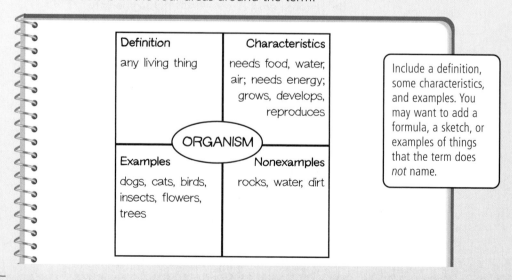

Include a definition, some characteristics, and examples. You may want to add a formula, a sketch, or examples of things that the term does *not* name.

Frame Game

1. Write a term in the center.
2. Frame the term with details.

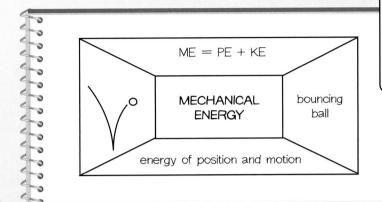

Include examples, descriptions, sketches, or sentences that use the term in context. Change the frame to fit each new term.

Magnet Word

1. Write a term on the magnet.
2. On the lines, add details related to the term.

You can also use phrases or sentences on the lines.

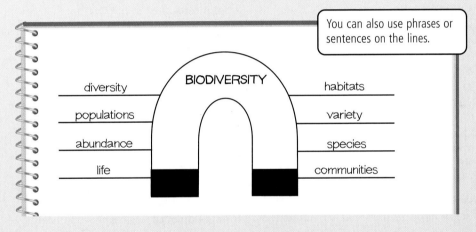

Word Triangle

1. Write a term and its definition in the bottom section.
2. In the middle section, write a sentence in which the term is used correctly.
3. In the top section, draw a small picture to illustrate the term.

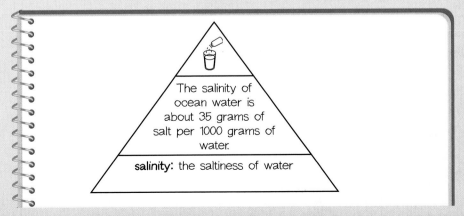

Glossary

A, B

acid
A substance that can donate a proton to another substance and has a pH below 7. (p. 126)

ácido Una sustancia que puede donar un protón a otra sustancia y que tiene un pH menor a 7.

alloy
A solid mixture composed of a metal and one or more other substances. (p. 134)

aleación Una mezcla sólida compuesta de un metal y una o más sustancias adicionales.

atom
The smallest particle of an element that has the chemical properties of that element. (p. xv)

átomo La partícula más pequeña de un elemento que tiene las propiedades químicas de ese elemento.

atomic mass
The average mass of the atoms of an element. (p. 17)

masa atómica La masa promedio de los átomos de un elemento.

atomic mass number
The total number of protons and neutrons in an atom's nucleus.

número de masa atómica El número total de protones y neutrones que hay en el núcleo de un átomo.

atomic number
The number of protons in the nucleus of an atom. (p. 12)

número atómico El número de protones en el núcleo de un átomo.

base
A substance that can accept a proton from another substance and has a pH above 7. (p. 126)

base Una sustancia que puede aceptar un protón de otra sustancia y que tiene un pH superior a 7.

bond energy
The amount of energy in a chemical bond between atoms.

energía de enlace La cantidad de energía que hay en un enlace químico entre átomos.

C, D

carbohydrate
A type of carbon-based molecule in living things. Carbohydrates include sugars and starches used for energy or as structural materials. Carbohydrate molecules contain carbon, hydrogen, and oxygen atoms.

carbohidrato Un tipo de molécula de los organismos vivos basada en el carbono. Los carbohidratos incluyen los azúcares y los almidones usados como fuente de energía o como materiales estructurales. Las moléculas de los carbohidrato contienen átomos de carbono, hidrógeno y oxígeno.

catalyst
A substance that increases the rate of a chemical reaction but is not consumed in the reaction. (p. 76)

catalizador Una sustancia que aumenta lel a ritmo velocidad de una reacción química pero que no es consumida en la reacción.

chemical change
A change of one substance into another substance.

cambio químico Un cambio de una sustancia a otra sustancia.

chemical formula
An expression that shows the number and types of atoms joined in a compound. (p. 43)

fórmula química Una expresión que muestra el número y los tipos de átomos unidos en un compuesto.

chemical reaction
The process by which chemical changes occur. In a chemical reaction, atoms are rearranged, and chemical bonds are broken and formed. (p. 69)

reacción química El proceso mediante el cual ocurren cambios químicos. En una reacción química, los átomos se reorganizan y los enlaces químicos se rompen y se vuelven a formar.

coefficient
The number before a chemical formula that indicates how many molecules are involved in a chemical reaction.

coeficiente El número anterior a una fórmula química que indica cuántas moléculas están involucradas en una reacción química.

compound

A substance made up of two or more different types of atoms bonded together.

compuesto Una sustancia formada por dos o más diferentes tipos de átomos enlazados.

concentration

The amount of solute dissolved in a solvent at a given temperature.

concentración La cantidad de soluto disuelta en un solvente a una temperatura determinada.

covalent bond

A pair of electrons shared by two atoms. (p. 50)

enlace covalente Un par de electrones compartidos por dos átomos.

cycle

n. A series of events or actions that repeat themselves regularly; a physical and/or chemical process in which one material continually changes locations and/or forms. Examples include the water cycle, the carbon cycle, and the rock cycle.

v. To move through a repeating series of events or actions.

ciclo *s.* Una serie de eventos o acciones que se repiten regularmente; un proceso físico y/o químico en el cual un material cambia continuamente de lugar y/o forma. Ejemplos: el ciclo del agua, el ciclo del carbono y el ciclo de las rocas.

data

Information gathered by observation or experimentation that can be used in calculating or reasoning. *Data* is a plural word; the singular is datum.

datos Información reunida mediante observación o experimentación y que se puede usar para calcular o para razonar.

density

A property of matter representing the mass per unit volume.

densidad Una propiedad de la materia que representa la masa por unidad de volumen.

dilute

adj. Having a low concentration of solute. (p. 118)

v. To add solvent in order to decrease the concentration of a solution.

diluido *adj.* Que tiene una baja concentración de soluto.

diluir *v.* Agregar solvente para disminuir la concentración de una solución.

E, F

electron

A negatively charged particle located outside an atom's nucleus. An electron is about 2000 times smaller than either a proton or neutron. (p. 11)

electrón Una partícula con carga negativa localizada fuera del núcleo de un átomo. Un electrón es como aproximadamente 2000 veces más pequeño que un protón o un neutrón.

element

A substance that cannot be broken down into a simpler substance by ordinary chemical changes. An element consists of atoms of only one type. (p. xv)

elemento Una sustancia que no puede descomponerse en otra sustancia más simple por medio de cambios químicos normales. Un elemento consta de átomos de un solo tipo.

endothermic reaction

A chemical reaction that absorbs energy. (p. 87)

reacción endotérmica Una reacción química que absorbe energía.

energy

The ability to do work or to cause a change. For example, the energy of a moving bowling ball knocks over pins; energy from food allows animals to move and to grow; and energy from the Sun heats Earth's surface and atmosphere, which causes air to move. (p. xix)

energía La capacidad para trabajar o causar un cambio. Por ejemplo, la energía de una bola de boliche en movimiento tumba los pinos; la energía proveniente de su alimento permite a los animales moverse y crecer; la energía del Sol calienta la superficie y la atmósfera de la Tierra, lo que ocasiona que el aire se mueva.

enzyme

A type of protein that is a catalyst for chemical reactions in living things. (p. 159)

enzima Un tipo de proteína que es un catalizador de reacciones químicas en organismos vivos.

exothermic reaction

A chemical reaction that releases energy. (p. 87)

reacción exotérmica Una reacción química que libera energía.

experiment

An organized procedure to study something under controlled conditions. (p. xxiv)

experimento Un procedimiento organizado para estudiar algo bajo condiciones controladas.

force
A push or a pull; something that changes the motion of an object. (p. xxi)

fuerza Un empuje o un jalón; algo que cambia el movimiento de un objeto.

friction
A force that resists the motion between two surfaces in contact. (p. xxi)

fricción Una fuerza que resiste el movimiento entre dos superficies en contacto.

G, H

gravity
The force that objects exert on each other because of their mass. (p. xxi)

gravedad La fuerza que los objetos ejercen entre sí debido a su masa.

group
A vertical column in the periodic table of the elements. Elements in a group have similar properties. (p. 22)

grupo Una columna vertical en la tabla periódica de los elementos. Los elementos en un grupo tienen propiedades similares.

half-life
The amount of time it takes for half of the nuclei of a radioactive isotope to decay into atoms of another element. (p. 32)

vida media La cantidad de tiempo que se necesita para que le toma a la mitad del núcleo de un isótopo radioactivo se en descomponganerse en átomos de otro elemento.

hydrocarbon
A compound that contains only carbon and hydrogen. (p. 163)

hidrocarburo Un compuesto que contiene solamente carbono e hidrógeno.

hypothesis
A tentative explanation for an observation or phenomenon. A hypothesis is used to make testable predictions. (p. xxiv)

hipótesi Una explicación provisional de una observación o de un fenómeno. Una hipótesis se usa para hacer predicciones que se pueden probar.

I, J

inorganic compound
A compound that is not considered organic. All compounds that do not contain carbon are inorganic, as are some types of carbon-containing compounds. (p. 148)

compuesto inorgánico Un compuesto que no se considera orgánico. Todos los compuestos que no contienen carbono son inorgánicos, al igual que algunos tipos de compuestos que contienen carbono.

ion
An atom or group of atoms that has a positive or negative electric charge. (p. 14)

ión Un átomo o un grupo de átomos que tiene una carga eléctrica positiva o negativa.

ionic bond
The electrical attraction between a negative ion and a positive ion. (p. 48)

enlace iónico La atracción eléctrica entre un ión negativo y un ión positivo.

isomer
Any of two or more compounds that contain the same atoms but that have different structures. (p. 152)

isómero Cualquiera de dos o más compuestos que contienen los mismos átomos pero que tienen estructuras diferentes.

isotope
An atom of one element that has a different number of neutrons than another atom of the same element. (p. 12)

isótopo Un átomo de un elemento que tiene un número diferente de neutrones que otro átomo del mismo elemento.

K, L

law
In science, a rule or principle describing a physical relationship that always works in the same way under the same conditions. The law of conservation of energy is an example.

ley En las ciencias, una regla o un principio que describe una relación física que siempre funciona de la misma manera bajo las mismas condiciones. La ley de la conservación de la energía es un ejemplo.

law of conservation of energy

A law stating that no matter how energy is transferred or transformed, all of the energy is still present in one form or another. (p. xix)

ley de la conservación de la energía Una ley que establece que no importa cómo se transfiere o transforma la energía, toda la energía sigue presente en alguna forma u otra.

law of conservation of mass

A law stating that atoms are not created or destroyed in a chemical reaction. (p. 79)

ley de la conservación de la masa Una ley que establece que los átomos ni se crean ni se destruyen en una reacción química.

lipid

A type of carbon-based molecule in living things. Lipids include fats and oils used for energy or as structural materials. (p. 156)

lípido Un tipo de molecula de los organismos vivos basada en el carbono. Los lípidos incluyen las grasas y los aceites usados como fuente de energia o como materiales estructurales.

M, N

mass

A measure of how much matter an object is made of. (p. xv)

masa Una medida de la cantidad de materia de la que está compuesto un objeto.

matter

Anything that has mass and volume. Matter exists ordinarily as a solid, a liquid, or a gas. (p. xv)

materia Todo lo que tiene masa y volumen. Generalmente la materia existe como sólido, líquido o gas.

metal

An element that tends to be shiny, easily shaped, and a good conductor of electricity and heat. (p. 27)

metal Un elemento que tiende a ser brilloso, fácilmente deformable moldeado y buen conductor de electricidad y calor.

metallic bond

A certain type of bond in which nuclei float in a sea of electrons. (p. 56)

enlace metálico Cierto tipo de enlace en el cual los núcleos flotan en un mar de electrones.

metalloid

An element that has properties of both metals and non-metals. (p. 30)

metaloide Un elemento que tiene propiedades de los metales así como de los no metales.

mixture

A combination of two or more substances that do not combine chemically but remain the same individual substances. Mixtures can be separated by physical means.

mezcla Una combinación de dos o más sustancias que no se combinan químicamente sino que permanecen siendo las mismas sustancias individuales. Las mezclas se pueden separar por medios físicos.

molecule

A group of atoms that are held together by covalent bonds so that they move as a unit. (p. 51)

molécula Un grupo de átomos que se mantienen unidos por medio de enlaces covalentes de tal manera que se mueven como una sola unidad.

monomer

One of many small, repeating units linked together to form a polymer. (p. 166)

monómero Una de muchas unidades pequeñas que se repiten y están enlazadas unas con otras para formar un polímero.

neutral

Describing a solution that is neither an acid nor a base. A neutral solution has a pH of 7. (p. 129)

neutro Que describe una solución que no es un ácido ni una base. Una solución neutra tiene un pH de 7.

neutron

A particle that has no electric charge and is located in an atom's nucleus. (p. 11)

neutrón Una partícula que no tiene carga eléctrica y que se encuentra en el núcleo de un átomo.

nonmetal

An element that is not a metal and has properties generally opposite to those of a metal. (p. 29)

no metal Un elemento que no es un metal y que tiene propiedades generalmente opuestas a las de los metales.

nucleic acid

One of several carbon-based molecules that carry an organism's genetic code. One of the nucleic acids—DNA—contains the information needed to construct proteins. (p. 161)

ácido nucleico Una de varias moléculas basadas en el carbono que llevan el código genético de un organismo. Uno de los ácidos nucleicos, el ADN, contiene la información necesaria para construir proteínas.

nucleus
The central region of an atom where most of the atom's mass is found in protons and neutrons. (p. 11)

núcleo La región central de un átomo donde se encuentra la mayor parte de la masa del átomo en la forma de protones y neutrones.

O, P, Q

organic compound
A compound that is based on carbon. (p. 147)

compuesto orgánico Un compuesto basado en el carbono.

period
A horizontal row in the periodic table of the elements. Elements in a period have varying properties. (p. 22)

período Un renglón horizontal en la tabla periódica de los elementos. Los elementos en un período tienen distintas propiedades.

periodic table
A table of the elements, arranged by atomic number, that shows the patterns in their properties. (p. 18)

tabla periódica Una tabla de los elementos, organizada en base a número atómico, que muestra los patrones en sus propiedades.

pH
The concentration of hydrogen ions in a solution; a measurement of acidity. (p. 129)

pH La concentración de iones de hidrógeno en una solución;, una medida de acidez.

photosynthesis
In green plants, the endothermic process in which light is absorbed and used to change carbon dioxide and water into glucose and oxygen. (p. 90)

fotosíntesis En plantas verdes, el proceso endotérmico en el cual se absorbe luz y se usa para cambiar dióxido de carbono y agua a glucosa y oxígeno.

plastic
A polymer that can be molded or shaped. (p. 167)

plástico Un polímero que puede ser modelado o deformadomoldeado.

polar covalent bond
The unequal sharing of electrons between two atoms that gives rise to negative and positive regions of electric charge. (p. 51)

enlace polar covalente El compartir electrones desigualmente entre dos átomos y que lleva a la formación de regiones de carga eléctrica positiva y regiones de carga eléctrica negativa.

polymer
A very large carbon-based molecule made of smaller, repeating units. (p. 166)

polímero Una molécula muy grande basada en el carbono compuesta de unidades más pequeñas que se repiten.

precipitate
n. A solid substance that forms as a result of a reaction between chemicals in two liquids. (p. 72)

v. To come out of solution.

precipitado *s.* Una sustancia sólida que se forma como resultado de la reacción entre sustancias químicas en dos líquidos.

precipitar *v.* Salir de solución.

product
A substance formed by a chemical reaction. A product is made by the rearrangement of atoms and bonds in reactants. (p. 71)

producto Una sustancia formada por una reacción química. Un producto se hace mediante la reorganización de los átomos y los enlaces en los reactivos.

protein
A macromolecule in living things that is made of smaller molecules called amino acids. (p. 158)

proteína Una macromolécula en organismos vivos compuesta de moléculas más pequeñas llamadas aminoácidos.

proton
A positively charged particle located in an atom's nucleus. (p. 11)

protón Una partícula con cargada positivamente localizada en el núcleo de un átomo.

R, S

radioactivity
The process by which the nucleus of an atom of an element releases energy and particles. (p. 30)

radioactividad El proceso mediante el cual el núcleo de un átomo de un elemento libera energía y partículas.

reactant
A substance that is present at the beginning of a chemical reaction and is changed into a new substance. (p. 71)

reactivo Una sustancia que está presente en el comienzo de una reacción química y que se convierte en una nueva sustancia.

reactive
Likely to undergo a chemical change. (p. 26)

reactivo Que es probable que sufra un cambio químico.

respiration
The exothermic process by which living things release energy from glucose and oxygen and produce carbon dioxide and water. (p. 94)

respiración El proceso exotérmico mediante el cual los organismos vivos liberan energía de la glucosa y del oxígeno y producen dióxido de carbono y agua.

saturated
Containing the maximum amount of a solute that can be dissolved in a particular solvent at a given temperature and pressure. (p. 118)

saturado Que contiene la máxima cantidad de soluto que se puede disolver en un solvente en particular a determinada temperatura y presión.

solubility
The amount of solute that dissolves in a certain amount of a solvent at a given temperature and pressure to produce a saturated solution. (p. 119)

solubilidad La cantidad de soluto que se disuelve en cierta cantidad de solvente a determinada temperatura y presión para producir una solución saturada.

solute
In a solution, a substance that is dissolved in a solvent. (p. 112)

soluto En una solución, una sustancia que se disuelve en un solvente.

solution
A mixture of two or more substances that is identical throughout; a homogeneous mixture. (p. 111)

solución Una mezcla de dos o más sustancias que es idéntica en su totalidad;, una mezcla homogénea.

solvent
In a solution, the substance that dissolves a solute and makes up the largest percentage of a solution. (p. 112)

solvente En una solución, la sustancia que disuelve un soluto y que compone el porcentaje mayor de la una solución.

subscript
A number written slightly below and to the right of a chemical symbol that shows how many atoms of an element are in a compound. (p. 43)

subíndice Un número que se escribe en la parte inferior a la derecha de un símbolo químico y que muestra cuantos átomos de un elemento están en un compuesto.

suspension
A mixture in which the different parts are identifiable as separate substances; a heterogeneous mixture. (p. 113)

suspensión Una mezcla en la cual las diferentes partes son identificables como sustancias distintas; una mezcla heterogénea.

system
A group of objects or phenomena that interact. A system can be as simple as a rope, a pulley, and a mass. It also can be as complex as the interaction of energy and matter in the four spheres of the Earth system.

sistema Un grupo de objetos o fenómenos que interactúan. Un sistema puede ser algo tan sencillo como una cuerda, una polea y una masa. También puede ser algo tan complejo como la interacción de la energía y la materia en las cuatro esferas del sistema de la Tierra.

T, U

technology
The use of scientific knowledge to solve problems or to engineer new products, tools, or processes.

tecnología El uso de conocimientos científicos para resolver problemas o para diseñar nuevos productos, herramientas o procesos.

theory
In science, a set of widely accepted explanations of observations and phenomena. A theory is a well-tested explanation that is consistent with all available evidence.

teoría En las ciencias, un conjunto de explicaciones de observaciones y fenómenos que es ampliamente aceptado. Una teoría es una explicación bien probada que es consecuente con la evidencia disponible.

V, W, X, Y, Z

variable
Any factor that can change in a controlled experiment, observation, or model. (p. R30)

variable Cualquier factor que puede cambiar en un experimento controlado, en una observación o en un modelo.

volume
An amount of three-dimensional space, often used to describe the space that an object takes up. (p. xv)

volumen Una cantidad de espacio tridimensional; a menudo se usa este término para describir el espacio que ocupa un objeto.

Index

Page numbers for definitions are printed in **boldface** type.
Page numbers for illustrations, maps, and charts are printed in *italics*.

INDEX

E, F

Einstein, Albert, 10
einsteinium, 10
electric current, 105
electrolysis, 71, *71*
electron cloud, *11*, 12, 34, *34*
electrons, **11**, *11*, 11–12, 106
  chemical bonds and, 47–48, 62
  discovery of, 105
  ion formation and, *14*, 14–15, *15*
elements, xv, 9–13
  atoms and, 11
  carbon (*See* carbon)
  compounds and, 41–45, 62
  density, trends of, 23
  atoms of, in Earth's crust, 10, *10*
  half-lives, 32, *32*
  halogens, 22, *22*, 29, *29*
  atoms of, in human body, 10, *10*, 16
  ion formation and periodic table, 48
  metalloids, 30, *30*, 34
  metals, **27**, 27–28
  names and symbols, 10
  noble gases, 29, *29*
  nonmetals, **29**, *29*, 34
  organization of, 17, 34, *34*
  periodic table of, 17–23, **18**, *20–21*, 26–32
  properties of, and compound properties, 41–42
  rare earth (lanthanides), 21, 28, *28*
  reactive, **26**, 27, *27*
endothermic reaction, **87**, *89*, 89–90, 100
  Chapter Investigation, 92–93
  photosynthesis, **90**, 90–91, 94, 95
energy, **xix**, xviii
  bond energy, 87, *88*, *89*, 100
  chemical, xviii
  and chemical reactions, 86–91
  electrical, xviii
  in endothermic reactions, *89*, 89–90, 90–91, 100
  in exothermic reactions, 87–88, *88*, 90–91, 100
  forms of, xviii
  law of conservation of, **xix**
  sources of, xix
  storage and release, 90–91
enzymes, 76, *76*, **159**
equations, chemical, 80–84
Europium, 28
evaluating, **R8**
  media claims, R8
evidence, collection of, xxiv
exothermic reaction, *87*, **87**, 87–89, *88*, 100
  Chapter Investigation, 92–93
  in living things, 88–89, *89*, 95
experiment, **xxiv**. *See also* labs.
  conclusions, drawing, R35
  constants, determining, R30
  controlled, **R28**, R30
  designing, R28–R35
  hypothesis, writing, R29
  materials, determining, R29
  observations, recording, R33
  procedure, writing, R32
  purpose, determining, R28
  results, summarizing, R34
  variables, R30–R31, R32

experimental group, R30
exponents, 33, **R44**
fact, **R9**
  different from opinion, R9
fatty acids, 127, *156*, 156–57
faulty reasoning, **R7**
Fermi, Enrico, 10
fermium, 10
fires and chemical reactions, 85
fluorine, 22
forces, **xxi**
  contact, **xxi**
  electrical, xxi
  friction, **xxi**
  gravity, **xxi**
  magnetic, xxi
  physical, xx–xxi
formulas, **R42.**
  See also chemical formulas.
fractions, **R41**
freezing point, 115
friction, **xxi**
fuel cell, hydrogen, xxvii, *xxvii*
fullerene, 59, *59*

G, H

gallium, 19
gases
  inert, 29, *29*
  studying, 104
Geiger counter, 30
glow sticks, 88, 94
glucose, 155–56. *See also* sugar.
  formula, 46
  model, *155*
  in respiration, 94–95
glue, 55
gold, 10, 12, *12*, 134
graphite, 59, *59*, 62
graphs,
  bar, 162, R26, R31
  circle, R25
  double bar, R27
  line, 77, R24, R34
gravity, **xxi**, xxiv
group, in periodic table, *20*, *22*, **22**, 26–30, 34, *34*
hair, 159, *159*
Hales, Stephen, 104
half-life, **32**
halogens, 22, *22*, 29, *29*
heat. *See* energy.
heat pack, chemical, 119
hemoglobin, 16, 159, *159*
hexane, 172
hormones, 157
human body, elements in, 10, *10*, 16
hydrocarbon, 96, *97*, **163**, 163–64, *165*
hydrochloric acid, 44, 126, 128, *128*, 129
  pH of, 129, *130*
hydrogen, 10, 16
  compounds of, 44–45
  fuel cells and, xxvii
  ions, 126, 128–31, *128*
hypothesis, **xxiv**, xxv, **R3**, R29

I, J

ice cream, 115
inert gases, 29, *29*
inference, **R4**, R35
infrared spectroscopy, 4
inorganic compounds, **148**, *148*
International Space Station, 138, *138*
International System of Units, R20–R21
Internet activity
    alloys, 109
    chemical bonding, 39
    chemical reactions, 67
    periodic table, 7
    polymers, 145
Investigations. *See* Chapter Investigations.
iodine, 22, 50, *50*
    molecular structure, 54, *54*
iodine clock reaction, 77
ionic bond, **48**, *48*, 48–49, *52*, 62
ionic compounds
    names of, 49
    properties of, 57–58
    in solutions, 114, *114*, 123, *123*
    structures of, 53
ions, **14**
    acids and bases, 126, 128–31, *128*, *129*
    formation, *14*, 14–15, *15*, 48
    negative, 15, *15*, *48*, 48–49
    periodic table and, 22–23, 48, *48*
    positive, 14, *14*, *48*, 48–49
isobutane, 152
isomers, **152**, *152*, 169
isotopes, **12**, 12–13, *13*
    atomic mass number and, 17
    half-life, 32, *32*
    radioactive, 30, 31–32

K, L

keratin, 159, *159*
Kevlar, 169, *169*
laboratory equipment
    beaker, R12, *R12*
    double-pan balance, R19, *R19*
    force meter, R16, *R16*
    forceps, R13, *R13*
    graduated cylinder, R16, *R16*
    hot plate, R13, *R13*
    meniscus, **R16**, *R16*
    microscope, *xxiv*, *R14*, R14–R15
    ruler, metric, R17, *R17*
    spring scale, R16, *R16*
    test-tube holder, R12, *R12*
    test-tube rack, R13, *R13*
    test tube, R12, *R12*
    triple-beam balance, R18, *R18*
labs, R10–35. *See also* experiment.
    equipment, R12–R19
    safety, R10–R11
Langmuir, Irving, 106
lanthanides (rare earth elements), 21, 28, *28*
laser, chemical reaction and, *xxiv*
Lavoisier, Antoine, 78–79, *79*
law of conservation of energy, xix
law of conservation of mass, 78–79, **79**, 100
    in chemical equations, 80, 81, 84
lemon, pH, *130*
Lewis, G.N., 106

lipids, **156**, *156*, 156–57, 172
lithium, 10
litmus paper, 127, 129

M, N

magnesium, 10, 27
magnetic force, xxi
mass, **xv**
math skills
    area, **R43**
    bar graphs, 162
    decimal, **R39**, R40
    describing a set of data, R36–R37
    formulas, **R42**
    fractions, **R41**
    line graphs, 77
    mean, **R36**
    median, **R36**
    mode, **R37**
    percents, 139, **R41**
    proportions, **R39**
    range, **R37**
    rates, **R38**
    ratios, 46, **R38**
    scientific notation, 33, **R44**
    significant figures, **R44**
    volume, **R43**, **xv**
matter, xiv–xvii, **xv**
    conservation of, xvii
    forms of, xvi–xvii
    movement of, xvii
    particles and, xiv–xv
    physical forces and, xx
mean, **R36**
measurement
    area, **R43**
    mass, **xv**
    volume, **R43**, **xv**
median, **R36**
medicine
    alloys and, 137, *137*
    from nature, 2–5
    radioactivity in, 31
Mendeleev, Dmitri, 18, *18*, 19
mercury, 27
metallic bond, **56**, 56–57, *57*, 62
metalloids, 30, *30*, 34
metals, 22, **27**, 27–28
    alkali, 27
    alkaline earth, 27
    alloys, 28, 109, **134**, 134–38, 140
    properties and bonds, 56–57
    reactive, 27, *27*
    transition, *27*, 27–28
methane, *44*
    bonding of, *50*, 50–51
    combustion, 81, *81*, 82, *82*, 88, *88*
    molecular structure, 54, *54*
metric system, R20–R21
    changing metric units, R20, *R20*
    converting between U.S. customary units, R21, *R21*
    temperature conversion, R21, *R21*
microchips, 98–99, *99*
microscope, *R14*, R14–R15
    making a slide or wet mount, R15, *R15*
    scanning tunneling (STM), *xxiv*
    viewing an object, R15
milk, pH, *130*
mixtures, 111. *See also* solutions.

INDEX

S, T

safety, R10–R11
salt, 131. *See also* sodium chloride.
saturated (solution), **118,** 118–19
saturated fat, 157
scanning tunneling microscope, 55, 107
science, nature of, xxii–xxv
scientific notation, 33, **R44**
scientific process, xxiii–xxv
semiconductors, 30, 33, *33,* 98
SI units. *See* International System of Units.
significant figures, **R44**
silicon, 98–99, *99*
   in Earth's crust, 10
soap, 127, *127*
   pH, *130*
sodium, 16, 27, *27*
   ion, 14, *14*
sodium azide, 84
sodium chloride, 49, *49, 52,* 140
   freezing point and, 115
   in solution, 114, 123, *123*
sodium hydroxide, 126, 128, *129*
   pH, *130*
solubility, **119,** 119–23, 140
   changes in, 120–23
   molecular structure and, 122–23, *123*
   pressure and, 122, *122*
   temperature and, 120–21, *121*
solute, **112.** *See also* solutions.
   change in solubility, 120–23
   concentration and, 117–18, *118,* 140
   dissolving, 114, *114*
solutions, 108–40, **111,** *113,* 140.
   See also solute; solvent.
   acidity, 129, *130*
   acids, 125–31, **126,** 140
   alloys, **134,** 134–38, 140
   bases, 125–31, **126,** 140
   concentrated, 118, *118,* 140
   concentration, **117,** 117–18
   dilute, *118,* **118,** 140
   gases, 112
   liquids, 112
   neutral, **129,** 140
   saturated, 118
   solid, 112, 134–38
   solubility, **119,** 119–23
   solvent-solute interactions, 114, *114*
   supersaturated, 118–19, *119,* 121
   types, 112
solvent, **112.** *See also* solutions.
   boiling point, 116
   changing properties, 115–16
   freezing point, 115
   interaction with solutes, 114, *114*
Space Station, International, 138, *138*
spectroscopy, 4
stainless steel, *135,* 136, 137
Standardized Test Practice
   analyzing descriptions, 103
   interpreting graphs, 143
   interpreting tables, 37, 65, 175
starch, 155, *155,* 156
steel, 136
   carbon, *135*
   stainless, *135,* 136, 137
subscripts, **43**
   in chemical equations, 83

   in chemical formulas, 43–44
sugar, 147, *148. See also* glucose.
   solubility of, *121*
   in solution, 114
surface area, in chemical reactions, 74–75, *75*
suspension, *113,* **113**
synthetic compounds, 4–5
synthesis reaction, *73,* **73**
technology
   alloys, 28, **134,** 134–139, *135*
   battery, 105
   carbon nanotubes, 153, *153*
   catalytic converter, 96, *97*
   chemical technology, 96
   electrolysis, 71, *71*
   electronic products, 98–99, *99*
   elements in industry, 27–30
   hydrogen fuel cells, xxvii
   microchips, 98–99
   nature of, xxvi–xxvii
   particle accelerator, 107, *107*
   particle detector, *xxii*
   petroleum, 164, *165*
   plastics, **167,** 167–168, *168*
   polymers, **166,** 166–169, *167*
   radioactivity in medicine, 31
   scanning tunneling microscope, xxiv, *xxiv, 55,* 107
   semiconductor, 30, 98
   spectroscopy, 4
Teflon, 168
temperature, 75, *75*
   reaction rate and, 75, *75*
   solubility and, 120–21, *121*
   unit conversion, R21, *R21*
thermite reaction, 87, *87*
titanium alloy, 137, *137,* 138
transition metals, *27,* 27–28
transportation, alloys and, 136

U, V

unsaturated fat, 157
vanillin, 150, *151,* 172
variables, **R30,** R31, R32
   controlling a, R17
   dependent, **R30,** R31
   independent, R30
vocabulary strategies, R50–R51
   choose your own strategy, 110, *110*
   description wheel, 40, *40,* R50, *R50*
   four square, 68, *68,* R50, *R50*
   frame game, 8, *8,* R51, *R51*
   magnet word, 146, *146,* R51, *R51*
   word triangle, R51, *R51*
volume, **xv, R43**
Volta, Alessandro, 105

W, X, Y, Z

water, **xvii,** *44,* 45, *45,* 51, *51, 52*
   electrolysis, 71, *71,* 89, *89*
   molecular structure, 54, *54*
   oil and, 122–23, *123*
   pH, *130*
   physical states, 70, *70*
   as solution, 124
   as solvent, 122–23, *123,* 126
   vapor, xvii
x-rays, 4

Acknowledgments

Photography

Cover © Photodisc/Getty Images; **i** © Photodisc/Getty Images; **iii** *left (top to bottom)* Photograph of James Trefil by Evan Cantwell; Photograph of Rita Ann Calvo by Joseph Calvo; Photograph of Linda Carnine by Amilcar Cifuentes; Photograph of Sam Miller by Samuel Miller; *right (top to bottom)* Photograph of Kenneth Cutler by Kenneth A. Cutler; Photograph of Donald Steely by Marni Stamm; Photograph of Vicky Vachon by Redfern Photographics; **vi** © Digital Vision/PictureQuest; **vii** From *General Chemistry* by P. W. Atkins, © 1989 by Peter Atkins. Used with permission of W. H. Freeman and Company; **ix** Photographs by Sharon Hoogstraten; **xiv–xv** © Larry Hamill/age fotostock america, inc.; **xvi–xvii** © Fritz Poelking/age fotostock america, inc.; **xviii–xix** © Galen Rowell/Corbis; **xx–xxi** © Jack Affleck/SuperStock; **xxii** AP/Wide World Photos; **xxiii** © David Parker/IMI/University of Birmingham High, TC Consortium/Photo Researchers; **xxiv** *left* AP/Wide World Photos; *right Washington University Record;* **xxv** *top* © Kim Steele/Getty Images; *bottom* Reprinted with permission from S. Zhou et al., *SCIENCE* 291:1944–47. © 2001 AAAS; **xxvi–xxvii** © Mike Fiala/Getty Images; **xxvii** *left* © Derek Trask/Corbis; *right* AP/Wide World Photos; **xxxii** © The Chedd-Angier Production Company; **2–3** © David Cavagnaro/Peter Arnold, Inc.; **3** Joel Sartore/National Geographic Image Collection; **4** © The Chedd-Angier Production Company; **5** © Colin Cuthbert/Photo Researchers; **6–7** IBM Research, Almaden Research Center; **7, 9** Photographs by Sharon Hoogstraten; **10** NASA; **12** © Pascal Goetgheluck/Photo Researchers; **13** Photograph by Sharon Hoogstraten; **16** © Cnri/Photo Researchers; **17** Photograph by Sharon Hoogstraten; **18** *left, right* The Granger Collection, New York; **24** *top* © A. Hart-Davis/Photo Researchers; *bottom* Photograph by Sharon Hoogstraten; **26** Photograph by Sharon Hoogstraten; **27** *left* © Charles D. Winters/Photo Researchers; *center* © Rich Treptow/Visuals Unlimited; *right* © Corbis Images/PictureQuest; **28** © Peter Christopher/Masterfile; **29** © M. Gibbon/Robertstock.com; **30** © Superstock; **31** *top* © Simon Fraser/Photo Researchers; *bottom* Photograph by Sharon Hoogstraten; **33** © Alfred Pasieka/Photo Researchers; *inset* © John Walsh/Photo Researchers; **38–39** © Digital Vision/PictureQuest; **39, 41** Photographs by Sharon Hoogstraten; **42** *left* © Rich Treptow/Visuals Unlimited; *center, right* © E. R. Degginger/Color-Pic, Inc.; **43, 45** Photograph by Sharon Hoogstraten; **46** © Lawrence M. Sawyer/Photodisc/PictureQuest; **47** © IFA/eStock Photography (PQ price control)/PictureQuest; **49** © Runk and Schoenberger/Grant Heilman Photography, Inc.; **52** © The Image Bank/Getty Images; **53** Photograph by Sharon Hoogstraten; **55** © Astrid & Hanns-Frieder Michler/Photo Researchers; *inset* © Volker Steger/Photo Researchers; **56** Photograph by Sharon Hoogstraten; **57** © David Wrobel/Visuals Unlimited; **58** © Rob Blakers/photolibrary/PictureQuest; **59** *left* © E. R. Degginger/Robertstock.com; *right* © C. Swartzell/Visuals Unlimited; **60** *top* © David Young-Wolff/Getty Images; *bottom* Photograph by Sharon Hoogstraten; **61** Photograph by Sharon Hoogstraten; **62** *left* © Rich Treptow/Visuals Unlimited; *center, right* © E. R. Degginger/Color-Pic, Inc.; **66–67** From *General Chemistry* by P. W. Atkins, © 1989 by Peter Atkins. Used with permission of W.H. Freeman and Company; **67, 69** Photographs by Sharon Hoogstraten; **70** © Daryl Benson/Masterfile; **72** *top left* © Science VU/Visuals Unlimited; *top right* © 1992 Richard Megna/Fundamental Photographs, NYC; *bottom left* © E. R. Degginger/Color-Pic, Inc.; *bottom right* © Larry Stepanowicz/Visuals Unlimited; **74** Photograph by Sharon Hoogstraten; **77** © Corbis Images/PictureQuest; *inset* © Andrew Lambert Photography/Photo Researchers; **78** © Wally Eberhart/Visuals Unlimited; **79** *top* The Granger Collection, New York; *bottom* Photograph by Sharon Hoogstraten; **80** © William Ervin/Photo Researchers; **82** © Maximilian Stock Ltd./Photo Researchers; **84** © Index Stock; **85** *left, inset* Courtesy of Chicago Fire Department; *center* Uline; *bottom right* Photograph by Sharon Hoogstraten; **86** Photograph by Sharon Hoogstraten; **87** *top* NASA; *bottom* © 1992 Richard Megna/Fundamental Photographs, NYC; **88** © Jeffrey L. Rotman/Corbis; **89** Thomas Eisner and Daniel Aneshansley, Cornell University; **91** © Harald Sund/Brand X Pictures/PictureQuest; **92** *top* AP/Wide World Photos; *bottom* Photographs by Sharon Hoogstraten; **93** Photograph by Sharon Hoogstraten; **94** © Runk and Schoenberger/Grant Heilman Photography, Inc.; **95** Photograph by Sharon Hoogstraten; **96** © Tom Yhlman/Visuals Unlimited; **97** *background* © Conor Caffrey/Photo Researchers; **98** © Arnold Fisher/Photo Researchers; **99** *left to right* © Bruce Forster/Getty Images; © Colin Cuthbert/Photo Researchers; © Fontarnau-Gutiérrez/age fotostock america, inc.; © D. Roberts/Photo Researchers; **100** © 1992 Richard Megna/Fundamental Photographs, NYC; **104** From Hales, *Vegetable Statiks* [1727]; **105** *top* The Granger Collection, New York; *bottom* Mary Evans Picture Library; **106** *top* AP/Wide World Photos; *bottom* © Dorling Kindersley; **107** *top, bottom* © David Parker/Photo Researchers; **108–109** © Stephen Frink/Index Stock; **109, 111** Photographs by Sharon Hoogstraten; **112** © Richard Cummins/Corbis; **113, 115** Photographs by Sharon Hoogstraten; **116** © Peter & Georgina Bowater/Stock Connection/PictureQuest; *inset* © 2001 Kim Fennema/Visuals Unlimited; **117, 118** Photographs by Sharon Hoogstraten; **119** *left, right* © 1990 Richard Megna/Fundamental Photographs, NYC; **120, 121** Photographs by Sharon Hoogstraten; **122** © Stephen Frink/StephenFrink.com; **123** Photograph by Sharon Hoogstraten; **124** © Thom Lang/Corbis; **125, 127, 129** Photographs by Sharon Hoogstraten; **130** *top left* © Martyn F. Chillmaid/Photo Researchers; *top right* © Chuck Swartzell/Visuals Unlimited; *center left* © E. R. Degginger/Color-Pic, Inc.; *center right* © Phil Degginger/Color-Pic, Inc.; *bottom left* © Stockbyte; *bottom right* © E. R. Degginger/Color-Pic, Inc.; **132** © Runk and Schoenberger/Grant Heilman Photography, Inc.; **132–133, 133, 134** Photographs by Sharon Hoogstraten; **135** *top to bottom* © Photodisc/Getty Images; © Greg Pease/Stock Connection/PictureQuest; © Stockbyte; © S. Feld/Robertstock.com; Jellinek & Sampson, London/Bridgeman Art Library; **136** © Joachim Messerschmidt/Bruce Coleman, Inc.; **137** *top* © Princess Margaret Rose Hospital/Photo Researchers; *inset* © Klaus Rose/Okapia/Photo Researchers; *bottom* Photograph by Sharon Hoogstraten; **138** NASA; **139** © IFA/eStock Photography (PQ price control)/PictureQuest; **140** © Joachim Messerschmidt/Bruce Coleman, Inc.; **144–145** © Jeff Greenberg/Index Stock/PictureQuest; **145, 147** Photographs by Sharon Hoogstraten; **148** *left* © E. R. Degginger/Color-Pic, Inc.; *right* © Charles D. Winters/Photo Researchers; **149** Photograph by Sharon Hoogstraten; **151** *top* © Claver Carroll/age fotostock america, inc.; *bottom left* © Fabio Cardoso/age fotostock america, inc.; *bottom right* Photograph by Sharon Hoogstraten; **153** *left* © S. J. Tans et al., Delft University of Technology/Photo Researchers; *right* Georgia Institute of Technology; **154** Photograph by Sharon Hoogstraten; **155** © Marcialis/StockFood; **156** © John Durham/Photo Researchers; **157** *top* © Meyer/StockFood; *bottom* © SPL/Photo Researchers; **158** Photograph by Sharon Hoogstraten; **159** *left* © Andrew Syred/Photo Researchers; *right* © SCIMAT 2000/Photo Researchers; **162** © Eising/StockFood; **163** Photograph by Sharon Hoogstraten; **165** *top* © Thomas Kitchin/Tom Stack & Associates; *center* © Superstock; *bottom left* © Bob Krist/Corbis; *bottom center* © Omni Photo Communications/Index Stock; *bottom right* © Gary Rhijnsburger/Masterfile; **167** *top* Image Club Graphics; *bottom* © 1994 CMCD, Inc.; **168** *bottom left* © J. Blank/Robertstock.com; **169** *left* © SuperStock; *right* © Cheryl A. Ertelt/Visuals Unlimited; **170** *top* © E. R. Degginger/Color-Pic, Inc.; *bottom* Photograph by Sharon Hoogstraten; **171** Photograph by Sharon Hoogstraten; **172** © SuperStock; **R28** © Photodisc/Getty Images.

Illustrations

Ampersand Design Group **85, 97**; Stephen Durke **11, 12, 13, 14, 15, 34, 48, 49, 50, 51, 52, 54, 59, 62, 64, 70, 71, 73, 88, 89, 97, 102, 114, 142, 148, 158, 159, 160, 172, 174**; Patrick Gnan **160**; Gary Hincks **124**; KO Studios **160**; Debbie Maizels **160**; Precision Graphics **165**; Dan Stukenschneider **R11–R19, R22, R32**.

ACKNOWLEDGMENTS